W9-BAM-887

Europe's Orphan

EUROPE'S ORPHAN

The Future of the Euro and the Politics of Debt

MARTIN SANDBU

PRINCETON UNIVERSITY PRESS
PRINCETON AND OXFORD

Copyright © 2015 by Martin Sandbu

Requests for permission to reproduce material from this work
should be sent to Permissions, Princeton University Press

Published by Princeton University Press,
41 William Street, Princeton, New Jersey 08540

In the United Kingdom: Princeton University Press,
6 Oxford Street, Woodstock, Oxfordshire OX20 1TW

press.princeton.edu

Jacket design by Faceout Studio

All Rights Reserved

ISBN 978-0-691-16830-2

Library of Congress Control Number: 2015944893

British Library Cataloging-in-Publication Data is available

This book has been composed in Adobe Garamond Pro
by T&T Productions Ltd, London

Printed on acid-free paper ∞

Printed in the United States of America

10 9 8 7 6 5 4 3 2 1

To Ana

CONTENTS

PREFACE

I moved from Europe to the United States a few months before the euro became the common money of eleven proud, old, nation states. I returned to work in the *Financial Times*'s London office in January 2009, shortly before the single currency was hit by a crisis that was dramatic in its own right and would be turned into an existential one by a series of tragic policy mistakes. If I had felt a little twinge of sadness at watching Europe's grand monetary experiment only from a distance in its first, seemingly successful, decade, I was granted a ringside view of the near-death experience that followed. For five years I wrote the FT's editorials about the eurozone sovereign debt crisis, in the course of which I gained the insights and developed the views that appear in the following pages. (These views, to be clear, should not be attributed to the FT but are mine alone.)

There are many people without whom this book would not have come about.

The most important is my wife Ana Marambio, whose simple question 'Why don't you write your book now?' at a stroke made everything possible. She supported me taking time off work, provided the space that any creative effort requires, and met the inevitable frustrations along the way with the tolerance and patience of a true life partner. I dedicate *Europe's Orphan* to her.

Two colleagues at the FT have been – and continue to be – particularly influential on my thinking and writing. One is David Gardner, who first recruited me to the paper and with whom I had the pleasure and privilege to work very closely in the leader-writing team. I could write at length about David's deep knowledge, exceptional clear-sightedness and beautiful writing, but I will sum it up simply by saying that he taught me what good journalism is. Then there is

Martin Wolf, who is so much more than an economics commentator and with whom every conversation is illuminating. Martin's willingness to engage with my ideas over the years is testimony to both his intellectual open-mindedness and his personal generosity.

I owe a great deal to the FT more broadly, and in particular to Lionel Barber, its editor. Not only did he entrust me with the job of being the paper's economics leader writer during the global financial crisis, but his acquiescence to my going on leave in 2013–14 allowed me to concentrate on the book project. Thanks also to James Lamont, the managing editor, and John Thornhill, the deputy editor, for facilitating my leave. The FT's decision to put me in charge of a new daily economics newsletter upon my return has kept my ideas about the euro sharp. Regular readers of *Martin Sandbu's Free Lunch* will no doubt recognise many of the ideas in the following pages.

Once I had decided to write the book, I had the good fortune that Sophie Lambert from Conville & Walsh wanted to represent me. A wonderful agent, she believed in the project from when it was little more than a sentence-long statement of a provocative idea. She has been the encouraging supporter that makes such a difference for a writer throughout the process – including when, during much of 2014, it seemed the eurozone crisis and any interest in a book about it had become things of the past.

A grant from the Norwegian government's *Finansmarkedsfondet* provided crucial financial support during my book leave, and I want to record my deep gratitude for the help. In the context of this support I gave several presentations to policy communities in Norway, which helped me formulate early ideas. I thank Morten Staude and Birger Vikøren for making this possible, and seminar participants at the Ministry of Finance and Norges Bank for their comments.

The book could not have found a better home than Princeton University Press. Everyone on the publishing team – and it really has the inclusive spirit of a team – has been impeccably professional and helpful. My editor Sarah Caro in particular has been tireless. She edited the first version of the manuscript with that elusive combination of firmness and tact – the book is much better as a result. Caroline Priday, Hannah Paul, Kathleen Cioffi and Andrew DeSio have all helped to bring the project from idea to reality, and then into public consciousness. The great professionalism of Sam Clark and Ellen White at T&T Productions has made the production process smoother than I ever thought it could be.

Dan Devroye, Catherine Fieschi, Philippe Legrain and my FT colleagues Tim Harford, Robin Wigglesworth and Giles Wilkes all read parts of the book and provided great feedback. Princeton also received five anonymous reviews of the manuscript. The reviewers' encouragements and comments made for a greatly improved final text. I am very grateful to everyone who gave their time to reading (sometimes rough) drafts.

I have been fortunate to learn from a large number of people. Among other FT colleagues, I'd like to mention fellow leader writers Chris Cook, Jonathan Ford, Ferdinando Giugliano, Peggy Hollinger and Alison Smith; economics editor Chris Giles; and the fabulous corps of European correspondents including Tony Barber, Anne-Sylvaine Chassany, Kerin Hope, Quentin Peel and Peter Spiegel. It is impossible to list all those who have enhanced my understanding in meetings at the FT or across Europe over the years since the crisis started. But even if I inevitably leave some people out, I would like to thank the politicians, officials, journalists and observers who have shared their views with me and who include Peter Altmeier, Gudmundur Arnason, Jörg Asmussen, Michel Barnier, Bertrand Benoit, Lorenzo Bini-Smaghi, Henrik Bjerre-Nielsen, Claire Brosnan, Marco Buti, José Manuel Campa, Nikos Chrysoloras, Panicos Demetriados, Hugo Dixon, Bertrand Dumont, Matthew Elderfield, Henrik Enderlein, Jonathan Faull, Marcel Fratzscher, Otto Fricke, Vitor Gaspar, Tim Geithner, José Manuel González Páramo, Charles Grant, Megan Greene, Daniel Gros, Ulrike Guérot, Luis de Guindos, Chantal Hughes, Steffen Kampeter, Martin Kotthaus, Bruno Maçães, Neil McMurdo, Nikolaus Meyer-Landrut, Mario Monti, John Mourmouras, Dan Mulhall, Álvaro Nadal, Nikos Nanopoulos, Jon Nicolaisen, Simon Nixon, Michael Noonan, Simon O'Connor, Øystein Olsen, Giorgos Papaconstantinou, Alfredo Pastor, Ken Rogoff, Elena Salgado, Andrea Sangiovanni, Wolfgang Schäuble, Matina Stevis, Jan Strupczewski, Simon Tilford, Jean-Claude Trichet, Shahin Vallée,

Herman Van Rompuy, Nicolas Verón, Norman Walter, Jens Weidmann, Thomas Westphal, Thomas Wieser, Guntram Wolff and Jeromin Zettermeyer.

I am only one of millions who have been transfixed by the eurozone crisis and the increasingly desperate politics of bringing it under control. But my personal vantage point is somewhat rare. There is a sense in which I, born and bred in Norway and a Norwegian citizen, have no dog in this fight. Norway has twice plumped for contented self-disenfranchisement outside the councils where Europe's future is made or unmade – but at least that gives it a claim to impartiality. At the same time, my family ancestry is from what Timothy Snyder calls the European 'Bloodlands'; my mother was born in Poland to a Polish father and a Ukrainian mother, who had met in forced labour in Nazi Germany. That background brings with it a visceral understanding of what European unification – or its failure – means. I know in my bones how much the European project matters.

I did not consciously set out to write a book that combines both attitudes: one of impartiality and one of deep engagement in the European cause. But now that I have finished writing, it looks to me that this is just what the book aspires to. Readers will have to judge if it succeeds.

Europe's Orphan

ONE
A Giant Historic Mistake?

SPINELLI'S PROPOSITION

THE MOST AMBITIOUS VISION of European unity was conceived in circumstances far more inauspicious than those putting it to the test today. The spring of 1941 was Europe's darkest hour, and Hitler's forces looked invincible. The Soviet Union was still allied with Nazi Germany; the United States stood on the sidelines of Europe's war. To believe that Europe might transcend national division would have taken extraordinary faith in humanity – or great naivety – most of all in the camps and prisons that held the opponents and victims of the continent's totalitarian regimes.

Yet at that very moment, in an eighteenth-century jail repurposed by Benito Mussolini on a volcanic rock off the tiny Italian island of Ventotene, Italian anti-Fascist prisoners were composing a programme for the political union of Europe after the Nazis' defeat. One of them was Altiero Spinelli, who would later become a European commissioner, a member of the European Parliament, and leader of the movement for a federal Europe.

In the 'Ventotene Manifesto', scribbled on cigarette paper and smuggled out to resistance movements across Europe, Spinelli and his fellow prisoners dismissed the relevance of old divisions between left and right. After the war, he wrote, the dividing line between the forces of progress and reaction would run right through traditional parties and pit those who aimed to restore the order of national sovereignty against those aspiring to a federated Europe:

> The question which must first be resolved, without which any other progress is mere appearance, is that of the definitive abolition of Europe's division into national sovereign states.

The Ventotene Manifesto did not specifically mention the abolition of national currencies. But of all the efforts to dismantle the
borders erected between the nations of Europe by two hot wars and
one cold, the euro is the most radical answer to Spinelli's call for an
end to the nation state. Rarely if ever has there been a greater voluntary concession of national sovereignty than Europe's Economic and
Monetary Union (EMU), created with the promise of greater prosperity and stability, and a convergence of both status and destiny. There
is no better test for Spinelli's proposition that Europe is best served by
ever closer union than the success or failure of EMU.

In response to the eurozone debt crisis, EMU's leaders have moved
towards sharing yet more sovereignty. They have pooled fiscal resources
in rescue funds for cash-strapped governments; they have centralised
control over policies through the conditions attached to the common
funds; they have handed power over their banks to the European Central Bank. But among ordinary Europeans, these moves have generated
resigned acceptance at best, and fierce rejection at worst, rather than
any Spinelli-like enthusiasm for deeper integration. Many more people
say things are going in the wrong direction in the European Union
(EU) than in the right one. Those who distrust the EU outnumber
those who trust it. Support for the single currency has weakened, as has
Europe's democratic legitimacy. In the euro's most crisis-hit countries,
less than one in four citizens believe that their voice counts in the EU
(the exception is Ireland, where 40 per cent do). Only 14 per cent of
Europeans say they trust political parties; the numbers are the lowest in
the countries worst hit by the eurozone crisis.[1]

The euro was supposed to strengthen the union between European
nation states by allowing the poorer 'peripheral' countries to catch
up with the richer core, increasing prosperity for all, as well as permanently channelling the growing strength of a reunified Germany
into a common European destiny. Instead, the periphery found itself
abandoned by financial markets and fell into an economic black hole.
The call for more German money put Berlin firmly in the driver's seat
of European policymaking. In the rest of Europe, voters, creditors
and debtors alike felt angry and disempowered. Rather than being
the crowning glory of Europe's successful reconciliation, the common

currency came to look more like a millstone around the continent's neck.

Much more is at stake than economic well-being. If a present-day economist had been able to go back in time and warn the Ventotene visionaries that Europe may not be an 'optimal currency area', that would have been the least of their concerns. Seven decades later, Angela Merkel, Germany's chancellor and Europe's most powerful politician, described the euro as a 'community of fate' in the same German parliament building that once housed the Ventotene prisoners' ultimate enemies:

> Nobody should think that another fifty years of peace and prosperity in Europe can be taken for granted. It cannot. This is why I say: if the euro fails, Europe fails. That must not be allowed to pass. We have a historic duty to protect by all means within our reach Europe's work of unification, which our forefathers set in motion more than fifty years ago after centuries of hatred and bloodshed. None of us can foresee the consequences, were we to fail.[2]

It would be naive to think that grand sentiments alone drive our leaders' decisions at times of crisis. But we should not be so cynical as to dismiss all their lofty rhetoric as cheap talk. Consciously or not, echoes of Spinelli's vision resonated through some leaders' minds when they conceded sovereignty to an extent unimaginable only a few years earlier.

The prospect of successful deeper integration in Europe depends not only on the euro's material success but also on a more fundamental fight over its political merit. Tragically, the policies now being pursued, ostensibly to make the euro work better, are grinding away the public support needed to achieve that goal. No pooling of sovereignty can save the euro if its users are left thinking the euro is not worth saving.

Since the crisis, this battle of ideas has been dominated by the sceptics. As the euro's detractors see it, the single currency has already been put to the test and failed. A striking number of the euro's supposed friends have unwittingly strengthened their case.

Vindication of the Sceptics?

Downing Street might seem an unlikely home for European federalism, but in the summer of 2011, David Cameron and George Osborne, the British prime minister and his chancellor, urged their euro area counterparts to 'get a grip' on the economic crisis by moving decisively towards sharing tax revenues and budget powers. If Britain's leaders channelled Spinelli, they did so in plain self-interest: the eurozone sovereign debt crisis was shattering their hopes of an export-led recovery at home. Even so, their intervention gave up a long-held foreign policy tradition of opposing any European configuration of power without the United Kingdom at the top table. Their lack of visible consternation at doing so demonstrates that they truly believed this was necessary for Europe's monetary experiment not to end in disaster. Osborne's pithy diagnosis was that a 'remorseless logic' points from monetary union to fiscal union.[3]

The 'remorseless logic' view is shared by many economists and policymakers, both within the eurozone and outside it. The general claim is that without some way of sharing economic resources, a monetary union is eventually bound to experience financial instability or economic depression, to the point where it will break-up. The broad inspiration for this view is the 'optimum currency area' (OCA) theory pioneered by Robert Mundell (who, interestingly, has strongly supported EMU) half a century ago.[4] The theory compares the benefits of monetary unification to those of using the exchange rate to maintain full employment in the face of economic disturbances. An OCA is a region in which the loss of this tool is outweighed by the gain of having fixed prices between countries. That will be the case when full employment can be achieved to a sufficient degree without exchange rate adjustments, e.g. through price and wage flexibility, easy displacement of workers and/or capital between regions of different economic fortunes, or private or government transfers between countries to insure against idiosyncratic economic disturbances. Those arguing in the OCA vein tend to doubt the presence in the eurozone of the required price/wage flexibility or worker/capital mobility, and therefore conclude that there is a need for some form of 'fiscal union' to cushion against unsynchronised swings in the economy. And for fiscal transfers to be politically acceptable, a 'political union' is also needed to establish shared control over how fiscal transfers are used.[5]

To create the euro without a fiscal transfer mechanism and a political union to govern it was 'a giant historic mistake', Harvard economics professor Kenneth Rogoff has said, and many other prominent commentators have made a similar assessment.[6] Some of those who thought the euro was a bad idea nevertheless take the 'remorseless logic' as a reason to push integration further rather than winding it back. As Martin Wolf puts it, creating the euro 'is the second-worst monetary idea its members are ever likely to have. Breaking it up is the worst.'[7] For hardened eurosceptics, the 'remorseless logic' leads to the opposite conclusion. Seeing deeper integration as either unachievable or as compounding the damage already done, they predict and even encourage the dismantling of the single currency. One of the more eccentric encouragements was a £250,000 prize offered by Lord Wolfson in 2012 for the best proposal to manage an exit from the euro. Others are more serious. A determined group of German academics have made it their cause célèbre to take the eurozone's anti-crisis policies, which they see as covert transfer mechanisms, to the German constitutional court. In the summer of 2015, German finance minister Wolfgang Schäuble broke a taboo by proposing that Greece should 'temporarily' leave the euro if it could not pass the policies its creditors demanded. Most sinister is the rise of fringe parties that make undoing the single currency a main rallying point. In Germany, the new *Alternative für Deutschland* (Alternative for Germany) party won seven seats in the European Parliament in May 2014. The neo-Fascist *Front National* is now France's biggest party. The comedian Beppe Grillo's protest party *Movimento Cinque Stelle* (Five Star Movement) commands up to a quarter of the Italian electorate for its anti-politics and anti-euro platform.

One might have expected those committed to European integration to stand up for the euro's merits against these condemnations. But what is their reply to the sceptics who want the euro gone or diminished? That if the euro fails, Europe fails; that letting the euro disintegrate would do more harm than good. This is true, but in political terms it amounts to a discreet parricide of the euro's founders by their successors. To say we must stick with the euro now that we have come this far, or all hell will break loose, is to say it would have been better not to have set out on this route to begin with. By capitulating to the view that design flaws in the euro caused the crisis, leaders gain a useful decoy for their own unforced policy errors but at the cost of their ability to formulate good policies and of voters' willingness to accept them.

The moves towards closer integration have been justified by the refrain: 'there is no alternative'. Through gritted teeth and holding their noses, political leaders have cajoled stunned electorates and bullied wary parliaments into lending money to crisis-hit neighbours (in creditor states) or accepting the disenfranchising conditions that come with the loans (in debtor states). Voters have been told there is no alternative but catastrophe to the financial rescues that shuffled loans in the hundreds of billions between governments, to draconian policy conditions extracted from the recipients of those loans, to a 'fiscal compact' that enshrines in international law German standards of fiscal discipline, or to new powers for Brussels to tell member states how to organise their economic affairs.

The currency bloc's official agenda is more of the same, even if the will to go through with it waxes and wanes. The road map to 'genuine' economic and monetary union, drawn up by the EU's highest officials at the behest of national leaders, accepts Osborne's remorseless logic in fact if not in name. It envisages, for example, that the single currency will be endowed with 'an appropriate fiscal capacity'. The plans have also endorsed the idea that countries should sign contracts that would legally prevent them from having second thoughts about reform promises, in return for more financial aid. The president of the European Central Bank has called for centralised powers over euro countries' structural economic policies.[8] These are all building blocks of fiscal and political union. But they labour under the paradox of their own justification: that more powers must be unified to fix the damage unification has already wrought. That argument is not only unconvincing, it is also dangerous.

A POLITICS OF BLACKMAIL

Eurosceptics get many things wrong, most of all their inability to imagine that people could ever adopt European as well as national identities. It is as if they do not merely disagree with Spinelli, they cannot even understand him. What eurosceptics lack in imagination, however, they make up for in tactical political instinct from which the supporters of closer union would do well to learn.

The sceptics have long lambasted the EU's centralising trajectory as undemocratic and illegitimate. They charge that the euro rode rough-shod over Europeans' resistance to giving up national sovereignty. European leaders do indeed have a disturbing tendency to harangue their peoples, sometimes through repeated referendums, until they make the right choice. The French approved the Maastricht Treaty with the thinnest of margins; the Danes only voted yes after they first voted no. The 2004 treaty on an EU constitution was rejected by referenda in both France and the Netherlands and had to be repackaged as the Lisbon Treaty (about which the two recalcitrant electorates were not asked to express an opinion).

The charge of illegitimacy is not wholly warranted – there is no authority in Brussels, Strasbourg or Frankfurt that was not vested there by democratic governments accountable to their national electorates. Still, making light of the need for popular consent is now exacting a price. The success of protest movements in many countries reflects a blowback against the political hubris with which European integration was pursued and a reaction against a political class that has presided over economic catastrophe. The former may be stronger in creditor states and the latter in debtor states, but either way, the management of the euro has unplugged classic wellsprings of populist protest.

Swathes of popular opinion object to the governing elite's chosen direction of travel. In creditor Europe, growing fatigue with financial aid is extinguishing the early willingness to help out neighbours in trouble. In debtor Europe, voters are hard put to say whether they resent the subordination to foreigners more than they despise their own political class. But the more that European politics concentrates on how to balance creditors' and debtors' interests, the more the trade-off itself – money from creditor states in return for control over debtor states – is taken for granted. Europe's politicians have almost without noticing it translated an economic conflict between classes (creditors and debtors) into a political conflict between nations. This cannot but undermine the broader solidarity the euro was meant to embody – a term, incidentally, which in the stultifying idiom of EU negotiations has been impoverished into a synonym for 'subsidy'.

As if it were not enough for Europeans to be told they are trapped in an imperfect monetary union that must be fixed, the substance of the alleged fix is the exact opposite of what they were promised when the euro was launched. Deficit countries were offered prosperity and equality with Germany; instead they have faced economic decline, social despair and political disempowerment. The Germans, and their fellow surplus countries, were promised they would never need to subsidise others, and even secured a treaty article they thought out-lawed such subsidies. While the eurozone's rescue policies have largely survived legal challenges, it is clear that both *political* promises have been broken. If Europeans feel betrayed by the euro, it is because everything they are told about it implies that they have been.

This offers anti-European populists and extremists prolific recruiting conditions, while renouncing any positive argument that mainstream political forces could use to counter them. The guardians of the single currency have had nothing to offer beyond trying to beat voters into resignation. But pushing for greater integration on the basis that the first time round we did not try hard enough will erode what solidarity and aspiration to unity remains in Europe. This is not the politics of common purpose; it is the politics of reciprocal blackmail. The logical destination is that the euro's governing elites follow in the direction they are driving their voters, and increasingly question whether monetary union is worth it. The bitterness of the Greek–German stand-off in the summer of 2015 sharply foreshadowed this future of disunity.

To break free from politics of blackmail, the first step must be to correct the misperception that there is no alternative within the euro. Unsettling that view is needed to open up a political space for those who want to achieve greater European unity through genuinely voluntary pursuits of mutual interests and not simply because they have their backs to the wall. That is the purpose of this book.

THE DISOWNED CURRENCY

By arguing that there is no alternative to their policies, lest the euro fails, eurozone leaders have produced a useful decoy for their own mistakes. But since the 'remorseless logic' endorses the notion that the euro was designed with dangerous and unsustainable flaws, these leaders have by the same token relegated their common currency to the status of an inconvenient foundling. Hard to love, quietly wished away by many, and all but impossible to expel, the euro has been disowned by its own kin. The loftiest aspiration Europe seems able to muster for its own creation is that a thorough reform of its character will make something good of it yet. But just as an orphan inconveniently dumped on its relatives arouses resentment and guilt rather than love, an orphaned euro cannot inspire loyalty or affection. Citizens of democratic societies expect to be authors of their collective destiny, not aimless elements of remorseless logic. The more often Europeans are told they have no choice, the more their resentment towards the euro will grow.

This book refutes the claim that there is no alternative, within the euro, to greater transfers of resources and more tightly centralised control over national policy autonomy.[9] It rejects the supposedly remorseless logic as being neither remorseless nor logical. Instead it aims to show that the disastrous political and economic experience of so many eurozone countries was caused by policymakers' entirely avoidable errors. The structure of the euro, as a monetary union without a fiscal union, did not force their hand: they retained alternative policy options that would have had much better results, economically and politically, than the ones they actually pursued. Had leaders made better choices, worries of a currency break-up would never have been awakened.

There are two ways in which the allegedly flawed structure of Europe's monetary union is blamed for a crisis that first erupted in US mortgages. One is its role in creating the crisis: because of their monetary union, so the charge goes, European economies racked up greater risks in the 2000s boom than they would have done had they kept their individual currencies. The other is in how it unfolded: whether or not the euro made a crisis more likely, it stands accused of taking out of policymakers' hands the best tools with which to fight it. Most of the rest of this book is devoted to the latter claim, but first, Chapter 2 addresses the former. It outlines the main ways people argue that the euro sowed the seeds of disaster and concludes that these arguments do not stand up well to scrutiny. Our best guess is that the excessive debt and credit build-ups that have been at the heart of the eurozone's near-death experience would have happened in much the same way without the euro.

In any case – and this is the theme of the rest of the book – the crisis was not preordained to develop the way it did because of the euro's construction. To make this argument, the next part of the book retells the main episodes of the sovereign debt crisis and shows that at key points, eurozone leaders made mistakes not because the euro left them with no alternative, but because of misguided ideas about what was needed – above all the idea that debt restructuring must be avoided at any cost. Chapters 3 and 4 tell the stories of the Greek and Irish sovereign debt panics and the two countries' 'rescues' at the hands of the eurozone. In both cases, the unwillingness to write down debts – of a sovereign in the former case and of private banks in the latter – was a key consideration, which in turn entailed further mistakes, both economic and political. The sanctification of debt into something that must be respected above all else led to unnecessarily severe fiscal consolidations and credit droughts. Politically, it required the suspension of national democratic autonomy.

If the book delves deeply into these two particular experiences, it is because far from being special cases, they set the precedent for broader policies. Chapter 5 explains how the intellectual principles behind the eurozone's approach to Greece and Ireland were generalised to guide policy in 2010–11 towards larger countries and to the currency union as a whole. The result was a disaster: a self-inflicted second recession, a poisoned politics, and a gratuitous existential threat to the euro itself. The costs of these mistakes are still being paid in ongoing economic suffering, political ill will and uncertainty. Chapter 6 tells the story of how the eurozone's leadership redeemed itself in 2012–13, though only very partially, by moving from an abhorrence of sovereign and bank debt restructuring to an embrace of both – from 'bail-out' to 'bail-in'.

The idea that underpins all these chapters is that this move could and should have happened sooner, more fully and more firmly. Chapter 7 offers the reader a dive into the alternative history in which the eurozone did the right thing from the beginning. As a denunciation of past mistakes and an admonition for future policy, it shows that restructurings could have been managed in ways that were as orderly as the bail-outs that actually took place, if not more so, and with much greater fairness. Europe's economic well-being and political health would have been vastly better as a result.

The final part of the book looks ahead. Some of the biggest questions raised by the euro – including its irreversibility (or not) – remain unsettled. Even so, the book's last four chapters aim to offer a modest guide to the future. Where is Europe's currency union headed now? Which course should it stake out? Chapter 8 defines the eurozone's three main economic challenges: completing the shift in policy attitudes from bail-out to bail-in to improve financial stability; vigorously boosting aggregate demand and preventing it from ever becoming so deeply deficient again in the future; and focusing in the long term on productivity rather than obsessing over export competitiveness. Chapter 9 reflects on the political imperative of establishing a coalition among eurozone countries and institutions that can achieve the economic goals just listed and articulate an alternative to the transfers-for-centralised-control paradigm that is driving voters to political extremes. Chapter 10 asks the taboo question that nevertheless matters to the future of Europe: doesn't the United Kingdom belong in the euro?

A book that sets out to refute claims about the euro's inherent flaws risks seeming overly defensive, so Chapter 11 concludes with the positive case for the single currency: reminding us what the euro is good for. The rest of this chapter, meanwhile, briefly tells the story of the euro's birth.

The Overlapping Goals of Monetary Unification

Before taking on the accusations against the euro, we must recall why countries adopted the common currency in the first place. Today, the idea that the euro is fundamentally flawed is so widespread that it is hard to imagine how Europe's old and jealous nations could ever have embarked on history's largest voluntary cessation of sovereignty. It is often said that EMU is the unsustainable product of a single commanding political vision that overruled any misgivings. It would be closer to the truth to say the problem was one of too many distinct (if overlapping) visions.

These overlapping motives have to be understood against the economic upheaval from which Europe was emerging in the late 1980s when, after several aborted attempts, a renewed push for monetary unification was gathering strength. The Bretton Woods system of fixed exchange rates, which had defined monetary stability in the postwar era, had unravelled in the early 1970s, causing lasting trauma to Europe's political economy. In the decades that followed, European finance ministers were on a Sisyphean quest to regain the monetary stability of the Bretton Woods years.

One country did retain its monetary moorings: Germany, whose inflation was low and whose Deutsche Mark became not just an international reserve currency but the political symbol of the West German people's quietly recovered self-confidence. Their central bank, the Bundesbank in Frankfurt, was admired at home, feared abroad and trusted everywhere. Germany's neighbours quickly realised that achieving stability in an economically open world meant they needed to track as closely as possible whatever monetary policy was set in Frankfurt. The alternative was to be forced, whenever financial markets smelled blood and picked off weaker currencies one by one, into serial devaluations and the high inflation and loss of international purchasing power that this produced – unless the Bundesbank itself could be implored to support exchange rates that the markets no longer found credible. Either way, the monetary independence so mourned by the euro's critics today revealed itself in the 1970s and 1980s as little more than the freedom to do what Frankfurt wanted.

Politically intolerable as this was for the rest of Europe, it was from Germany that the decisive impetus for currency union came, a fact often forgotten today in Germany itself. Hans-Dietrich Genscher, West Germany's liberal foreign minister for nearly twenty years, relaunched the momentum for monetary unification after earlier false starts by calling for a single currency in 1988. It may seem ironic today that Genscher's reason for wanting a single currency was to secure economic stability – a shelter from the ravages of fluctuating exchange rates and soaring inflation in many countries. But in light of the push for a single market in financial services – one from which Germany, that fount of surplus savings, stood to benefit significantly – the violent currency swings of the post-Bretton Woods years were a serious obstacle.

Meanwhile, for Germany's partners – France above all – monetary union promised an end to the humiliating inferiority of their own currencies to the Deutsche Mark, the anchor of Europe's financial system which it seemed necessary yet never quite achievable for the others to tie themselves to.

Greece, Spain and Portugal had joined the European Communities (as they were then called) in the 1980s. For these newly restored democracies of southern Europe monetary unification was both a means of exiting a cycle of inflation, depreciation and low productivity growth so as to catch up with their economically more advanced neighbours, and a powerful emblem of their elevation to a higher political status. Their accession to the euro would prove they had joined the ranks of Europe's stable democracies for good, and that any return to their bad old ways – politically or economically – had been institutionally bricked up.

Then the Berlin wall fell, opening the prospect of a truly unified Europe. This did not fundamentally transform the motives for currency unification; rather it updated them. With a reunified Germany, the fear of German dominance – de facto if not intentional; economic if not political – was even stronger than before. A single currency came to be seen as the solution to Europe's old 'German problem' of one country being too big and mighty to be kept in check in a stable balance of powers. For Germany, meanwhile, melding the Deutsche Mark into a larger common currency helped to reconcile its neighbours to reunification. Not that they could really have stopped it. But Genscher and Helmut Kohl, the chancellor, had no desire to undo decades of building a 'European Germany'. Jacques Delors, then European Commission president, once said: 'Kohl sensed his partners' unease. He knew that economic and monetary union gave him an instrument to calm them down. And so he used that instrument.'[10]

A more general political wave also carried the project forward. The European Community was fresh from the success of making good – more or less – on the promise of the 1957 Rome Treaty to create a single market for goods and services. This paved the road for the euro in two important ways. One was the economic logic of complementing the single market with a single currency: 'one market, one money', as the slogan went. The other was political: the achievement of the Single European Act meant that the political momentum for unification – the spirit of Spinelli – was strong.

Neither argument, of course, provided conclusive reasons for replacing national currencies with a single international one. Currency union is not a sine qua non for a prosperous trading relationship – but it does help.[11] Political momentum is also far from self-justifying. The feeling that progress towards an exalted vision is possible does not necessarily mean the vision is one that ought to be pursued.

It would be frivolous to call the euro a lowest common denominator – the extraordinary pooling of sovereignty that currency union involves went beyond the limits of what many would have thought possible. But a common denominator it certainly was (perhaps the highest rather than the lowest). Conversely, no single idea could on its own make a conclusive case for the euro. A reduction in economic volatility does not inspire enthusiasm in the hearts of the average citizen. Nor does the idea of counterbalancing Germany's power in post-cold war Europe. Had the euro not seemed to serve a number of different political imperatives simultaneously, it would never have been born.

A Currency Designed by Economists

It is sometimes said that the euro was a political project that ignored economics. But economic thinking was central to the creation of the euro. The group charged with designing the common currency was made up largely of technocrats. Although it was chaired by Delors, whom no one would mistake for an apolitical bureaucrat, it comprised the governors of the all the EU's national central banks. Central bankers are, of course, political animals, but they also pride themselves on their economic expertise. They were, moreover, the ones with the most to lose from monetary union, since the key function of the national central banks they headed – setting monetary policy – would cease to exist. Though collectively they would regain this power as members of the Governing Council of the common central bank, they would also be left exposed if the project turned out to be a failure. If anyone had an incentive to find reasons against monetary union, it was the Delors committee. Yet its report – the euro's blueprint – ensured that the political motives enumerated above doubled up as genuine economic considerations as well.[12]

The most obvious economic effect of the euro is the elimination of exchange rate fluctuations. Currency volatility has real economic costs. It discourages international trade and investment by making their profitability more uncertain. It makes cross-border financial flows potentially more destabilising. It is in the nature of exchange rates to change violently and excessively. In part this is because, when prices and wages take time to react to changing economic circumstances, exchange rates, which can adjust instantaneously, overcompensate relative to their long-term equilibrium.[13] Double-digit appreciations or depreciations within a period of months are not unusual, and such large, rapid changes in relative prices disrupt the economies that suffer these swings. A sudden shift in relative prices does not have to be enormous before it completely undermines a previously solid business plan. The measures that people can take to shield themselves are costly. Hedging against currency risk – that is, buying insurance against exchange rate swings – adds another cost of doing business, and is in any case only available for short periods or at a high price, especially for the smaller businesses that create the most jobs. Alternatively, businesses can simply avoid activities that are sensitive to exchange rates, but that makes the economy more closed to international trade than it could ideally be. 'One market, one money' was not merely a catchy slogan – it contained a respectable economic logic.

Monetary union also brought the promise of better macroeconomic policy. Since for many, monetary stability in practice required shadowing the Bundesbank, much of Europe was originally bound to a policy that was designed to suit only Germany. A pan-European central bank would instead choose the best policy for all. Moreover, the Delors committee's central bankers – reclaiming collectively some of the power they were to lose individually – ensured that the new European Central Bank (ECB) would inherit the Bundesbank's independence from political control as well as its single-minded focus on keeping inflation at bay. The French had never warmed to the idea of central bank independence and a narrow focus on inflation, but this was the condition set by a German government confronted with grumbles about the currency project at home. And for the countries most plagued by high inflation and volatile exchange rates, German-style monetary stability was attractive in its own right.

It is worth noting in retrospect how workaday these benefits can seem. While monetary union was an enormous political undertaking, the direct economic consequences it promised – in brief, better business conditions through more predictable prices and cheaper credit – were rather pedestrian. These ambitions hardly matched the calibre of the Ventotene Manifesto.

There was, however, one big economic aspiration: that membership of the euro would encourage governments to undertake policies to improve productivity. Competitive devaluation – letting the exchange rate fall to shift demand from other countries' exports to one's own goods and services – would now be a thing of the past. Without resort to this quick fix, it was hoped, laggard economies would be forced to put in place genuine productivity improvements to improve long-term growth, rather than just address slowdowns with temporary demand boosts that did nothing to improve the economy's capacity.

This indirect effect was the only route by which the euro was ever going to solve Europe's real economic problems, which were not at their root monetary. Whether an economy thrives or stagnates in the long run is only partially determined by the currency and monetary regime under which it operates. The desire for more stable exchange rates was an eminently reasonable one, and eliminating volatility took one foot off the brake on the engine of growth. Making the engine run faster was, however, an altogether different thing. By creating better conditions for trade and capital flows, it was hoped that the euro would broaden the opportunity and, over time, intensify the need for its member economies to become more productive.

Misplaced Misgivings

Monetary union obviously presented economic risks as well as opportunities. The euro's founders were far from blind to them, though their vision may be said to have been partial. Not so much because they were unimpressed by OCA theory, which by then had failed to keep up with decades of macroeconomic understanding,[14] but because they were concerned to the point of obsession with the implication of leaving fiscal deficits and debts in the hands of national governments.[15]

Fiscal policy in one economy influences economic activity in the economies it trades with because national aggregate demand fluctuations spill across borders through the trade balance. Capital movements can amplify this interdependence as well as create interdependence on their own. Since investors treat different governments' bonds at least partly as substitutes, one government's decision to alter its borrowing directly influences the cost of credit to others, in addition to any monetary and credit consequences of the aggregate demand repercussions through trade.

As a consequence of these spillovers, uncoordinated fiscal policy is inefficient, since national governments decide their budgets without taking into account the economic costs (or benefits) to other countries. More generally, a lack of coordination makes it difficult for the region as a whole to have the right size of fiscal deficit or surplus. This is not a problem caused by monetary union but a consequence of economic integration generally, though a single currency makes it more important to address. The problem is far more general than suggested by the cliche of a profligate government exporting instability to others. Indeed, imprudently large deficits in one country can be *beneficial* to trading partners whose domestic demand falls short of supply; and insufficient deficits (or excessive surpluses) can cause damage in the same situation. A good case can be made that these two patterns characterise the most significant spillovers in the eurozone's first decade and a half. Before the crisis, public- (and private-) sector deficits in other euro members helped sustain Germany's exports while domestic demand stagnated there; after the crisis, fiscal consolidation by Berlin held back the already sickly aggregate demand in the eurozone as a whole. In the run-up to the euro, however, only the spillovers from excessive deficits were a politically salient concern.[16]

Deficits aside, the *stock* of public debt was a preoccupation in its own right. The fear was that if a state within a monetary union ran into difficulties refinancing a large debt burden, others might prefer to bail it out rather than let it default. Foreshadowing the feeling of blackmail that would sour eurozone politics in 2010, the European Commission warned that in such a situation 'markets cannot be expected to behave as if solidarity across Community Member States were completely ruled out, since concerns for solidarity are integral to the philosophy of the Community'.[17] The unstated assumption – that it would be more pressing for EMU members to show such solidarity than for the rest of the Community (i.e. non-euro EU countries) – is crucial for how events were to unfold. This is a strange assumption, however. No one has ever suggested that in the pre-euro area, 'solidarity' (i.e. subsidies) was the required response to a government having to reduce the real value of its debt by the then commonly used method of printing money. Why was there a greater need for 'solidarity' to help it avoid a debt reduction through default? Here was an unquestioned *moral* premise about monetary union – that the prospect of a member defaulting on its debt should be avoided as a matter of joint responsibility, in a way that a country's inflating away its debt had never been. It would play a big role in the decisions made for Greece in 2010.

Amid the general momentum towards making the single currency a reality, the especial pessimism on these issues was striking.[18] This came above all from Germany, which saw itself as most likely to have to pay for the lax public finance practices of other countries if their deficits threatened stable prices or their debts made them ask for financial aid. Attention was focused disproportionately on the costs of excessively loose policy, to the neglect of the potential harm from excessive tightness. The risks of deficits and debts in the public sector were feared while the risks of those in the private sector were disregarded. The concern was more with financial outcomes themselves than with the deeper economic ailments of which they were the symptoms. All this incoherence would be on vivid display during the crisis.

The proposed solution was single-minded too in its disproportionately legalistic approach, which was to prevent a problem by proscribing it. The Maastricht Treaty was fitted with a prohibition on monetary financing of government budgets as well as the so-called no bail-out clause. The latter was a politically significant misnomer. It prohibits the assumption of a member state's liabilities by others – it makes it illegal, in other words, to treat the obligations of one as the obligations of all after the fact. That still leaves room for voluntary intergovernmental lending, which the eurozone resorted to when the sovereign debt crisis exploded in 2010.

Maastricht also created a 'stability and growth pact' (SGP) of supposedly mandatory public finance conditions to govern a country's entry into the euro and its behaviour once admitted. Among the rules were prohibitions on deficits above 3 per cent and public debt levels above 60 per cent of annual national income. The rules were never applied all that stringently before the crisis. Belgium, Italy and Greece were all admitted with debt levels far above the limit. As for the deficit rule, Greece barely met it thanks to some creative accounting. And Germany of all countries saw to it that the pact was definitively defanged by breaking the deficit ceiling with impunity in 2004. The lesson drawn by Germany's policymaking establishment – as much, perhaps, because of its own violation of the pact as those by others – was that it needed to be more strictly enforced.

As a set of entry criteria, though applied with a great deal of latitude, the SGP did some good in motivating the more incontinent of

Europe's public treasuries to regain a measure of self-control. Before the single currency's 1999 launch, deficits fell, public debt tapered off, and inflation slowed down abruptly in the countries that had been most plagued with these ills of economic mismanagement. The reward, in the form of lower interest rates, followed swiftly. Investors found monetary unification credible, even if many academic experts on OCA theory did not.

Europe's Economic Drift

The disproportionate focus on public finances was understandable, and not just because of German sensitivities. When the single currency was being designed, the public debt stocks of most of its prospective members were on a sharply upward trajectory. In the decade to 1990, their average public debt-to-gross domestic product (GDP) ratio doubled, as Figure 1.1 shows.

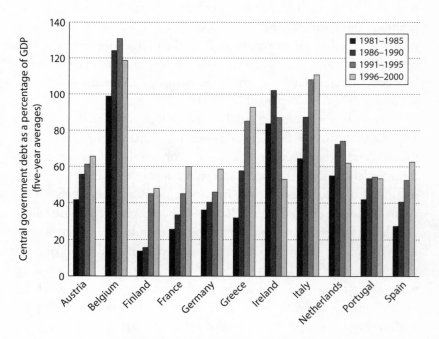

Figure 1.1. The rise of public debt, 1981–2000.
Source: EC Annual Macroeconomic Database.

This development followed the economic earthquakes of the 1970s – the collapse of the Bretton Woods system of fixed exchange rates and Opec's quadrupling of oil prices – which marked the death of the post-war period of monetary stability and fast progress in productivity.[19] In its place came a new era of volatile prices and fitful, unevenly distributed growth. The result was a slow undoing, that is still continuing, of the great levelling that happened during social democracy's heyday in what the French call *les trente glorieuses* – the three decades after the war in which the West rose from the ashes and when, for the first time, all its castes and classes rose together.[20] (See Figures 1.2 and 1.3.) Rather than curing this economic ailment – admittedly no easy task – most European governments indebted themselves much faster than their economies grew in order to fund increasingly expensive welfare states.

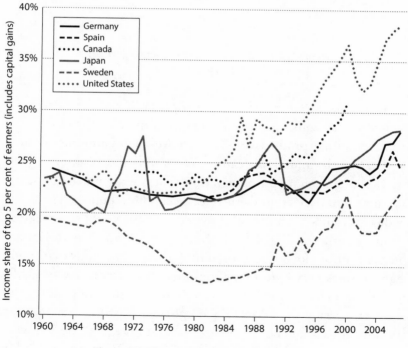

Figure 1.2. The return of income inequality.
Source: World Top Incomes Database.

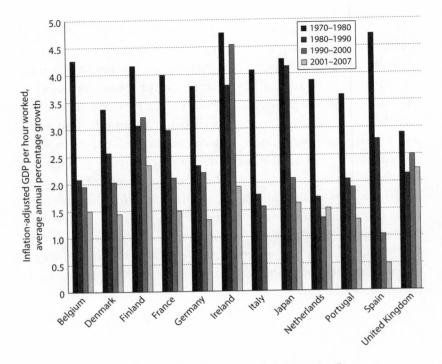

Figure 1.3. Europe's slowing productivity growth.
Source: OECD.

It was clear that maintaining prosperity by rapidly rising state indebtedness could not go on forever. But it is difficult – and can be counterproductive – to remove the symptoms without addressing the underlying causes. What were these causes? Angela Merkel often makes an observation that reveals much about the German mindset around European economic policy: 'If Europe today accounts for just over 7 per cent of the world's population, produces around 25 per cent of global GDP and has to finance 50 per cent of global social spending, then it's obvious that it will have to work very hard to maintain its prosperity and way of life', she likes to say, adding 'All of us have to stop spending more than we earn every year.'[21] Merkel's numbers are striking, suggesting an imbalance that cannot possibly be sustained. 'We do not want a German Europe,' says her finance minister Wolfgang Schäuble, 'but we want a Europe that can compete... [Europe's] strategy aims to overcome imbalances by improving the competitiveness of all eurozone countries.'[22]

Clearly Europe's redistributive systems and public welfare provision are more generous than those in any other region on earth. But that has nothing to do with whether the region is 'competitive' enough against other parts of the world. As Paul Krugman pointed out decades ago, economies are not like companies, for which competitiveness is (or should be) a requirement for profitability, and without which they (should) go out of business. A country does not go 'out of business'. The question is simply: can it offer enough exports to the world for what it wishes to import; or, in financial terms, can it pay its bills.[23]

The eurozone as a whole pays for what it consumes – and then some – and has done since the euro's birth. To think that Europe is not selling enough abroad is to be blinkered by mercantilism. And even in countries that did live beyond their means during the boom and were struck by the sovereign debt crisis when it stopped, loss of export competitiveness was not the central factor it is often made out to be, as Chapter 2 will show.

If Europe's social model is under economic pressure, it is not because of 'competitiveness'. Rather, it is because of productivity – how much each hour of labour or each unit of capital produces in absolute terms, regardless of whether it is more or less than other countries. European productivity is not keeping up with the cost of welfare states having to respond to ageing and costlier medical provision. The productivity predicament is not confined to the old world – in the United States, too, productivity has slowed sharply since the 1970s and only temporarily rebounded in the 1990s. The response to this situation of trying to maintain living standards with the aid of debt has been broadly shared too, as Raghuram Rajan has persuasively argued.[24] The United States also applied the credit card palliative, trying to make the fruits of prosperity available even if prosperity itself was elusive. The main difference with Europe lay in who was using the credit cards. In Europe, it was governments that increased their borrowing from the 1980s on, and several had not kicked the habit before the global financial crisis hit. In the United States, policies encouraged the private sector to do the same, particularly in the 2000s through ballooning mortgage debt used to fund living standards that borrowers could not actually afford.[25] Some European countries followed the US example. Instead of old-style government deficit spending (which, however, persisted in Greece and to a lesser extent elsewhere), the Spanish and Irish economies, for example, were inflated through private credit bubbles.

The euro had the great misfortune of being born into the greatest private credit bubble of all time. This made it possible for the eurozone economies to postpone their reckoning with accumulated public debts and to allow new private debt mountains to build up. Later, it also afforded them a *post hoc ergo propter hoc* argument: blaming the euro for their mess. But rather than being a consequence of monetary union, Europe's credit binge was merely the local outbreak of a global disease: an unholy bargain between governments and financial markets to enjoy credit-driven but unsustainable growth – from the United States and the United Kingdom to Iceland, Spain and Greece.[26] The next chapter explains why the single currency should not be held responsible.

TWO
Before the Fall

A Honeymoon for the Single Currency

Notwithstanding the pre-euro misgivings, for a blissful decade the magic was working. The doubts hovering over the marriage between eleven national currencies – which quickly became twelve with the addition of the Greek drachma in 2001 – gave way to a honeymoon period.

Germany got the stability it wanted: from the single currency's birth until financial market turbulence started in 2007, euro-zone-wide inflation averaged 2.05 per cent, barely above the 'below but close to 2 per cent' the ECB set as its target. The other countries got their longed-for monetary policy parity with Germany, symbolised in France's case by its successful battle to install French central bank governor Jean-Claude Trichet as president of the ECB after a truncated inaugural term for Dutchman Wim Duisenberg.

For most of Europe, the 2000s were good economic times. After initial gripes about price gouging when marks, francs and lira were converted into the new coinage, the public's scepticism was soothed by a consumption boom. Growth rates were solid, though no higher on average than in the years preceding the euro's birth. While some economies were expanding fast, others, like Portugal and Italy, flatlined. Economic well-being nonetheless increased markedly in the new monetary union and across Europe as a whole. Jobs became more plentiful – especially in the peripheral catch-up nations – and unemployment dropped. Even if growth did not necessarily accelerate after the national currencies were welded together, people made the most – and then some – of what growth there was. Consumption (and often investment) in most countries was growing faster than before – sometimes much faster. However cool citizens

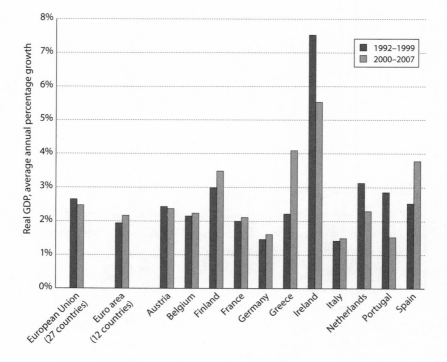

Figure 2.1. GDP growth before and under the euro.
Source: EC Annual Macroeconomic Database.

had been toward the euro beforehand, it was now summertime, and the living was easy. (See Figures 2.1 and 2.2.)

Too easy, as is now clear. The fact that in many countries consumption was accelerating even if income was not proves that their booms were bought on credit, just like that of the United States and many non-euro countries within Europe. But a boom does not feel less good for being debt-fuelled, and it temporarily shielded the single currency from any serious recriminations from the public. As for the elites, self-congratulation was the order of the day. In light of what was to come, Trichet's celebratory speech for the euro's tenth anniversary in January 2009 today sounds naive:

In recent months we have seen another benefit of the euro: the financial crisis is demonstrating that in turbulent financial waters it is better to be on a large, solid and steady ship rather than on a small

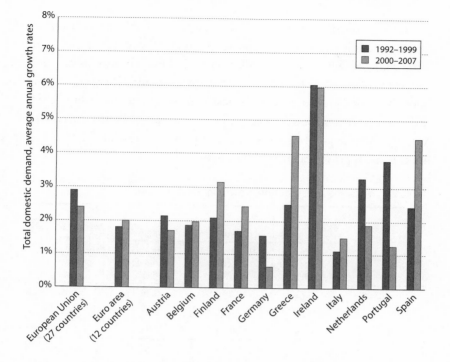

Figure 2.2. Domestic demand before and under the euro.
Source: EC Annual Macroeconomic Database.

vessel. Would Europe have been able to act as swiftly, decisively and coherently if we did not have the single currency uniting us? Would we have been able to protect many separate national currencies from the fallout of the financial crisis?[1]

The best times, however, eluded one important country. Germany entered the euro in a state of economic malaise, burdened by high unemployment and the cost of reunification. In the early 2000s, a social democratic chancellor, Gerhard Schröder, pushed through the 'Hartz plan' that shook up the labour market with reforms that are today used as an example of what the crisis-hit countries need to do. The truth is more complex: decentralised bargaining and deunionisation prepared the ground for the Hartz reforms to boost economic activity.[2] German growth benefited from the tailwinds of a favourable international economy, and the increasingly flexible labour market encouraged businesses to hire. The result was faster growth on the back of rising exports. But the weakening of workers' protections also changed what sort of work was available. Job growth came in the form of precarious and part-time employment. There were more jobs, but their greater precariousness kept wages down. Adjusted for inflation, German hourly wages did not rise at all in the euro's first decade.[3] While good times were rolling over the rest of Europe, German consumption was turgid (see Table 2.1).

Table 2.1. Wage and consumption growth in Germany.

	Average annual growth in real daily wages			Average annual growth in consumption per capita (%)
	Tradable manufacturing (%)	Non-tradable sectors (%)	Tradable services (%)	
1995–1999	0.73	0.10	0.46	1.49
1999–2003	0.96	0.00	0.47	1.00
2003–2007	0.28	–1.13	–1.23	0.60

Source: Dustmann et al., Journal of Economic Perspectives 28(1): 167–88 (Table A2).

Since German workers were not benefitting from this export boom in terms of higher wages, where did the profits end up? They were largely salted down in German banks, which found few better uses for their increased funds than lending them out abroad. German wage repression, then, was an important source of the credit flows that were soon to destabilise the newly minted currency union. Germany's trade surplus with the rest of the eurozone ballooned as workers' consumption stagnated, while trading partners, drenched in credit, imported Mercedes cars like never before.

THE EURO AND THE GENESIS OF THE CRISIS

Most of this book is devoted to refuting the claim that the euro tied policymakers' hands so that they could not properly handle the financial crisis. Monetary union undeniably shaped the form the crisis would eventually take, but it is simply not true that the euro was either a straitjacket or a burning house whose owners had thrown away the key, both metaphors that are frequently thrown around in the policy debate.

In this chapter my aim is the more limited one of suggesting that the euro played at most a minor role in how the crisis arose in the first place. There is a widely shared view that the structure of the monetary union made a crisis more likely. The factors invoked to blame the euro include the destabilising effect of a single interest rate for the entire eurozone; the misalignment of real exchange rates when nominal exchange rates could no longer adjust; the ability to run current account deficits that were too large and lasted too long; and, finally, the fact that debt was accumulated in a currency that could not be printed at will by national central banks. In what follows, I argue that all these factors have been commonly misunderstood. In each case, either the supposed problem is less of a problem than is often thought or it would have been just as likely to occur without the euro.

One Size Fits None

In August 2012, with Spain heading into a second recession, the socialist deputy Francisco González Cabaña wrote the following on his blog:

> For a while now we Spaniards have got used to living with the *prima de riesgo* [risk premium] which has, from being a complete unknown, turned into our daily bread. Its rises, its falls, its effects on our everyday life have become the daily concern of our conversations.[4]

The Spanish were not unique in their newfound appreciation of capital markets. In Ireland in late 2010, one would not be surprised to overhear conversations about bond spreads between people that nobody would mistake for finance professionals. Throughout Europe's crisis-hit periphery, financial sophistication was spreading almost as fast as the market fluctuations to which people now gave the attention they normally reserve for things on which their lives – or in this case, their livelihoods – depended.

Before the unthinkable happened and financial markets closed their doors on one European state treasury after another, these spreads and risk premia had been a non-issue. Not only had they not imposed themselves on the consciousness of ordinary citizens, they had as good as disappeared from financial markets themselves. In the euro's early years, sovereign spreads narrowed to vanishing point. For the first time, the government in Athens was paying the same rate to borrow as that in Berlin. (See Figure 2.3.)

Early on, this was taken to be a good thing. With the euro, other countries saw Germany's credibility rub off on themselves. Today, it is seen as a problem. The euro is accused of artificially engineering a 'one-size-fits-all' interest rate for countries that differ in the monetary conditions that their specific circumstances call for. In a simple mechanical sense, this is true. The ECB sets a single set of policy interest rates to keep average inflation across the eurozone under control. But average price stability camouflages the widely varying inflation rates in the national economies of the eurozone. Only Belgium saw its prices rise at about the eurozone average pace. France averaged a 1.78 per cent annual rate in the pre-crisis euro years (from its inception up to December 2007); Germany's rate was 1.57 per cent. Austria and Finland recorded similar below-average rates. In the periphery, meanwhile, prices leapt ahead. Italy's average pre-crisis euro inflation was 2.3 per cent, while Greece and Ireland recorded 3.4 per cent and Portugal and Spain were not far behind.

Unless the business cycles of member economies are perfectly synchronised, the common ECB rate is not what each of the national central banks might ideally have chosen as most appropriate for their domestic economy. Academic research suggests that ECB interest rates during the boom were generally appropriate for European core economies on average, which means they were somewhat too tight for Germany and far too lax for the periphery.[5]

Such a mismatch between the common rate and local conditions may have been increasingly destabilising over time. In a country at the height of its economic cycle (such as Spain), an insufficiently high interest rate makes inflation rise, which lowers the *real* interest rate even further. (The real interest rate adjusts for the way inflation

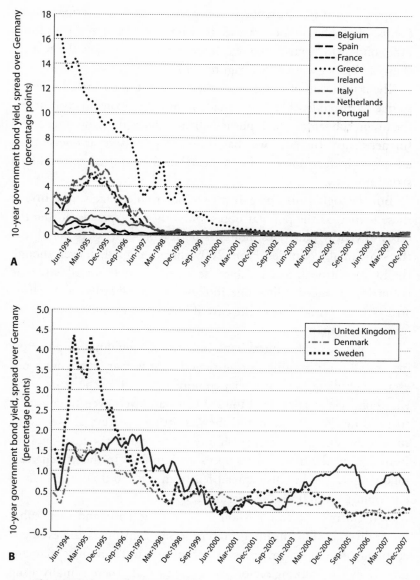

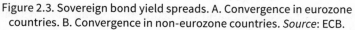

Figure 2.3. Sovereign bond yield spreads. A. Convergence in eurozone countries. B. Convergence in non-eurozone countries. *Source*: ECB.

erodes the purchasing power of the borrowed amount by the time it is repaid.) That reinforces the original boom by encouraging yet more credit-driven spending. Conversely, in an economy that is depressed compared with the currency union average (such as Germany), the excessively high common rate leads to lower demand and thus lower inflation – which raises the real interest rate and makes the relative sluggishness yet worse.[6] (See Figure 2.4.)

The unification of monetary policy, this critique concludes, was a source of instability because it made nominal borrowing costs across the union the same, which pushed already-diverging economic cycles further apart. The euro was based on the premise that one size fits all, when in fact one size fits none. That does indeed sound like a structural flaw.

But the logic runs up against two inconvenient facts. The first of these is that, as the popular obsession with yield spreads during the crisis so vividly illustrates, nominal borrowing costs were *not* always the same in all countries. From 2009 spreads exploded, even though the ECB continued to set a single set of policy rates for all eurozone countries. A one-size-fits-none interest rate can hardly be a self-destructive structural flaw of the euro if interest rates can as a matter of fact come in many sizes.

If having a single central bank interest rate could not stop borrowing costs from diverging during the crisis, it was arguably not a necessary ingredient in their earlier compression. Before the crisis, sovereign bond yields converged toward German levels even in countries that did not join the euro and showed little indication of ever doing so. The average spread of British interest rates over German ones fell from 2.32 in the fifteen years up to 1998 to 0.48 in the fifteen years following it. The Swedish spread fell from 2.88 to 0.20; the Danish one from 2.34 to 0.21. (See Figure 2.3.)

What drove the compression in borrowing costs and their subsequent divergence? Non-financial businesses, consumers and even governments do not borrow money at central bank's main refinancing rate. Only the banking sector has access to that. There is many a slip between central bank cup and real economy lip, and the rates paid by end borrowers vary with the willingness and ability of private lenders to extend credit to them. The internal workings of financial intermediaries such as banks, and the policies and regulations that govern this intermediation, matter as much as monetary policy decisions.

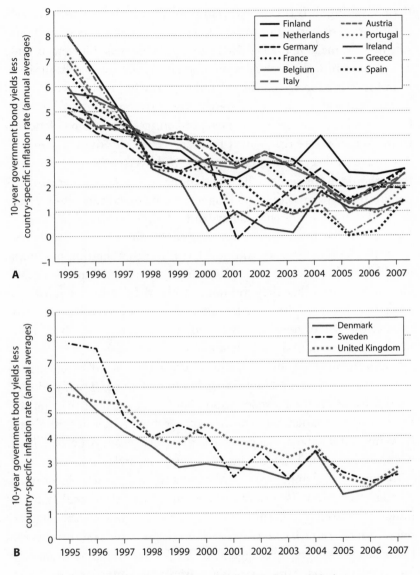

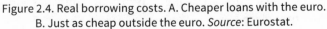

Figure 2.4. Real borrowing costs. A. Cheaper loans with the euro.
B. Just as cheap outside the euro. *Source*: Eurostat.

From the late 1990s, banks and other financial institutions throughout the world – not just in the eurozone – engaged in an enormous
ramp-up of lending which governments did little to restrain. More

than anything, it is this global credit bubble that is to blame for the compression of borrowing costs everywhere, inside the euro and outside it. If financial markets priced a loan to Athens as if it were as safe as one to Berlin, this was because financial actors got caught up in a hunt for returns in which they abandoned any sensitivity to risk.

The euro is sometimes blamed for this because it removed Greece's ability to devalue, thus protecting international lenders from exchange rate risk. But if markets' generosity towards Greece did indeed reflect a rational response to lower exchange rate risk, they should have reacted just as rationally to the greater risk of default once Athens could no longer print its own money to service debt. That means they should have differentiated between high-debt, high-deficit borrowers like Athens and medium-debt, low-deficit ones like Berlin. But they did not. Claiming that lending practices would have been less reckless without the euro attributes a rationality to investors that they did not actually display in the eurozone or elsewhere. Their irrational exuberance would have led them to neglect the risk of devaluation outside of the euro as surely as they neglected the risk of default inside of it.

Euro membership did not remove the ability of policymakers to rein in these excesses, despite what is often claimed. True, national central banks in the currency union could not set their own policy rates to offset market exuberance, but we should be sceptical about how much monetary independence there ever was to be had in a world of free capital movements. Academic research shows that even with floating exchange rates, smaller central banks track bigger ones to a surprisingly large extent[7] and financial cycles in smaller economies are strongly determined by monetary policy in the biggest ones.[8] Small countries' freedom to use central bank rates to smooth financial cycles is greatly exaggerated. The ineffectiveness of monetary independence was, after all, a big reason why countries joined the euro in the first place.

Moreover, national authorities have tools other than the official interest rate for restraining credit. Nothing in the euro's structure would have stopped Irish and Spanish authorities from limiting lending by banks headquartered in their countries, had they wished to do so. They could have imposed heavier capital requirements or stricter collateral policies, made bankruptcy laws more favourable to debtors, even taxed banks in proportion to their overreach. Lending by foreign-based banks could have been addressed by rules on resident borrowers: it was entirely possible for national authorities to pass laws limiting how detached mortgages could become from incomes or historical house prices, for example. And it goes without saying that profligate governments like Greece's could have chosen to borrow less, and seemingly prudent ones like Spain's and Ireland's could have saved even more to offset private sector overborrowing. In short, there were plenty of tools available to control the credit bubble.[9] The eurozone's more sluggish economies, for which the ECB policy rate felt too tight, could have used national policy measures to loosen credit conditions to stimulate demand. To blame the euro's design for the mispricing of credit is to dress up national failings as national impotence.

THE 'EXPORT COMPETITIVENESS' CONUNDRUM

If it is wrong to blame the euro for the compression in borrowing costs, the compression nonetheless happened. And since governments failed to use the available policy tools to moderate the divergent economic cycles, inflation rates consistently differed between countries, as discussed above. The fact that prices in peripheral economies outpaced those in the core has been taken to show that the euro generates 'competitiveness' problems. When countries that had little tradition of cost discipline were welded to countries that had a lot of it – above all Germany, which put that experience to use with the Hartz reforms – it had to go wrong, or so the argument goes. It is an argument that comes in different versions, with different moral tinges. Some blame the dissolute countries of the periphery for neglecting the cost competitiveness of their exports, pricing themselves out of global markets. Others put the onus on Germany for undercutting the rest of the eurozone through policies that held wages down when competitors could no longer respond by devaluing. Either way, the euro gets blamed for divergences in export competitiveness because the nominal exchange rate can no longer offset them.

Countless charts of how real exchange rates and labour costs diverged after the introduction of the euro have been used to illustrate this export competitiveness argument. The real exchange rate measures how much goods and services cost in one country compared with another, taking into account both the prices in local currency and the nominal exchange rate. Inside the euro, of course, the nominal exchange rate becomes irrelevant – a euro is a euro – and only relative local price levels matter. Compared with trading partners outside of the eurozone, the real exchange rate is affected by the euro's moves against other currencies. As Figure 2.5 shows, the real exchange rates of the peripheral countries took off relative to the core during the boom.

It is important to note, however, that higher price and wage inflation in the periphery is not necessarily bad. The poorer members of the euro were those with the greatest potential for catching up economically – indeed it was hoped that the euro would help bring this about. If tighter economic integration resulting from the euro led to increased productivity in traded goods and services, and more so in the poorer countries than in the more mature economies, then one would expect to see higher inflation in the former than in the latter for entirely benign reasons. Economists call this the Balassa–Samuelson effect, according to which productivity gains in the traded sector (whose prices are largely set in international markets) push up prices, wages and investment returns in the non-traded sector too, as the gains are spent across the economy. The result would be higher economy-wide inflation rates in the growth period, but rather than signs of trouble these could be the marks of success.[10]

This benign interpretation would only be warranted, however, if the higher wages were really paid for by greater economic output per worker or per hour of work. This was not the case. Where prices and wages rose the most, they also grew faster than productivity. This is clear in the evolution of unit labour costs. The unit labour cost is how much an individual company, industry or entire country pays the labour engaged in producing one unit of the output in question. At the industry level, for example, one can measure the unit labour cost in car manufacturing, which would be the total wage bill for the labour involved in making a single car. When calculated for the

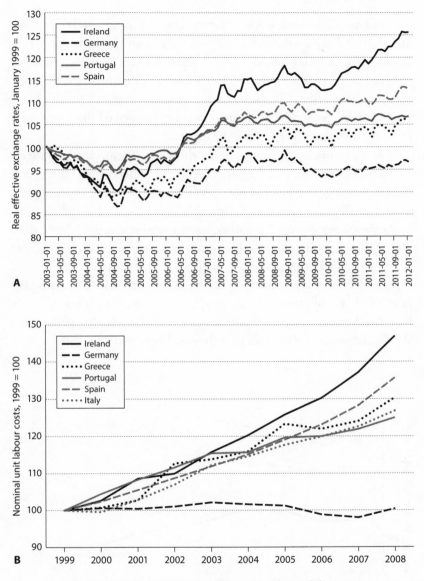

Figure 2.5. A. Real effective exchange rates. B. Unit labour costs.
Sources: A, Bank for International Settlements via St. Louis Fed; B, OECD.

whole economy, it is defined as the wage costs spent in producing one
unit of aggregate real economic output: a euro-worth of inflation-adjusted GDP.[11]

As Figure 2.5 shows, the unit labour costs of Greece, Ireland, Spain and Portugal diverged dramatically from Germany's in the euro's first decade. This is often taken to mean that workers in these countries received wage increases far beyond what could be justified by more efficient production. The euro's critics conclude that, as a result of this, the exporting sectors in the periphery countries priced themselves out of foreign markets by the time the crisis hit.

But this conclusion does not fit the facts. While the peripheral countries' economy-wide labour costs did indeed rise, there was nothing wrong with their export performance. Greece's exports grew as fast during the boom as Germany's; Spain's and Ireland's as fast as Austria's. As Figure 2.6 shows, each periphery country's share of global merchandise exports was roughly the same in 2007 as it was in 2000 (with the exception of Ireland, which was shifting toward a more service-based economy at the time). Spain's and Portugal's market shares slipped a little, but that was because their exports happened to be concentrated in sectors and markets that grew more slowly. Adjusting for the fact that they had been dealt a worse hand in

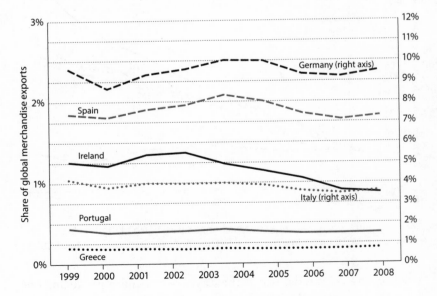

Figure 2.6. The periphery's export performance.
Source: EC Annual Macroeconomic Database.

terms of what they exported, these two countries actually held on to market share better than Germany.[12]

So there is simply no sign of an export underperformance in the periphery's traded goods sectors. How can this be reconciled with the steep growth in unit labour costs? The answer is, by measuring them separately for the sectors that produce traded goods and services (manufactures and such services as tourism, for example) and those that are not traded (such as public services and construction). Doing this reveals that the traded sectors of the peripheral economies did not in general experience excessive inflation. The cost increases blamed for these countries' supposedly poor export performance occurred in activities that are not sold abroad at all. Blaming the euro for deteriorating export competitiveness in the periphery is to blame it for a problem that did not occur.

THE EURO'S LOPSIDED CAPITAL FLOWS

What did occur was that wages and prices in the public and non-traded sectors went up very fast in the periphery. This was, however, a symptom not a cause. It reflected a borrowing binge to pay for imports, not a withering away of exports.

The eurozone as a whole was neither a net importer nor a net exporter in the boom years. Even if a global net capital glut from China and commodity-producing countries inundated the world economy in the early 2000s, capital flows in and out of the eurozone were roughly matched; on a net basis, Europeans lent largely to one another. But within the eurozone, it mattered hugely who lent to whom. Money flowed from the hard-saving core of the monetary union – above all Germany, but also the Netherlands, Austria and Finland – largely but not solely to the union's poorest member states. German savings and Dutch North Sea gas windfalls were being recycled into Greek and Portuguese consumption and Irish and Spanish housebuilding. (Italy, it is often forgotten, was no longer living much beyond its means, but its past history of doing so meant that its budget surpluses before interest expenses were more than eaten up by debt service.)

It was not simply that the euro inaugurated a shopping spree for imported goods. In several periphery countries, the increased borrowing in the 2000s replaced steep losses of foreign income in the 1990s. In 1990, Ireland, Greece and Portugal received more than 5 per cent of their national income in transfers and remittances from abroad. By the time the euro was introduced, these were drying up. Rather than adjusting to this one-off fall in purchasing power, the extraordinary financial loosening that happened at the same time as the euro came into being allowed the countries to stave off a reckoning by substituting foreign credits for the lost income. While net trade balances (exports minus imports) deteriorated somewhat, much of the borrowing took place simply to maintain pre-existing trade deficits to which the countries were accustomed.

This borrowing showed up in increasingly lopsided current account balances. A country's current account measures the difference between the resources it produces every year and those it uses to consume or invest – it is the best measure of whether an entire economy is living within its means. Current account deficits need to be financed by foreign capital (or by running down foreign savings). But the capital flows that cover the deficit can take place entirely between private hands. That was largely the case everywhere in the eurozone except Greece, whose government continued to run substantial deficits throughout the boom to fund public sector wage and pension increases.

The largest current account deficits, and thus the most cross-border loans, were racked up by Greece, Cyprus, Portugal, Spain and Ireland, in that order. (See Figure 2.7.) It is no coincidence that these were the countries that ended up receiving eurozone rescue loans. What they had in common was not excessive public borrowing but large-scale borrowing by the economy as a whole. (See Figure 2.8.) Public finance numbers were therefore a poor guide to the risk posed by excessive credit flows. Madrid and Dublin, two of the sovereign borrowers worst affected by the subsequent market panic, ran smaller deficits and had less debt than Berlin. Even if Germany and France had not rendered it toothless in 2004, the stability and growth pact would not have sounded the alarm about Spain or Ireland.

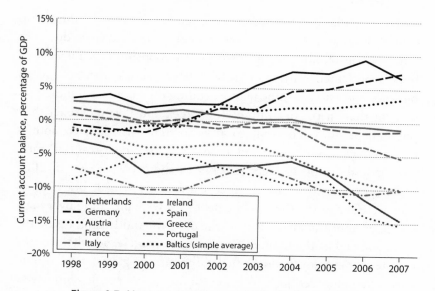

Figure 2.7. Macroeconomic asymmetries in the eurozone.
Source: Eurostat.

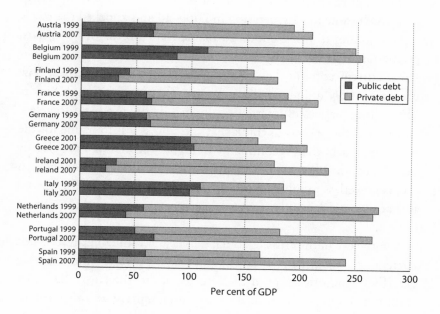

Figure 2.8. Private debt bubbles.
Source: Eurostat.

The fact that private credit accounted for most of the intra-euro capital flows and that some governments borrowed little does not, however, mean public finances were run responsibly. The huge credit bubble presented Europe's highly indebted states with a windfall, but they chose to consume it away, ending the boom with more public debt than at the beginning. The Greek and Portuguese let their public debt stocks continue to grow in step with their economies or faster. Even Germany and France let their debt-to-GDP ratio rise from about 60 per cent in 1999 to about 65 per cent in 2007. Other governments looked superficially more frugal, but even as they were shrinking their public debt they were presiding over huge increases in private debt. This is true of Spain and Ireland inside the eurozone and of the United Kingdom outside it. And wherever the private sector enjoyed a debt-fuelled boom, the government should have taken more seriously its responsibility to counter it aggressively. Surpluses should have been built up in good times to cushion the blow when the economic cycle turned.

Here lies the main cause of the eurozone crisis: huge flows of capital, which came to a sudden stop in 2009–10 and knocked the receiving economies to the ground. To blame the euro for this, we must presuppose that the credit flows would have been smaller without it. Large current account deficits and balance-of-payments crises, however, are hardly unique to the eurozone. They recur through history like visiting plagues of internationally mobile finance. And there are two important reasons to think that the euro is less to blame for the build-up of debt than is commonly thought. The first we have already mentioned: membership of the single currency did not render governments powerless to mitigate or influence the credit flows. The second is that very similar build-ups of debt happened outside the eurozone as well.

On the eve of the crisis, Estonia, Latvia and Lithuania all recorded current account deficits as large as Greece's; Bulgaria's was even bigger. These countries pegged their currencies to the euro (the Baltic countries have now adopted it), but gaping current account deficits could also be found in Iceland and Turkey, which did not. Since huge capital flows into these countries happened without euro membership, there is little reason to think things would have been different for the peripheral euro members if they had stayed out. One could argue that it was a mistake for non-euro countries to fix their currency to the euro. But if that is so, it is a mistake that the hypothetically non-euro Greece, Ireland or Portugal would have been equally likely to make. The same reasons that made these countries join the euro in the first place would have motivated them to peg to it (or to the Deutsche Mark if the euro had never seen the light of day) as their second-best alternative. And in any case, capital rushed into floating-rate countries as well.

It is likely, therefore, that the countries that borrowed too much inside the euro would have acted in much the same way had they been outside it. Consider this thought experiment: if Greece had not been a member of the euro, would markets not have offered it cheap finance? Given how lenders were throwing money at American house-buyers with no income, or Icelandic banks with no investment record, it is hard to believe that they would, uncharacteristically, have had qualms about lending to a European government with no continence (or to the country's local banks, which in turn could have funded the government). With or without the euro, cheap money would have been as available to the eurozone rim states as it actually was for countries outside of the euro. Easy credit reflected the global desire of money managers to shift enormous amounts of capital out of the world's economic centres, not the composition or even the existence of Europe's monetary union.

Besides, we should qualify how much of a problem current account 'imbalances' are. When investors estimate risks responsibly, monetary unification probably does encourage money managers to invest across borders in greater amounts and at lower rates than they would if national currencies persisted. But if the risks are indeed responsibly estimated, large capital flows need not be a bad thing. The word 'imbalance' implies something that cannot be sustained. But current account deficits that fund productive investments are a tool for economic catch-up and growth, which make debts easier to service and balance-of-payments crises less likely. 'Asymmetries' is a more neutral, and better, word.

In an integrated regional economy like Europe's, it is improbable that every country is able to offer just the right investment opportunities to match the country's own savings. Countries that want to save more than they invest need to find a productive outlet for their savings. Countries that can productively invest more than they are willing or able to save must find funds from the outside. And so long as the funds that flow across borders are invested well, such flows can benefit lenders and borrowers alike. Indeed, large asymmetries are not only compatible with efficient economic development but they can be vital for making it happen: Norway's current account deficit reached 14 per cent of GDP in the late 1970s, but the capital it imported enabled it to build up one of the world's largest oil industries.

That is why the goal of lifting the constraint on poorer European countries' balance of payments was the right one – even if the constraint returned with a vengeance in the crisis. Allowing capital to shift more easily between countries was the point. Faster development of the periphery thanks to excess savings from the core was the promise of the euro. If the promise failed, it was not because of the credit flows themselves but the use to which they were put. In Spain and Ireland they financed housing projects that would never be worth what was spent on them; in Greece, Portugal and Cyprus they were not invested at all but rather squandered on public spending that felt good while it lasted but produced no permanent benefit. The result was that one part of the eurozone sank with frightening speed into grotesque levels of indebtedness to another part, centred on Germany and other northern members.

The form of capital flows matters as well how they are invested. Why did Bulgaria, which ran up larger current account deficits in the 2000s than Greece, exit its crisis swiftly, whereas Greece remained in crisis in 2015? A good case can be made that it was because Bulgaria's foreign financing largely took the form of foreign direct (equity) investment rather than bank loans or bond sales. Since this form of capital exposes the investor more directly to the failure or success of the investment, it may have encouraged better investment of the proceeds. But even if it did not, it made a sudden stop more manageable. Since equity investors, unlike creditors, cannot demand their money back, a balance-of-payments crisis puts less of a squeeze on an economy that has funded itself with equity rather than debt flows.[13] A similar point can be made about much of central and eastern Europe, whose capital inflows largely came as private capital between headquarters and local subsidiaries of foreign banks. These banks could manage the crisis in less disruptive ways than a panicked bond market.[14]

The failure to channel funds to productive uses during the boom, or even to encourage safer forms of capital than debt, was not unique to the eurozone. There, like elsewhere, it resulted from the meeting of reckless borrowers with irresponsible lenders in a collective haze of punch-drunk optimism, blessed by poor national policies for resource allocation. To blame this on monetary unification is a backhanded compliment if ever there was one: it assumes far too much about what a currency regime by itself determines. The responsibility remains with national governments, which could have directed the capital to productive investments but failed to do so.

Losing the Printing Press

Even if unsustainable capital flows would have been just as likely without the euro, there is one more argument to be addressed about why a common currency may have exacerbated the risk of balance-of-payments crises. Governments tend to borrow at relatively short maturities (5–6 years on average) and roll over loans when they fall due. But if creditors, for whatever reason, refuse to refinance, they can push even a solvent but illiquid borrower into default – and the fear of this happening can justify their refusal to refinance in the first place. The likelihood of such self-fulfilling defaults may depend on the currency regime. A sovereign borrower with its own currency, the argument goes, always has the whip hand against creditors, because it can print money to honour any payment due. Therefore, it cannot be forced into a default by a self-fulfilling run on government debt in which panicked investors refuse to roll over loans. If, however, the ability to repay depends on access to hard currency, the borrower's credit-worthiness erodes when that access, rightly or wrongly, is in doubt. There is evidence that eurozone membership – which means giving up the printing press – increases the scope for such bad self-fulfilling outcomes.[15]

I will discuss in later chapters how the sovereign debt crisis was shaped by the inability of sovereign debtors to print money to service their obligations. Here I would like to make three points.

First, that the disadvantage of giving up the domestic printing press is not as stark is it is sometimes claimed. Even a government that can print money to service its debt must weigh the relative benefit of doing so over defaulting on creditors, and the political costs of the exchange rate and inflation fallout that could ensue from debt mon-etisation might outweigh the costs of default. When this is the case, self-fulfilling runs on sovereign debt are possible even when that debt is issued in a currency the government can print at will. Sovereign default on such domestic debt is, after all, a common occurrence.[16]

Second, giving up the printing press was a large part of the euro's attraction for the previously high-interest, high-inflation countries. Part of their goal was precisely to reassure foreign lenders that they would not print their way out of debt any more. One may argue that this was a mistake. But given these countries' evident desire to trade the money press for Germanic monetary stability, it is likely that they would have tried to achieve the same outside of the euro by issuing more foreign-currency-denominated debt, as many rich-country gov-ernments already do in modest amounts (Greece, for example, has had small yen-denominated bonds).

Third, in most cases, the excessive debts built up in the boom were private transactions channelled through banks, and the experience of many non-euro countries is that banks borrowed large amounts in foreign currency.[17] If the European periphery countries had stayed out of the euro, foreign-currency-funded banks would have been the biggest buyers of domestic-currency sovereign debt. The possibility of a debt crisis would not, in such a situation, have gone away: it would merely have moved from the public to the private sector, and the ability to print domestic money would not have helped an economy whose banking sector was funding itself in foreign currency. It would have relied on help from foreign central banks to deal with a sudden stop in lending just as much as eurozone economies rely on the ECB.

The Euro's Innocence

To sum up: the four main claims that the euro made a crisis more likely do not hold up to proper scrutiny. First, the compression of borrowing costs may have caused economic cycles to diverge – but the euro can hardly be blamed for this since the same phenomenon happened everywhere, and eurozone governments in any case retained (but neglected) the ability to influence domestic access to credit. Second, prices and wages did develop very differently in the core and the periphery, and nominal exchange rates could not offset this. But this did not really happen in the traded sectors, so the euro cannot be accused of destroying export competitiveness. Third, huge intra-euro capital flows permitted current accounts to develop dangerously large asymmetries and finance unsustainable import binges. But this, too, happened outside the euro as much as inside it. In any case, the real problem is not external financing per se but the form it takes and the uses to which it is put, both of which national governments were in a position to influence. And fourth, while peripheral eurozone economies indebted themselves in a currency their government could not print at will, so did many non-eurozone countries through their banking systems. It is likely that the peripheral economies with the most unstable monetary history would have done the same outside of the single currency. Besides, the ability of such countries to print their way out of debt was as likely as not to itself become a destabilising factor in a balance-of-payment crisis; this is why they had chosen to give it up.

All these arguments are about the *genesis* of the crisis. The euro did, however, undeniably alter the *form* the crisis took and the way it unfolded. So the bigger question to which we must now turn is: did the euro make the crisis worse because it made it harder for policymakers to handle it? The answer is no: the eurozone's lamentable performance in the crisis has little to do with inherent features of the single currency and everything to do with a series of unforced errors by its leaders. To see why, the next part of the book chronicles the crisis, starting in Greece.

THREE
Greece and the Idolatry of Debt

THE PROMISE OF EUROPE

GREECE ONLY MAKES UP one-fiftieth of the eurozone economy. The problems it has caused the monetary union, however, are out of all proportion to its size. Greece is where the sovereign debt crisis started; and at the time of writing it is the one eurozone economy where conflagration again threatens. This is not because Greece is a 'special case', although the problems it faces are uniquely big. It is, on the contrary, because the handling of Greece is emblematic of the principles that have governed the eurozone as a whole since the financial crisis began. That is why a detailed examination of Greece's travails is the right place to start a retelling of Europe's crisis. It reveals just how stubbornly the eurozone has stuck to the goal of trading financial transfers for more centralised power – from the first crisis in early 2010 to the stand-off between Greece and the rest of the eurozone after left-wing radicals won power in Athens in January 2015.

The forerunners of the EU were created in order to secure peace in Europe. But the forms of unification that actually developed were at first largely economic in nature. When the original six members – France, Germany, Italy and the Benelux countries – began to integrate key economic sectors in the 1950s, it was to aid their recovery from the devastation of World War II and to align their commercial interests so as to make economic self-interest inimical to renewed conflict. If the desire to avoid war made the pooling of sovereignty politically possible, the nature of the pooling itself was economic. Commercial logic also motivated the accession of Denmark, Britain and Ireland in 1973.

Greece's entry to the European Economic Community in 1981, seven years after ridding itself of a military junta, marked an important change. It was underlined in short order by Spain and Portugal, which had also emerged from fascist militarism, and again two decades later by post-communist central Europe. For countries emerging out of the wasteland of dictatorship, the institutional transformation inherent in the European project entailed something beyond market access and a share in the continent's prosperity. Important though these were, 'joining Europe' meant cementing newly recovered democratic foundations and locking in regimes that would be both politically more accountable and economically more responsible than what had gone before. The single currency was the culmination of this ascent. It marked the final graduation to the status of a modern European nation. This must at least partly explain the continued strong support for the euro in all the recent democracies in Europe's south (and the ambivalence in Italy, whose experience with Fascism ended in 1945).

But Greece failed to modernise itself. It embarked on a huge expansion of its patronage state in the 1980s, just when most of western Europe was busy undoing heavy-handed systems of state economic control that were often captured by special-interest groups. These had worked wonders in the post-war era, but they blocked the sort of reforms other countries found they had to undertake after the economic shocks of the 1970s. In contrast, the Greek state remained organised around networks of patrons and clients. Politicians of the two main parties would heap benefits on powerful special-interest groups (speaking very loosely, public servants for the centre-left Pasok, and the professional classes and the military for the centre-right New Democracy) in return for key electoral support, which ensured a political duopoly centred around a handful of powerful families and reinforced by oligarchic corporate and media sectors. This perpetuated a deeply inefficient allocation of resources and a politicised distribution of jobs and rewards, not to speak of outright corruption.[1]

Absurd stories from the Greek economy are legion. Licensing requirements for an interminable list of professions have meant that those lucky enough to come by a permit, often through family-based political connections, could rely on high incomes without the inconvenience of pleasing customers or clients. Virtually no new licences for long-haul trucking, for instance, were issued for decades before the crisis. The predictable result was that extant permits were traded for hundreds of thousands of euros, which any aspiring new trucker would have to cough up. More sinister for the economy was that transport from Athens to Thebes cost more than from Athens to Rome, ten times the distance. Similar effects flowed from laws requiring minimum fees (for lawyers and notaries, for example) or profit margins (for pharmacists), as well as geographical restrictions on where and when professionals could practice. As for the public sector, every new government would swell the payroll with its supporters after taking office. Much of the deteriorating fiscal deficit in Athens in the years before the crisis is accounted for by more spending on public sector salaries. All this did away with the incentive to improve products and services, in both the public sector and the protected segments of the private sector. Instead it encouraged people to compete for access to politically allocated privileges – what economists call rent-seeking. Other countries, too, retained such distortions, but none on the same scale as Greece.

I have called these privileges absurdities, but for those on the wrong side of them, a better word is indignities. The greater the benefits for those lucky enough to be inside the favoured groups, the higher the price outsiders need to pay in the form of lower salaries, exclusion from jobs reserved for relatives and acolytes of the powerful, and the ubiquitous *fakelaki* (the envelopes of cash required to obtain supposedly publicly provided services from, for instance, doctors and teachers). The whole system effectively imposed a giant tax on outsiders to pay for the privileges of insiders. Again, other countries' laws enforce unfair and inefficient barriers between insiders and outsiders, but Greece has long been the worst offender.

Running an economy this way while trying to catch up with European living standards was unsustainable. Long before the euro, this much was proved by the huge government budget gaps, filled by unfettered money-printing. In 1990, Athens's deficit reached 15 per cent of GDP, and annual inflation was as high as 24 per cent. Then, just as the lure of euro membership convinced the Greek government to contain its profligacy – both the deficit-to-GDP ratio and the inflation rate fell to about 3 per cent in 1999 – along came the global credit bubble. It temporarily but lethally suspended the fiscal discipline the euro was intended to bring. Greece's unreformed system of government survived past its natural life only because easy credit once again permitted the state to create the appearance that everyone was benefitting.

A COUNTRY RUNS OUT OF CREDIT

By late 2009, even as the rest of the world was crawling out of recession, it was obvious that Greece faced dire economic challenges. A decade of heady growth had gone into reverse in early 2008, and the sagging economy revealed a fiscal time bomb. Public spending had always exceeded government revenues; with the downturn, the gap became terrifying. George Papandreou's newly elected government shocked its European counterparts in October 2009 by throwing open Athens's opaque government accounts to reveal a deficit of 12.9 per cent of national output (later revised to an even more abysmal 15.6 per cent). For every three euros of Greek public spending, one was borrowed rather than raised in taxes, and credit was quickly becoming harder to obtain. As 2009 drew to a close, the government's total debt reached 130 per cent of the nation's yearly production.

The counterpart to public profligacy was not, as in some other countries (notably Italy), a hard-saving private sector. The funds financing wasteful government spending were ultimately lent by foreigners, as shown by Greece's current account deficit, which touched 15 per cent of GDP in 2008. The balance-of-payments constraint refused to vanish as the European Commission had predicted, and an exceptionally painful belt tightening was on the cards. As Chapter 2 explained, this cannot be blamed on the euro. In the non-euro Baltic states drastic spending retrenchments were already underway as balance-of-payments crises led to fiscal crises. Sticking to the drachma would not have spared Greece the cuts that were soon to come.

When the sources of credit began to run dry, the Greek state faced two challenges. One was how to pay for the living standards to which

Greeks – particularly those with jobs in public administration or favoured industries – had become accustomed. How to distribute the unavoidable pain was a political problem as much as an economic one – one shared, albeit rarely to the same extent, by almost every European state.

The second challenge was how to service the mountain of obligations to creditors who now reeked of fear. The crucial deadline was May 19, when Athens – already some €25 billion short of meeting its budgeted 2010 expenses – had to repay €8.1 billion borrowed ten years earlier. In normal circumstances, a government issues a new bond to refinance the old one at a similar cost. But by early 2010 bond buyers looked likely to accept new bonds only at prohibitively high interest rates, or not turn up to the bond auction at all. Investors who had hitherto blithely poured money into Greece were now blanching at the sheer scale of the country's fiscal challenge. Apart from at the end of wars, eliminating double-digit fiscal deficits in a handful of years had never been done before. That was nevertheless what Papandreou's finance minister, Giorgos Papaconstantinou, promised his counterparts that Greece would do.

But in the financial markets, the gears of self-fulfilling pessimism had already begun to turn. Investors contemplating the possibility that Athens might run out of cash increased the rate at which they would hold its bonds. Every time borrowing costs rose, the amounts Athens would need to save to service its debt were recalculated at ever higher and less realistic levels, prompting prudent money managers to demand yet higher risk premia and give the vicious cycle another spin. It was a colossally high-stakes game of Old Maid, as Keynes memorably described[2] the dynamics of financial markets, in which no one wanted to be stuck with investments that all others shunned.

European leaders reacted with incredulity to the scale of Athens's budget shortfall, and with a sense of betrayal at being caught by surprise. Papandreou and his ministers took the opportunity to air the state's financial and dirty laundry while they could still blame their predecessors for both the mismanagement and its cover-up. In their counterparts' eyes, however, the exposure of Greek accounting tricks confirmed suspicions that had threatened Greece's entry into the euro in the first place. In February 2010, Eurostat, the EU's statistics agency, declared that the numbers submitted by Athens for years could not be relied on. It also emerged that the deficit had been artificially lowered under the Maastricht threshold through derivatives trades facilitated by Goldman Sachs – itself seen as a villain of the global financial collapse. These revelations strengthened the feeling that the Greeks could not be trusted, regardless of the government at the helm.[3]

The challenges confronting Papandreou's government, in domestic politics and international finance, were indisputably gargantuan. But they were Greece's problems, and Greece is a small country. Its economy makes up 2 per cent of the eurozone whole; it is a backwater of the global financial system. If there was disbelief that Greece could destabilise Europe's entire monetary union – and with it all of world finance – it is because disbelief was warranted. Indeed there was not enough of it. Eurozone leaders increasingly came to think that they, and not just Athens, were responsible for averting a Greek sovereign default. But what was presented as axiomatic – 'there is no alternative' – was in reality a choice to treat the unfortunate problems of one small, mismanaged country as a common threat to all the euro's users. Why this should be so was a question that should have been posed with greater insistence, for both the cost of financial aid for Greece and the political obstacles to it were massive.

The Difficulty of Putting Your Money Where Your Mouth Is

A Greek default would, of course, have far-flung consequences: both outright losses for foreign investors and possible repercussions in financial markets everywhere. But these consequences were hardly confined to other eurozone countries. The United Kingdom, in particular, was vulnerable given its large financial industry and the exposure of global banks – of which Britain hosts a disproportionate share – to Greece. When a sovereign rescue was first broached in EU discussions, there was an expectation in continental Europe that the United Kingdom would take part. The United States, too, was keen to avoid upsetting financial markets just as it was nursing its own banks back to health. But they and others pushed the view that this was 'a eurozone problem' and that the euro countries should shoulder the burden of fixing it. Her Majesty's Treasury in particular worked hard to prevent the Greek crisis from being cast as an EU-wide challenge. That is understandable: it meant non-euro countries would benefit from a solution without having to pay the cost. What is strange is that the eurozone so easily agreed, especially given how high the cost was. Nearly 50 per cent of Greece's annual GDP was pledged in the first rescue loan; more than 100 per cent when the second is counted in. On top of that came eventual creditor writedowns, and central banks' purchases of Greek bonds from the market.

Then there were the political costs for all involved. The traditional port of call for a state in fiscal distress is the International Monetary Fund (IMF). But no country resorts to the IMF without experiencing it as a national humiliation. Although the IMF was originally created for west European states with temporary balance-of-payments problems, no such state (except tiny Iceland) had had recourse to it since the 1970s. In the United Kingdom, one of the last rich countries to seek help, the memory of going cap in hand to the IMF in 1976 remains politically potent. For Greece, a recent democracy burdened with both national insecurities[4] and statist traditions, the prospect of becoming a ward of the 'neoliberal' IMF seemed intolerable.

The humiliation of an IMF rescue was dreaded not just by Greece. Those with a certain idea of Europe – France above all – recoiled at the idea of their monetary union being associated with the kind of banana republic they saw as the stereotypical IMF client. The Italian member of the ECB's executive board, Lorenzo Bini-Smaghi, warned about the 'image of the euro' if the IMF was involved, which would 'be that of a currency that is only able to survive with the support of an international organization'.[5] To keep things in the family, European leaders toyed with the notion of setting up a European Monetary Fund (EMF).

The IMF itself was in a political tight spot: its large emerging-market members, with good reason, resented the idea of helping out countries many times better off than they. Directors representing them, as well as important segments of IMF staff, thought Greece should restructure its debt before any aid could be given – for its own sake as well as for theirs.[6]

In the event, practical considerations put paid to the idea of Europe taking matters into its own hands. The time and expertise needed to set up an EMF were lacking, and once it became clear that Berlin wanted the IMF's participation, and that Washington was willing to let it happen, there was nothing Gallic or Hellenic pride could do to stop that happening.

All this shows just how unlikely a rescue loan was until the moment it became a reality. Eurozone leaders hoped to calm the market without having to put their money where their mouths were. As winter turned to spring 2010 they made increasingly expansive statements of confidence that Greece would not default. In February finance ministers offered a vague, unquantified, promise of financial aid for Greece if necessary. In April this had finally been pinned down to a €30 billion rescue loan if necessary, but hedged with reassurances that Athens had not asked for it. Yet every new attempt to cajole investors back to Greece achieved less than the previous one. Even promises of financial support far beyond what would have been imaginable only months earlier were so unequal to the task that investors took them as proof Europe would not bail them out. So what leaders intended as a call to order became the investors' cue to run for the hills. Greek interest rates continued to rise. The market whose influence Mitterrand and his contemporaries had wanted the euro to domesticate was now calling their successors' bluff.

Three Great Morality Plays

By trying to talk markets into submission in early 2010, the eurozone had staked its reputation on Greece not 'failing' – that is to say, defaulting on its debt. This bid up the political cost of a Greek default for the other euro countries collectively. Their pledge to prevent it, which they hoped would not be tested, unnecessarily aggrandised the bankruptcy of one country into a failure for them all.

It was still quite possible to say no after saying yes. The loss in eurozone credibility from letting Greece hang would have been manageable. A German veto would have sufficed, which Berlin could have justified under the so-called no bail-out clause of the EU Treaty, dear to German voters. Other countries could blame German recalcitrance. Why did the monetary union nevertheless decide, against all the economic and political odds, to 'rescue' Athens from default? Greece's fate, and the precedent it set, was shaped by the collision of three great political morality plays.

The first was an idea of solidarity, championed in particular by France and the southern European countries. Letting a eurozone government be toppled by a market run was a betrayal not just of a fellow member of the common currency but of the principle that politics, not market forces, must steer the destiny of countries. Pascal Bruckner, the French thinker, has put it well: 'The idea that the nation's prosperity is not a pure governmental decision and that private actors can overturn the rules of the economic game unsettles some of our deepest convictions.'[7] Denying speculative attacks an arena in which to play was a big part of Mitterrand's vision for monetary unification and it continues to motivate the French push for 'economic government' in the eurozone.

This was solidarity infused with both self-interest and conceit. Several other countries – especially Ireland and Portugal, and to a lesser extent Spain and Italy – sensed nervousness in their own sovereign debt markets. France had its banks to worry about. Of all non-Greek institutions holding Greek government bonds, French banks were the largest national group, with over €20 billion of claims on Athens directly and more than €80 billion at stake in the Greek economy overall.[8] There was also offence at the idea that a fellow eurozone member might not honour its debt – 'honour' being the operative word, since it reflected national pride as much as hard-nosed interest.

More self-assured countries, in particular Germany, were not unduly worried that a Greek default would bring them shame. In terms of financial self-interest, however, Berlin knew that German banks were vulnerable too, even though their follies had been directed more at Irish and American loss makers than Greek ones. And everyone vividly remembered how the Lehman Brothers bankruptcy had sent the global financial system into cardiac arrest. But Merkel hesitated to endorse financial aid for Athens. A very different morality play governed the analysis in Berlin.

German public opinion saw its government as the guardian against the euro turning into a 'transfer union' in which some countries permanently subsidise others. There was genuine uncertainty in Berlin's austere chancellery building as to whether the courts would accept a financial rescue of Greece. Aside from legal complications, the so-called no bail-out clause captured the political promise on which the euro had been sold in Germany: that it would not have to pay for other countries' misfortunes or mismanagement.

That promise was not just about shielding taxpayers in richer countries. It was also the manifestation of a broader German view that the monetary union should be one of solid economies. The membership of Greece and Italy, with their history of incontinent fiscal and monetary policy, had always jarred with this vision. Any mutualisation of liabilities, any bailing out of the excessive by the prudent, would encourage continued misbehaviour and, ultimately, instability. Avoiding the economists' dreaded 'moral hazard' had been a German priority from the start. In the years that followed, Merkel would publicly question the wisdom of having let Greece join, given her European policy goal of making the euro a 'stability union'. By 2015, her government would openly propose Greece's suspension.

For all these reasons, in 2010 German leaders were at least willing to contemplate a Greek restructuring. There was a natural alliance to be formed between Berlin and the IMF. But the Fund's French managing director Dominique Strauss-Kahn, widely thought to have designs on the presidency of France, sided with his compatriots' aversion to debt writedowns in Europe.[9]

At the same time, Berlin was tied by the European Council's earlier attempts to talk markets into obedience by vaguely promising that Greece would be helped even though there was no agreement as to how. Then there were the political incentives for Merkel, who despite being the leader of Europe's greatest power was mostly in a minority in the councils of the EU and the eurozone. One person close to German policymaking has put it thus:

If you go along with the majority you're on the safe side. If you are the one blocking the decision you can either be a hero (but usually joined by many others) or you're the villain of the whole story because you are blamed for the consequences. If they are described as catastrophic and there is a very small risk of a catastrophic event then [in terms of] your incentives as a politician it takes a lot of courage to stand up and say I don't care – it's much easier to play safe.

If there was one person who could instil fears of catastrophe, it was Jean-Claude Trichet, the imperious ECB president. With the backing of most of his central bank colleagues, he took it upon himself to spur politicians into action. In a momentous European Council on Friday 7 May, Trichet thundered to the assembled government chiefs that their indecision could trigger a market collapse similar to the Lehman crisis. They needed, he insisted, to douse the fire by putting enough money on the line to remove any doubt about the 'sovereign signature' of all eurozone governments – something on the scale of the $700 billion that the US government pumped into American banks during the post-Lehman chaos. This compliment to the Americans was returned with strong US lobbying for Trichet's cause. The view in Washington was that the United States had saved the world by decisively bailing out the banks, and it was now Europe's turn to bail out its own systemic basket cases. US pressure on the eurozone, and on Merkel in particular, to bail out rather than restructure would be applied on several crucial occasions in the years that followed.[10]

Trichet should not, however, be understood as appealing merely or even mostly to an economic cost–benefit comparison of a Greek rescue with a sovereign bankruptcy. The former governor of France's central bank was steeped in the French principle of government's primacy over markets. As former chair of the Paris Club (the grouping of official creditors to developing countries), he was acutely attuned to the asymmetry between those who can pay their debts and those who cannot. His unwillingness to countenance restructuring – which persisted even after governments belatedly adopted one for Greece eighteen months later – left him trembling with indignation at the thought that not paying one's debt should be a policy option. This insistence that the 'sovereign signature' must be sacrosanct was a piece of political ontology: it was about what sort of country a eurozone member is.[11]

In the contest between the Gallic call for solidarity against 'speculators' and the Teutonic predilection for self-help and just rewards, this third moral idea – the abhorrence of bankruptcy – tipped the balance. Leaders resolved to lend €80 billion to Greece and put up €500 billion more to buttress other states losing market confidence. With IMF participation, the amounts reached €110 billion and €750 billion, respectively. For once, an EU summit went beyond expectations. But in the event, the eurozone was paying up for a policy that would make things worse.

The Costs of Compromise

Nothing happens in the EU except by compromise. To secure Berlin's acquiescence, two features had to be built into the policy edifice that was hurriedly being erected. One was rhetorical: fiscal aid for Greece could only be justified as a last resort. Merkel's chancellery needed the rescue policy to be acceptable both to the German constitutional court and to the Bundestag, where many members of Merkel's own coalition were more sceptical than her about coming to Greece's aid. To forestall their rejection of an inevitably contested decision, Merkel's chancellery developed the doctrine of *ultima ratio* – aid would only come as a last resort to save the common currency.

This had harmful consequences. It committed Merkel's government to dragging its feet until disaster was on the doorstep. It also meant justifying crisis-fighting policies to the public in terms of there being no alternative, rather than as the considered choice between several possible visions for Europe.

Merkel's second requirement was that 'solidarity' must have its desired effects. Money lent in aid should not be wasted, nor should it help sustain the unsustainable, which would only make more aid necessary in the future. In Greece's case, money would be lent but on strict conditions of radical policy reforms supposed to ensure that it would be repaid and that Athens would not run into similar trouble again. Thus, along with loans came the 'troika', a mission representing the ECB, the IMF and the European Commission. It drew up the policies Athens must undertake, and would scrutinise the government's compliance at regular reviews before authorising each new disbursement. Their guiding document was the rescue loan's 'memorandum of understanding', a term that quickly became hated in Greece.

German policymakers at the highest level have remained remarkably faithful to this model of cash for control – not just for Greece but for the monetary union as a whole. They consistently express a willingness to go further in the pooling of financial resources – including issuing debt in common – but in return insist that other states must give up significantly more sovereignty. In the words of one, joint 'eurobonds' only become thinkable when Brussels can overrule Paris on the retirement age of French workers. Non-German observers often dismiss this as bad faith, a rhetorical delaying tactic to shift the onus away from Europe's most powerful state. The simpler explanation is that they mean what they say. Finance minister Wolfgang Schäuble's tireless agitation for a eurozone budget, finance ministry and parliament should be understood through this prism. So should the troika's introduction – and, in 2015, the converse insistence that Greece should leave the euro if it does not comply with creditors' demands.

The creditors' need for reassurance about Greece's ability to repay was rooted in understandable mistrust. But as a consequence, the policy programme was loaded with contradictions. The deepest one was that between the fundamental need to reform Greece's political and economic system – of which Berlin rightly perceived that the fiscal crisis was merely a symptom – and the external imposition of policies intended to make reform happen. Overcoming the crisis was not just a question of cutting spending, it would require an overhaul of the entire social model, which could only be done with a deep cultural and political commitment to change. That commitment, however, is nigh-on impossible to generate when the policies to be pursued are decided upon and imposed from the outside. Foreigners have only ever successfully reformed political cultures in cases where a country has been defeated in war – post-war Germany being the prime example. In less extreme circumstances, outside forces can impress on a nation that change is necessary, but the motivation must be forged in the interaction between those who govern and those who are governed – that is to say, in domestic politics. The humiliation of having the troika breathing down their neck was not going to make the Greeks more enthusiastic about putting in place measures they were never keen on in the first place.

Another contradiction was that the eurozone's rejection of a debt restructuring gave the Greek political class an incentive to drag its feet. Since the eurozone had so clearly demonstrated its fear of a Greek default, it could be expected to cough up even if Athens fell short of its commitments. In due course, each 'slippage' on the part of the Greek government was eventually followed by extra money, but only after delays and quarrels that exhausted both sides and the public. There was a degree of complicity here: when people complain that Greece did not do what it promised, recall that the creditors signed off on progress reviews to release fresh loans as many as five times.

This only deepened the mistrust that had motivated the intrusive monitoring regime in the first place. When the troika was later supplemented by a 'task force' to ensure that Greek bureaucrats did what they were supposed to, Brussels managed to exceed its usual reputation for a political tin ear by appointing a German as its head. Greek leaders, more concerned with their own political manoeuvring than with the country's future, mostly did as one might have expected: they framed government policies not as being necessary for the sake of the country but as a burden imposed by their creditors. Domestic political choice was narrowed to the preferred degree of obstructionism against the troika. The Greek people's opportunity to reshape their destiny as a modern European country instead became the cause for resentment of their creditors.

The concrete upshot of all this was a list of required actions that grew more and more detailed over time. The disempowerment of ordinary Greeks grew in lockstep with the extraordinary degree of troika micromanagement.[12] So did their economic suffering. For the political contradiction between demanding policy actions and disempowering the sources of legitimacy needed for them was matched by substantive contradictions in the policy programme itself.

Economic Tragedy

The ostensible purpose of the rescue loan was to tide Greece over until it regained market access, which would supposedly happen once Athens had tightened its belt sufficiently. However, Greece was not locked out of markets because of its admittedly huge deficit but because of its overhang of outstanding debt. Markets will finance even a budget gap of 15 per cent of GDP for a state with no prior liabilities. To lend to a state whose existing debts exceed what it can repay, however, is to throw good money after bad even if it has no deficits at all and merely needs to refinance old debts. In the jargon, the stock of debt is more important than the flow of borrowing. The eurozone's policy of eliminating the flow (cutting the ongoing deficit) rather than the stock (writing off the accumulated debt mountain) undermined its own stated goal of restoring Athens's access to financial markets.

Protecting existing debt made it necessary to cut the deficit at a historically unprecedented pace. Most of the rescue lending had to cover repayments and interest, leaving little to fund ongoing government spending. An interest bill originally of some €12 billion per year, which was set to rise in line with growing debt until the budget gap was closed, required Athens to aim for not just balancing its books but running a primary surplus. (The primary surplus or deficit is the difference between government revenues and expenditures before counting interest expenses.) Since the debt was ultimately to foreigners, this meant getting the national economy to a point where as much as 7–8 per cent of GDP would be extracted from it in on a regular basis.[13] But history teaches that an economy buckles under such pressure, so that this rate of extraction can destroy the very capacity to produce goods and services to be extracted. In Weimar Germany, whose huge war reparations Berlin should have remembered, the consequence was hyperinflation; in Greece, which could not print its own money, it would be a deflationary depression in which the deficit was cut at the cost of a much heavier debt burden relative to the economy's size. (See Figures 3.1 and 3.2.) As the IMF has since admitted, the creditors badly underestimated how much spending cuts and tax rises would damage the economy.[14]

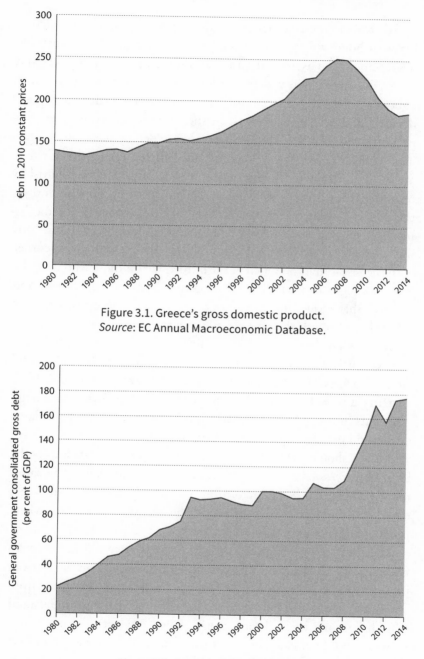

Figure 3.1. Greece's gross domestic product.
Source: EC Annual Macroeconomic Database.

Figure 3.2. Greece's debt mountain.
Source: EC Annual Macroeconomic Database.

The troika's policy programme also suffered from a contradiction between honouring old debts and reforms to promote 'competitiveness', understood as a fall in prices and wages. But falling prices and wages do not lighten a debt burden fixed in euro; they worsen it. Labour market liberalisation in particular can also reduce aggregate demand and hold back growth in the short term.[15] The direct economic downside of such reforms is compounded by their difficult politics. Policies to lower wages, politically difficult at the best of times, are even harder to push through at a time of widespread hardship resulting from extreme fiscal austerity. By insisting on dismantling the collective-bargaining system, the troika also removed a mechanism for forging a consensual and fair distribution of burdens. This was a general pattern: each interest group was left to fight its corner, with the result that too much of the burden fell on those who were the least privileged to start with.[16] The protests and strikes, sabotage and violence that ensued in turn harmed economic activity further and delayed any growth the reforms might eventually bring.

There is no doubt that Greece, like many other peripheral eurozone countries, needed to increase competition in both product and labour markets. But the right priority would have been to limit fiscal austerity until reforms had been implemented. Meanwhile, although wage cuts in the public sector were inevitable (they had been inflated far beyond private wages in the credit bubble), the priority for the private sector should have been to make product markets (including the licensed professions, where product and labour are really the same) more competitive before reforming labour markets to push wages down. I include in 'product markets' the licensed professions, where product and labour are really the same.

The IMF's own research – which unfortunately did not seem to find its way to its team on the ground – finds big positive effects from product market liberalisation but only weak and uncertain ones from structural reforms in labour markets.[17] It is not hard to understand why that should be so. Product price falls would be associated with increased production as a result of firms competing harder for market share. In contrast, wage falls induced by labour reforms would at first be associated with easier firing rules and less employment, and cause a downward pressure on demand that it would be better to postpone until growth returned. The troika policies did the opposite, and made labour markets more precarious while prices remained rigged above competitive levels – squeezing living standards without expanding production. (See Figure 3.3.) This was compounded by successive Greek governments' choice to protect existing vested interests – in particular public sector employees and the licensed professions – and shift the bulk of the burden onto the unprotected parts of the private sector, where taxes went up and wages down.

An obsession with 'competitiveness' and whole-economy unit labour costs biased the rescue programme towards measures to reduce wages. This was misguided, as we saw in Chapter 2. The cost inflation in the boom reflected capital as well as labour costs, not an increasing share of the economic pie going to workers. Moreover it was mostly confined to the non-traded sector: there never was an erosion of export competitiveness that had to be reversed. The huge current account

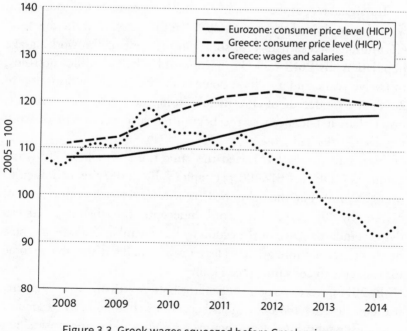

Figure 3.3. Greek wages squeezed before Greek prices.
Sources: ECB, Eurostat.

deficit was largely driven by an import binge. Of course increased exports could help close the deficit, but a lack of cost competitiveness is not what has been holding exports back: despite huge wage cuts in the traded sectors since 2009, foreign sales have barely picked up.

Rather than cutting wages, the strategy for expanding exports should have aimed to improve the productivity of tradeable goods and services. That would most urgently have required boosting public and private investment, keeping credit flowing, and making it easier to move resources from unproductive sectors to productive ones. The memorandum policies actively harmed the former two: leaving the debt overhang in place forced cuts to public investment, while the deep recession and continued uncertainty over public finances paralysed Greek banks. A deep, policy-inflicted credit crunch made it harder for companies to avail themselves of whatever flexibility was being gained in labour markets.

The result of all this has been a double tragedy: the shattering of Greece's aspirations to both democracy and prosperity.

The signal fact of the economy is that it is produces less today than when Greece joined the euro in 2001. In the last year of the drachma, 4.1 million Greeks had jobs, some 56 per cent of the working-age population. By 2013 only 3.6 million did – half a million jobs lost in twelve years, and a million down from the peak of 4.6 million in 2008. After a decade of euro membership, the employment rate was lower than it had been at the beginning: just under half of working-age Greeks had jobs.

National income has traced the same rise and fall. In 2001, the country's GDP was €17,400 per capita.[18] By 2008, this had risen to over €20,000, but then slumped back to exactly the same level of €17,400 by 2012. And this record understates the true fall in Greeks' living standards. Even as the economy has shrunk, the share of it now needed to service foreign debts leaves a yet smaller disposable income for residents to consume. (See Figure 3.4.)

By 2014 Greece was bouncing off the bottom – thanks to a temporary pause in austerity and better global economic conditions. The economy was quickly submerged again, however, by renewed uncertainty and radical liquidity shortage in 2015. The social debris from a destruction of

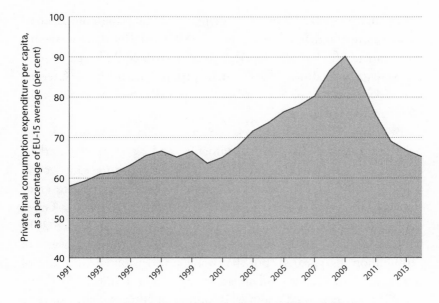

Figure 3.4. Greece's consumption catch-up unravelled.
Source: EC Annual Macroeconomic Database.

productive capacity unparalleled in peacetime European history remains wherever you care to look: in the middle classes' descent into poverty, in the emigration of those who can secure a job abroad, in the growing number of people taking their own lives, and in the stirring of hatred for foreigners – both poorer immigrants thought to prey on impoverished Greeks and rich Germans blamed for the country's economic collapse. Average incomes have fallen by nearly 40 per cent. A third of households have annual incomes below €10,000; almost half rely on a pension as the main or only source of income.[19]

Solidarity, prosperity and democracy: on each of the three values European integration was meant to secure, Europe has fallen short, and nowhere more so than in Greece. Whatever the loan agreed against all odds in May 2010 was meant to achieve, it was surely not this.

The Alternative That Could Not Be Named

If the eurozone's record in Greece is to count as a 'rescue', we are entitled to wonder from what fate Greeks were delivered by this supposed salvation. Virtually the entire eurozone policymaking elite asserted there was 'no alternative' except to leave the euro. But there was: eurozone leaders who huddled together in May 2010 could have endorsed a sovereign writedown. That a managed restructuring of Greece's public debt was feasible is clear from the fact that one was successfully completed two years later.

By summer 2011, the Greek economic collapse was making the debt less rather than more sustainable, and a return to markets seemed more distant than ever. In return for agreeing to a second round of official refinancing, Germany insisted that private creditors would have to take losses on their remaining holdings of Greek debt. This 'private sector involvement' was carried out in March 2012 without a glitch. At the stroke of a pen, debts with a face value of €100 billion disappeared. But that was too little, too late. Billions of private investors' claims had already been paid back in full. By February 2012, Greece owed about €110 billion to eurozone governments and EU institutions (including central banks) and €20 billion to the IMF, out of a total debt of some €350 billion. When the markets first closed their doors on Greece, virtually the entire debt of (then) some €300 billion had been in private hands.

The belated restructuring shows just what an opportunity was wasted by not daring to restructure at the outset. Chapter 7 analyses in detail how a more courageous policy would have played out. The following paragraphs simply give an idea of the magnitudes that could have been saved.

Suppose that the early months of 2010 had been spent designing a private sector restructuring that suspended redemptions and debt service. Freed of a €12 billion-a-year interest burden, Athens would only need to finance new primary deficits. Assuming Greece had stuck to its actual primary deficit reduction path, it would have needed about €25 billion over the following five years.[20] That financing requirement compares to a total of about €230 billion in the first two rescue packages combined, plus another €50–€80 billion or so being negotiated at the time of writing.

The lesson to draw is not that an immediate restructuring would have allowed the same austerity with less official financial aid but that it would have created room for a slower pace of deficit reduction while still requiring much less financial aid.

Eliminating the deficit more gradually – for example to reach primary balance by 2015 instead of 2013, but with the same front-loaded cuts in 2010 – may have required a total official financing package of about €40 billion.[21] Greece would have been lent over five years a third of what it was offered over three in the first rescue – and that would have got the job done. This counterfactual, moreover, is conservative to a fault: it does not allow for the economy performing better than it did by being squeezed significantly less. From the slower but probably more successful schedule suggested here, a depression may still have resulted – but it is likely that tens of thousands more Greeks would have kept their jobs, and hundreds of thousands fewer fallen into poverty.[22]

These simple calculations ignore two important questions. One is what one would have done with the suspended debt. It could, in theory, have been written down to close to zero. But while restructuring sovereign debt is not as radical as Europe made it sound in 2010, a complete writedown would have been virtually unprecedented. Some portion of the debt would no doubt have remained – to be serviced at some point in the future. But much could be done to avoid a looming overhang, such as stretching the maturities out evenly over thirty or fifty years or even longer, and above all by linking debt service to the level and growth rate of GDP. This would have prevented debt service from counterproductively eroding the ability to pay, since it would be payable only (or predominantly) when the economy was doing well.[23] It took five years before this idea was put on the table by the left-wing government elected in January 2015 – only to be dismissed out of hand by eurozone governments that had, by then, become Greece's biggest creditors by far.

The second question involves the Greek banks, which a restructuring would have bled dry of capital. In 2010 Europe was still wedded to the doctrine that governments must ultimately pay to prop up banks. When the eurozone, two years too late, wrote down some of Athens's debt, a €40 billion bill for recapitalising Greece's banks was passed on to her taxpayers. That doctrine was always flawed, and would soon cause great damage in Ireland, as the next chapter recounts. Antici-pating that argument, Greek banks too could have been restructured at the outset. This would have hurt their creditors, but it would have kept banks lending and minimised the credit crunch and its impact on growth, all without adding to government debt.

Some will say it is going too far to suggest that the eurozone could have freed itself from not just one but two taboos in one go (restruc-turing the debts of both the sovereign and private banks). They will conclude that the capital needed to keep the Greek banking system alive would always have had to come from the government. This, of course, concedes the point that ideological opposition to debt restruc-turing made things worse for Greece. But even including extra money to make banks whole after a sovereign writedown, the total amount Greece would have needed from its creditors could still have been sig-nificantly less than the financial support that has actually been given.

An Escape from the Euro?

What about that other alternative, 'Grexit', the ugly name for Greece's exit from the single currency? Early on in the crisis, if the eurozone's political leaders mentioned Grexit at all it was to underline the una-voidability of their policies: the alternative was too horrible even to contemplate, was the argument. If not quite a *reductio ad absurdum*, it was a *reductio ad horribilem*. They were right about this: at least for the eurozone as a whole, the departure of any member would cast a permanent shadow over all the others. This would have been an invitation to financial markets to speculate on who would be next – a return to precisely the monetary precariousness (but even worse) which, for France in particular, the euro was intended to overcome. Only in 2015 would some eurozone governments openly suggest Grexit might be the least bad option.

But since long before then, a large corps of professional econ-omists and economic commentators, incongruously flanked by insurgent populist politicians, have taken the *reductio* to work the other way.[24] They think that the social and economic consequences of policies designed to fix the currency union's problems mean the euro is maintained at the cost of keeping Greece – and perhaps other members – shackled in depression. In this view 'Grexit' is the key to recovery, not a monster with which to scare the children. 'They saved the eurozone; they just forgot to save the people', one US commentator has scoffed.[25] More moderate critics accept that undoing the euro would now be costlier than keeping it together – but they express regret (and sometimes *Schadenfreude*) that Europe went down this track at all.

The calls for Grexit seem not to go away. So it is worth asking: how exactly is Greece supposed to benefit from leaving the euro, or from never having joined it in the first place? The previous chapter showed that there is little reason to think that the debt build-up (and the associated real exchange rate misalignment) would have been avoided in the bubble years even outside the euro. The argument, therefore, must hinge on how much euro membership incapacitated Athens when the balance-of-payments crisis broke out.

The immediate effect of 'Grexit' would have been a plunge of the new drachma, multiplying the burden of Greece's debt (taken out in euros) relative to its tax base (now in devalued local currency).[26] A default would have been impossible to avoid. Those who think the euro is bad for Greece may reply that such a default would have been a thoroughly good thing. That may be true, but then why not just default within the euro – what is bought by leaving the single currency as well? A within-euro default would be less destabilising than default-with-devaluation. The latter would drastically alter the status of most private-sector debts as well, even those that were perfectly payable before. And just establishing which debts should or should not be redenominated would cause huge legal and economic disruption. Formal restructuring is better than default-through-devaluation because it targets the relevant overstretched borrowers instead of effectively writing down all debts indiscriminately.

What if Greece had never joined the euro at all? Domestic debts denominated in drachma could then conveniently be inflated away. But even if drachma-denominated debt would, in such a situation, be spared formal default, the required amount of inflation would still mean a hugely destabilising redistribution – in favour of the government in particular (since the point would be to mimic a sovereign default), but also between private creditors and debtors wholly unrelated to the government's problems.[27] It was precisely these sorts of distortions Greece and other countries wanted to put behind them by joining the euro. And, as Chapter 2 argued, it is highly unlikely that all or even most debts would be drachma-denominated. The banks, in particular, may well have funded themselves with euro debt.

So much for the 'stock' problem of accumulated debts. That leaves the 'flow' problem. Outside of the euro too, of course, the huge gap between Greece's imports and its exports would have to be closed in a balance-of-payments crisis. Indeed, it would have to be closed more abruptly than within the euro, since less financial aid would presumably have been available. Grexit advocates' most important argument is that it would be easier if Greece left the euro: the ability to devalue would allow Greece to price itself back into export markets and reduce imports faster.

To this there are three things to say, apart from the fact that Greece never priced itself out of export markets to begin with (see Chapter 2). First, devaluation does not always work in practice. As I discuss further in Chapter 10, sterling plunged in 2008 but the UK trade deficit did not narrow, while Spain's exports boomed despite the lack of currency flexibility. And despite a sharp internal devaluation – Greek private sector wages have fallen by 20–30 per cent relative to other European countries – exports have barely picked up. It is reckless to advocate the chaos of currency break-up without explaining how Grexit would change whatever makes Greek exports unresponsive to cost cuts now.[28]

Second, even in theory, devaluation 'works' by making people poorer. In the oft-cited example of Argentina, default and devaluation was followed by growth less because of increased 'competitiveness' than because of a highly regressive redistribution of wealth (as well as the lucky strike of a commodities boom). The rich, who disproportionately held foreign assets and redenominated domestic debts, enjoyed a windfall which prompted them to invest domestically.[29] In the European context, Grexit would probably make the lure of a foreign wage all the more tempting, and encourage those who can find jobs elsewhere (typically the most productive) to emigrate. Emigration, in turn, would worsen debt burdens and threaten the productivity and export prowess of those who stayed behind.

Finally, if one really wants to shift the cost of domestic production relative to foreign prices, there are ways to do this within the euro. So-called fiscal devaluation can be achieved by raising indirect taxes (which are levied on imported goods as well as domestic ones) and lowering payroll taxes (which only affect domestic production). This increases the price of imports and lowers the cost of exports and domestic import substitutes. This can be done in a revenue-neutral way so as not to undermine public finances, and can be designed to replicate exactly the effects of any desired nominal exchange rate devaluation.[30]

In short, not only are the alleged benefits of leaving the euro dubious, they are available inside the euro anyway.

Killing Democracy in Its Cradle

On a Monday night in late October 2011, prime minister Papandreou announced to his stunned cabinet that the Greek people would be asked in a referendum whether they approved the terms of a second loan programme with eurozone governments and the IMF. The dramatic week that followed sealed the fate of his country as well as of his political career. It cemented most of the errors in the first 'rescue'. Almost everything that happened in the renewed stand-off between Athens and its creditors in 2015 followed the pattern set in late 2011.

It had been clear for some time that the €110 billion package from May 2010 would not get the job done. The first year had been promising: Athens reduced its deficit by a third (€12 billion, or 5 per cent of annual output) at the cost of a manageable recession. By late 2011, however, the economy was sliding into a depression and Greek society was on the verge of breakdown. A general strike paralysed the economy; parades on the national day were cancelled when protesters hurled accusations of treason against the president and other officials.

In the last days of October, Papandreou's government had concluded negotiations on a new rescue package with Europe and the

IMF. It was an ambitious agreement. The additional money was significant: another €130 billion was offered to Greece on top of the initial €110 billion. Equally important, it gave Greece a second stab at reforms after months of foot-dragging. Above all, the new package included a writedown of debts that Athens still owed to private investors – precisely the approach that had been adamantly ruled out a year and a half earlier. (Chapter 6 describes this change of heart in detail.)

Financial markets and world leaders – just about to gather for a G20 summit in Cannes – were caught off guard by Papandreou's referendum stunt. It knocked over the political building blocks that had delicately been balanced over a period of months to create a semblance of design for Greece's hapless economy. As of that Monday night, all bets were off – and not just bets on Greece. A new Lehman moment seemed to loom over the entire global economy. Most worryingly, Spanish and Italian borrowing costs were rising fast.

The reactions came fast and furious. Merkel felt betrayed. French president Nicolas Sarkozy was piqued when his G20 extravaganza was overshadowed by a new eruption of the Greek problem. Like angry schoolmasters, they summoned Papandreou first to Paris and then to Cannes. Joined by José Manuel Barroso and Jean-Claude Juncker, the presidents of the European Commission and of the 'eurogroup' of eurozone governments, 'Merkozy' bullied Papandreou into agreeing that any referendum had to be not on the terms of the loan, but on the bigger question of whether the Greek people wanted to stay in the eurozone. (They were helped by the fact that Evangelos Venizelos, a Pasok grandee who had replaced Papaconstantinou as finance minister, had his own designs on the top job.)

The verbal manhandling of a small country's prime minister was not just undignified, it was also a political mistake of deep strategic importance. It consecrated the 'there is no alternative' narrative: if Greeks could not be allowed to pronounce on the policy programme without putting in question their place in the euro, the programme had surreptitiously become the de facto precondition for continued membership. The only thing that changed when another Greek prime minister called a referendum four years later was that the surreptitous became explicit. The ECB's cap on liquidity for Greek banks during the 2015 referendum campaign showed beyond any doubt the willingness to expel from the euro a country that did not toe the line.

Insisting on a poll about euro membership rather than the updated memorandum policies defeated any democratic legitimacy a plebiscite might have generated. As one Greek commentator remarked, 'one does not present the people with a choice where one option is suicide'. Instead, the preference consistently expressed by the vast majority of Greeks throughout the crisis, and still today, is to keep the euro but reject the troika's demands. To the extent that the European debate has acknowledged this preference at all, it has been to dismiss it as economic illiteracy, or as a preposterous demand for permanent subsidies by Greeks who want to keep living beyond their means. But this was always wrong – Greece could have stayed in the euro, albeit very uncomfortably, without fiscal support. Why did European leaders remove this option from democratic consideration? In part because they believed their own propaganda that a Greek rejection of the rescue programme would necessitate 'Grexit'. In part because of something altogether more sinister: a willingness to make this claim true, and force the break-up of the euro in order to force Greece and other recalcitrants into line.

Papandreou dropped his referendum plan. A modicum of legitimacy was instead provided by a parliamentary vote of confidence. Losing the vote would have meant no further financial aid; the 'no alternative' narrative that had killed the referendum was enough, just, to carry the day in parliament after Papandreou himself had promised to resign. He was replaced by an unelected technocratic government led by Lucas Papademos, Greece's erstwhile central banker. It marked the sorry state of leadership in Athens that the prime minister could only win a so-called confidence vote by acknowledging that he no longer enjoyed the country's trust. And it was a sad verdict on democracy in its historical cradle that a technocratic government was installed, at the behest of outsiders with the connivance of domestic politicians, over the heads of citizens just when political legitimacy was most needed.

Disenfranchisement without Respite

Curiously enough, when the commotion subsided after Papandreou's departure, the sound and fury turned out to have changed very little. The planned second programme survived intact, and with it the principle of trading loans for belt tightening and 'competitiveness' policies. There was one significant difference: Greece's remaining private sector creditors were pushed into 'voluntarily' accepting a debt swap that shrank Athens's debt burden – but it was too little, too late. After Greek banks were compensated with new government capital for their losses on the writedown, only about one-fifth had been shaved off the face value of Athens's debt.[31]

Something else survived, too: the determination to insulate policy choices from any democratic deliberation. It was, at best, an infantilisation of the Greek people at the hands of Europe's and Greece's own political elite: until citizens were mature enough to support actions to which there was 'no alternative', the correct choice would be made for them. This attitude – not so much the primacy of politics over markets as the dominance of technocracy over democracy – would define relations between Greece and the eurozone on two more occasions in the following years.

The first was after consecutive elections in May and June 2012, when the unelected Papademos government had finished its job of shepherding the debt restructuring through and got some reforms going. The May election wiped out Papandreou's Pasok, while Syriza – a radical left-wing movement campaigning on rejecting the memorandum – came first. With no party able to form a majority coalition, a rerun election was held six weeks later. Across the globe, a decisive Syriza victory was feared as the catalyst of Grexit, a fear no doubt encouraged by some of its outdated rhetoric, which was of the extreme-left firebrand variety. Few bothered to take note that Alexis Tsipras, Syriza's leader, was adamant he did not want Greece to leave the euro. And eurozone politicians, as they would continue to do, did their utmost to redefine the choice facing Greek voters to one of whether or not to keep the single currency.

The propaganda may have worked: in the rerun election, Syriza was pipped to the post by the centre-right New Democracy, whose leader Antonis Samaras cobbled together a coalition with the rump of Pasok. In opposition, Samaras had not lifted a finger to help implement the first memorandum, and he, too, had campaigned against the troika demands. Once in office, however, he gave in to eurozone pressure and accepted the troika's policy programme. Samaras's elected government embodied the democratic will of Greek citizens little more than Papademos's technocratic interlude.

Samaras, like Papandreou, dragged his feet on structural reforms but persisted with deficit cutting. By the end of 2013, for the first time in decades, the Greek state kept non-interest spending below its own revenues. In 2014, with interest rates falling around the world, Athens even managed to re-enter bond markets temporarily. But Greece's ravaged politics turned the winds again. In May Syriza came first in the European election, and in January 2015 it won a snap election recklessly called by Samaras. It was a momentous victory: it marked the first time a eurozone country was ruled by a party that not only challenged the 'no alternative' narrative rhetorically, but even seemed to mean it.

It is quite clear what the voters who put Syriza in power wanted: to stay in the euro but to end the troika's austerity and reform policies, as well as the overlordship of the troika itself. As for reforms, Syriza promised to take aim at the oligarchs controlling much of Greece's monopolistic economy, while restoring protections for average workers. There was serious reason to doubt that Syriza had either the competence or the coherence to fulfil its promise of a break with the past: it may well offer only a path back to the immiserising clientilism of old. The doubts have only been reinforced by the movement's bumbling record in office. But what matters more is that Greece's eurozone 'partners' have been doing everything they can to prevent it from trying. Whether Syriza's policies are good or bad for Greece, the rest of Europe have succeeded in taking the choice out of Greek voters' hands and into their own.

The main threat by which the eurozone is enforcing their preferred policies is not that of stopping official budget financing. For

Greece, the primary surplus means it can get by without more loans if it delays debt service to the troika. Default within the eurozone would be painful but, in itself, manageable. The chokehold by which Europe ultimately coerced Athens into signing up to its demands is on Greece's banks. These are kept alive thanks to enormous flows of emergency liquidity from the eurozone's central banking system. When the ECB decided to stop extending these lifelines in June 2015, the banks would no longer have access to cash to meet accelerating deposit withdrawals. The capital controls Greek authorities had to impose as a result meant people could no longer withdraw money from their accounts on demand. Even this need not force an exit from the euro: as Chapters 6 and 7 discuss, judicious controls on capital movements are possible and manageable for some time. In Greece they could even be used to shift the cash-based economy into electronic payments, which would help combat tax evasion. But over time capital controls almost as harmful for economic activity as restricting the circulation of blood is for the human body. The tougher are the limits on liquidity and the longer they last, the greater is the temptation for Athens to start printing its own money.[32] In this way it is the ECB's choice whether to push Greece out of the euro.

The draconian threat to strangle the banking system has only become widely understood by the public after Syriza's in-your-face challenge to the eurozone consensus. But it is nothing new. The ECB has applied this particular chokehold repeatedly since the start of the crisis. Its willingness to use it to disempower Greek popular opinion was made clear in 2012 when Jens Weidmann, Bundesbank chief and high priest of Germany's religion of monetary rectitude, used several interviews between the two Greek elections to underline the point that, if a new administration rejected the eurozone's policy demands, central bank lifelines to Greek banks might stop. Though a two-thirds majority of the ECB's Governing Council has to agree to limit emergency bank liquidity, Weidmann's remarks showed that such a vote – effectively on forcing Greece out of the euro – was conceivable already early on in the crisis. In 2015, of course, the Governing Council made good on the threat.[33]

How the current stand-off between Athens and the other euro-zone governments and institutions is resolved will pivot on the ECB's decisions on liquidity for Greek banks. (At the time of writing, Syriza has seemingly capitulated to the creditors' demands, despite their landslide rejection in the referendum.) But it would be wrong to see this as a *sui generis* question for Greece, let alone one that is caused by Syriza's radicalism. The ECB has applied the same threat repeatedly since 2010, but at first it did so to enforce another taboo. This was a taboo not on sovereign default, but on letting even private banks go bankrupt. And it was not in Greece, but in Ireland.

FOUR

Ireland: The Private Is Political

AN INTERVIEW OUT OF THE ORDINARY

THE LISTENERS WHO TUNED IN to the *Morning Ireland* radio programme one Thursday in mid November 2010 knew the Irish economy was in a bad state. Even so, the interview with Patrick Honohan, the governor of Ireland's central bank, was shocking enough to chill their morning coffee.

It was six months after Greece had been subjected to the troika's tutelage in return for a vast bridge loan, and the eurozone had set up a rescue fund in case other euro states lost access to market funding. Dublin's deficit was on course to hit an incredible 31 per cent of GDP, most of it due to the cost of bailing out collapsing Irish banks. Rumours were rife that Ireland was about to become the first to apply to the new European Financial Stability Facility (EFSF) for financial aid, which would place Irish economic policy, too, under the troika's whip. But even with Dublin's borrowing costs soaring and IMF officials spotted in the capital, one frazzled government minister after another denied that a eurozone rescue was imminent, all the way up to finance minister Brian Lenihan and the Taoiseach (prime minister), Brian Cowen, himself.

Honohan's interview had come about in an unusual way. Usually it is journalists who chase officials to get them to comment – especially when the topic is as sensitive as whether Ireland would have to follow Greece into the arms of the troika. But Honohan himself had phoned in from Frankfurt, where he was about to sit down with ECB colleagues. Ireland's top financial technocrat had something he wanted to tell the Irish people, and he was in a hurry.

His message was that the rescue loan was coming. It would be in the tens of billions of euros, he told stunned Irish listeners; he confirmed that much of this would be for the purpose of putting yet more capital into private banks – to put 'beyond question' that the government had whatever funds they might need. A 'substantial outflow of funds' by foreign institutions from Irish banks had created a need for 'exceptional funding' from the central bank, he admitted.[1]

It was astounding to have a central bank governor announce the country's helplessness live on air, but even more extraordinary were the ongoing struggles that the interview exposed: struggles between Honohan and the government, between Ireland and its eurozone counterparts (particularly the ECB), and between two ideas about how to resolve Ireland's crisis.

Honohan's public intervention came after a lengthy tussle in private. Unbeknownst to the public, ECB officials were urging the government to apply for a rescue loan, a stance Honohan supported and to which he lent all his weight. The night before, he had privately pressured Lenihan to call together the cabinet so it could resolve to apply for an EFSF loan. Lenihan had baulked; the government was determined to avoid the humiliation of a Greek-style rescue. Next morning's interview, however, masterfully upstaged the elected government. Once the expectation of a rescue loan had been publicly established by someone with Honohan's authority, rejecting it would have provoked a complete market panic around Ireland and its banks. Within days, the government applied for the rescue. Lenihan, already terminally ill (he would die from cancer less than a year later), sounded a broken man as he recollected his return from Brussels after signing away Dublin's policy autonomy: 'No Irish minister has ever had to do this before. Now hell was at the gates', he said later.[2]

To bounce the Irish government into its eurozone–IMF rescue loan may have been a victory of competence over bungling – Cowen and Lenihan were responsible for some of the most awful policy decisions of any European country in the foregoing years – but it was also the subjection of representative democracy to technocratic rule. It marked the imposition of a particular view of how to deal with Europe's sickly banks. Despite being one of Europe's worst perpetrators of bank bail-outs, Dublin was belatedly creeping towards 'bail-in' – the policy of recapitalising banks by forcing their creditors, rather than taxpayers, to absorb the losses their investments had generated. Strong-arming Dublin into the eurozone rescue operation halted this progression back to financial policy sanity.

This was not, of course, how the victors put it. European Commission and ECB officials, Honohan included, remained adamant that the aid was necessary, as was putting more government money into banks to protect their creditors' investments. And the official narrative has stuck. Here is how the presenter of the BBC's *Hardtalk* programme introduced an interview with Honohan in 2014: 'Three years ago Ireland was a zombie economy, crippled by broken banks and bad debt, kept alive only by an emergency bail-out from the EU and IMF.'[3] In fact, the bail-out prevented the writedown that both growth and public finances needed more than anything else.

One Letter and Six Months

How, as the Irish put it, did they lose the run of themselves? The country had entered the crisis as the eurozone's star pupil. When a new Irish ambassador arrived in Berlin in 2009, he was seen as the representative not of an imminent trouble spot but of a government that had just secured a referendum victory on the Lisbon Treaty, which Irish voters had initially turned down.

Seen through the lens of Maastricht, Greece and Ireland up to 2008 were like night and day. While Athens had been the eurozone's worst fiscal delinquent by a wide margin, Dublin came into the crisis as the single currency's star performer. Public finances in Ireland were in much better shape than in not only Greece, but most euro countries including Germany. In 2008, the government's debt amounted to just 25 per cent of GDP; its deficit was negligible.

By 2013, the public debt burden had quintupled, to 124 per cent of GDP. But unlike with Greece, it cannot be argued that lax policing of the stability and growth pact helped cause the problem. None of the things that went wrong in Ireland can be blamed on breaking the eurozone's fiscal rules, for Dublin satisfied them all. Fiscal irresponsibility did not lead Dublin into a Greek-style policy programme – it was the other way round. By indenturing the Irish taxpayer for the sake of Irish banks' creditors, the 'rescue' programme took the government debt stock from the lowest in the eurozone to one of the highest.

Ireland did share some similarities with Greece, but they were not fiscal. In the 1980s and 1990s Ireland had thrived from EU membership by building up a successful low-tax hub for international manufacturers, taking the 'Irish tiger' from being one of the union's poorest members to one of its richest. But in the 2000s sprightly growth rates came to be driven not by productive business developments but by foreign credit. On the eve of the crisis Ireland's current account deficit neared 6 per cent – not Greek levels, admittedly, but the model of borrowing one's way to unsustainable living standards was the same.

The better comparison, however, is with Iceland. The Irish, who will always be rich in humour when all else turns against them, recognised as much in a joke doing the rounds when Iceland's banking sector spectacularly collapsed: 'What is the difference between Ireland and Iceland? One letter and six months.' Like its neighbour to the north, Dublin's boom had consisted of inflating the country's lenders with cheap loans from international markets that were then pumped into ever more swollen real estate deals at home. The final destination for this 'investment' was down the drain of reckless property development. But the employment and tax revenues this temporarily generated financed fast-growing wages and spending that could not be sustained – including on housing, which inflated the bubble further. In the first eight years of the euro, Irish house prices rose by 155 per cent; in the first decade, public sector wages doubled.[4] When the financial crisis hit and cross-border lending between banks abruptly stopped, Irish institutions owed an amount totalling many times the country's annual national income, while their revenues were plummeting alongside a punctured housing market. The situation was ripe for a balance-of-payments crisis.

The policy pursued by Ireland until 2008 (though the term 'policy' is an overly generous term, implying as it does a greater degree of rationality than the facts bear out) was the same as Iceland's; it is best described as not looking a gift horse in the mouth. The horse in both cases was a rapidly growing banking sector that bankrolled one tax windfall after another. The mouth, as both countries' leaders would have discovered if they had just been willing to look, was full of sick teeth in the form of extreme risk taking, lack of control and thread-bare capital buffers. But they chose not to look, preferring to ride the boom unreined. The high rollers greased politicians' palms and egos alike, with everything from campaign donations to the sort of lavish private spending that casts glitter over formerly drab surroundings (witness Reykjavik's rocketing status in both subculture and celebrity culture).

Ireland's and Iceland's metastasised banking systems (see Figure 4.1) were extreme, but they were not exceptional. Every European island state has turned itself into a giant hedge fund. After Luxembourg, the top five European countries ranked by the size of their banks' balance sheets as a multiple of the economy's annual production are Iceland, Ireland, Cyprus, Malta and the United Kingdom – all of which have banking systems more than five times bigger than

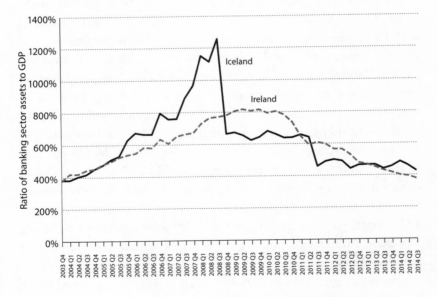

Figure 4.1. Not looking a gift horse in the mouth.
Sources: Central banks of Iceland and Ireland, Statistics Iceland.

the country's annual GDP. And this is just the most exaggerated manifestation of a broader European addiction to banks.

Europe's Banking Addiction

What are banks? At their core, they are a link between savers and borrowers. In their purest form, banks match deposits from those whose resources exceed their immediate spending needs with loans to those with investment projects too big for their own funds. More broadly, they raise funding for the loans they grant from many sources, including bonds sold in financial markets, and invest some of their funds not in loans to households and businesses but in financial securities or with other banks.

Linking those who want to save and those who want to borrow is crucial for economic efficiency and productivity growth. But banks are not the only way to match up borrowers and savers. It can be done through capital markets, where companies raise money from investors by issuing securities such as stocks and bonds. Another alternative are non-bank financiers, such as investment funds or private equity firms, which mimic what banks do well enough to merit the neologism 'shadow banks'. And new methods are appearing for peer-to-peer-lending, where saver and borrower cut out the middleman altogether.

Ever since Europe invented banking in the late middle ages, Europeans have seemed determined to stick to that method of allocating credit (although Britain makes relatively greater use of capital markets, which *it* largely invented). If you look at all the financial claims in the European economy, more than half can be found on the balance sheet of banks. Only 12 per cent take the form of company shares; bonds – tradable debt contracts – make up the bulk of the difference. The eurozone is even more lopsided in favour of banks than Europe at large. (See Figure 4.2.)

Comparing these numbers with the United States reveals just how inordinately bank-heavy the Old World is. The total amount of financing in the American economy is comparable to Europe, but the banks' share of financial claims is only 22 per cent, less than the 25 per cent share accounted for by stock market funding.

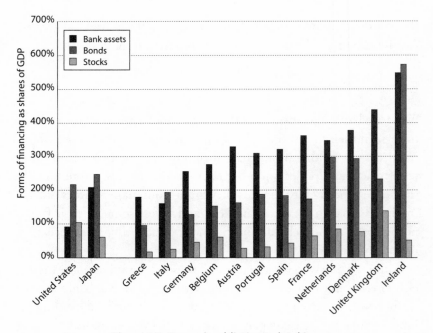

Figure 4.2. Europe's addiction to banking.
Source: IMF Global Financial Stability Review 2014.

Europe's love affair with banks makes for gargantuan banking systems, compared with other forms of finance and with the size of the physical economy. The total assets of banks in both the euro-zone and the EU as a whole are about three and a half times the regions' annual GDP. Europe's top ten banks alone hold assets worth €15 trillion, or 122 per cent of EU GDP; in the United States, that ratio is 44 per cent (and all US bank assets put together only reach 78 per cent of US GDP). The overgrown stature of Europe's banks looks even worse compared with the financial wherewithal of their individual national domiciles. Each of the biggest European banks has enough debts on its own to match or exceed its home country's annual GDP.[5] A recent expert report to the European Systemic Risk Board – the body responsible for spotting risks to the financial system as a whole – concluded that the banking system has grown to a size where it harms economic activity rather than boosting it.[6]

So banks and banking weave through the European economy like they do in no other part of the world. We should not be surprised to find them just as entangled with the region's political fabric. Politicians inevitably take an interest in the institutions that control the flow of credit; they would be negligent not to. But in most of the rich world, and almost everywhere in Europe, the connection between politics and banking go far beyond this. I am not making claims here about outright corruption in which political and regulatory favours are bought and sold, although such claims can be made. The point that matters most is that Europe's overdimensioned banking sector causes problems for politicians' ability to distinguish the interests of banks from those of the state, let alone the population.

In many countries banks are institutionally conjoined with the political sphere. Local savings banks such as Spain's *cajas de ahorro* or Germany's *Sparkassen* and *Landesbanken*; Italy's banking foundations; and Dexia, the Franco-Belgian lender to those countries' municipalities – all these are examples of banking structured so as to function as an extended branch of political power. And whenever an institution has become a political instrument, it is in the logic of power itself to make that institution's permanence a political goal.

Even where banks are largely owned by private shareholders – as in Ireland before the crash – the tell-tale signs of symbiotic relationships are evident. They can be seen in the banks' disproportionate investment in their own governments' sovereign debt[7] or in governments' extreme unwillingness to let one of 'their' banks succumb to market forces. Such a muddling of interests is natural, given the social proximity of banking and political elites everywhere. But it gives rise to the intellectual and moral error of confusing what is good for banks with what is good for the country.

Too Big to Fail

The most insidious route by which this error takes hold of a governing elite is through another conflation, this one between the banking system and the individual banking institutions that constitute it at any one time.

No modern economy can work without a basic well-functioning banking system (though it need not be gigantic in size, as the United

States shows). Apart from making decisions about where credit should flow, banks provide the essential means of storing value safely through their deposit accounts, and they manage the electronic payments system. These services are indispensable.

It does not follow that every bank that delivers them is indispensable. On the contrary, a strong banking system is one whose functions are perpetuated regardless of the fate of specific banks. It is useful to draw the analogy with a public utility – which banking should also be, in addition to whatever else it does. While an uninterrupted supply of electricity or water is obviously vital, that does not mean the same power or water companies must always own and operate the plants; indeed, the system is stronger the less power generation and water provision depend on the health of individual operators. If the continuity of essential social functions cannot be separated from the survival of existing for-profit enterprises, bad business decisions by individual companies take entire societies hostage.

Two characteristics of banking make this separation more difficult than in other vital industries. One is that in banking, the finances of the 'operators' and the service that is provided are to a large extent the same thing. A bank thought to be insolvent will very quickly lose its ability to carry out any banking functions at all as creditors and depositors hurry to redeem their funds: ATMs can run out of cash, business clients may lose their credit lines, the banks' trading commitments may not be honoured. Even a suspicion that this is possible can trigger a run on a bank, as the example of Northern Rock in the United Kingdom showed.

This fate can befall even a bank with more than enough assets to cover its debts, since depositors and creditors may demand their money back much faster than assets can be converted into the cash needed to pay them. Without liquidity, a bank can become dysfunctional within days. Normal corporate bankruptcy procedures are far too slow to wind down a failing bank. Long before competing claims on the bank's assets could be settled, the bank's operation would have collapsed, causing much bigger damage in the process.

The second complicating characteristic is contagion. If one bank goes down, every other bank suffers from the blow to public confidence. Fears that another bank will be next can be self-fulfilling if depositors or creditors act on it by rushing to pull their money out.

These are the reasons why politicians so often see banks, in the phrase that has penetrated the public consciousness to the point of cliche, as 'too big to fail'. More accurately (since it goes for small banks too), they see them as being too important to the financial system as a whole to be allowed to fail. A threat to individual institutions is seen as a threat to the system as a whole.

This belief has informed European policymaking from the beginning of the crisis, and policymakers felt confirmed in their conviction by the horrific scenario of the Lehman Brothers collapse (even though Lehman was not a deposit-taking bank – its big role was in the trading of financial securities). When the mega-bank was thrown into the pit of the ordinary US corporate bankruptcy process, it not only killed Lehman's business instantly but paralysed the global financial system and thrust the world economy into deep recession by upsetting all the expectations on which financial and physical business decisions were made. For years, nobody knew how much – if anything – they would get back from what had once seemed safe investments with Lehman.

But are banks actually too big to fail? It is not beyond the wit of man to set up what are now called 'special resolution regimes' for banks. These are emergency bankruptcy schemes that slice a bank up over a weekend to ensure that it can maintain its essential functions. They aim to dispel any self-fulfilling fears that it might not be able to by backing these and only these functions with a sufficient share of the bank's good assets. Other claimants are then left to share whatever assets are left over, in due time and according to ranks prescribed by law and contract. Their compensation can be shares in the new, healthier bank carved out from the wreckage of the old. In the United States, the Federal Deposit Insurance Corporation (FDIC) has operated such a system for deposit-taking banks since the 1930s.[8] As for Europe, a reformed UK Banking Act created a template for such a system as early in the crisis as February 2009.[9]

What about contagion? A proper resolution regime, while keeping the banking system safe from the losses of an individual business, might trigger fears that other banks with similar problems would be resolved in the same way. But if done according to an orderly process that keeps banking services functioning, bank resolution would not mean the unravelling of the system. The affected banks would be restructured, and new owners would take the old ones' place, but there is no reason to see this as a societal problem. Common conversions of banks' debt into shares in new and better banks would simply be the normal course of the banking industry. (Chapter 7 further pursues what a more restructuring-friendly banking system would look like.)

A deep scepticism about banking resolution and restructuring, however, has made European governments drag their feet. It has taken the whip of an EU directive to make governments set up mechanisms to enable orderly resolutions (the Bank Recovery and Resolution Directive, which I discuss in Chapter 6). Years were wasted before Europe grudgingly began to accept that banks should not be protected from market forces. Instead, states have put breathtaking amounts of taxpayer money into Europe's banks to keep them alive – a total of four and a half trillion euros in guarantees, capital injections and other subsidies in the three years after the Lehman bankruptcy[10] – never questioning whether they deserved to survive.

When Irish banks' loss-making investments caught up with them in 2009–10, each eurozone state was still treating its banks as an extension of itself, to be preserved come what may.

Pulled Down by a Helping Hand

The most glaring financial excrescence on any European body politic was Anglo Irish Bank. This small-sized lender had challenged larger Irish banks by lending aggressively into the housing bubble. It bore a significant responsibility for the inflating of property values – as well as of the price of its own stock. When house prices started sliding in 2007, Anglo was in the middle of the conflagration as investors took flight and debtors struggled to honour their claims. To camouflage its problems, Anglo gave loans to well-connected business people for them to buy shares in the bank to prop up its market value.

This and other questionable behaviour was possible because of Anglo's place in what seemed an extraordinary Irish success story. Its overly friendly relations with the government – epitomised by the shoulder rubbing and fundraising between bankers, property developers and Fianna Fáil politicians at the annual Galway Races – had earnt it their loyalty. Anglo's political capital would be the last of its funds to run dry.

The rankness of the banks' chummy relations with politicians was particularly intense in Ireland, but the phenomenon exists in other countries, inside and outside the euro. The single currency was not responsible for the lackadaisical regulation that led to overgrown banking systems. While Dublin did not set its own interest rate, all the levers of credit regulation it might wish for were at its disposal. It could have restrained Irish banks' ability to lend; it could have made it harder for Irish residents to borrow. The government chose not to do any of this.[11] There is no reason to think that being outside the euro would have made Ireland behave any less like Iceland, or that the international markets would have been less eager to fund it.

The single currency did, however, shape the country's options once the game was up. Again, this is not because monetary union robbed it of tools to tackle the crisis. If anything, the euro prolonged the ability to continue making bad choices when financial markets seized up, and the rest of the eurozone piled pressure on Dublin to perpetuate its mistakes. It was Ireland's peculiar misfortune to have enough rope to hang itself with and to be a member of a club where others expertly tied the knot.

This was the decisive difference between Ireland and Iceland when the world's banks abruptly stopped lending to one another after Lehman's bankruptcy in September 2008. Iceland's financial firms could not be helped. Any regulator would agree that the country's three big banks, accounting for virtually the entire domestic market, were too big to fail. But they were also too big for Reykjavik to bail out; their hard currency liquidity needs were far beyond the means of Iceland's tiny central bank. No one should harbour illusions about the quality of Icelandic banking policy before the crisis, but when the crunch came, Reykjavik – left with a choice between chaos and radical change – made a virtue of necessity. It swiftly dismembered the three big banks, separating the domestic from the foreign entries on their balance sheets. The domestic bits were nationalised into new entities to keep banking services functioning for Iceland's imploding economy. The foreign parts were sent into bankruptcy, chips falling where they might. It was an improvised but orderly act of bank resolution. The old banks were dead, but the system survived. An economy that had been powered entirely by the banks' lending inevitably suffered a big fall, but banking services remained available and people continued to access their (however shrunken, and no longer internationally convertible) savings and salaries.

If Iceland made virtue out of necessity, Ireland kept evading both necessity and virtue alike. Irish banks were largely funded in Ireland's own currency – the euro – and could post their assets against cash with one of the world's biggest central banks. This gave them a seemingly endless lifeline when interbank lending dried up. Moreover, the original health of its public finances encouraged Dublin to think it could restore confidence in the banks by backing them with the public purse. In the last days of September 2008 it did just that. In the same week as Reykjavik owned up to the reality that it must save the country from the sinking banks, Dublin determined that the banks – which, we must remember, had all been private companies – should not face the market storm on their own and instead be steadied by the ballast of a sovereign guarantee. For two years Irish taxpayers would back some €440 billion of private obligations that creditors could cash in at Ireland's public treasury if the debtor bank defaulted.

The Irish blanket guarantee, amounting to almost three years' worth of national income, was a folly. But for a while it seemed to do the trick. The outflow of capital from Irish banks temporarily reversed, to the ire of Ireland's neighbours, who feared Dublin's lavish guarantee would draw funds away from their own quivering banking systems. But it was really just the most indiscreet expression of a pan-European sentiment: that every government must stop 'our banks' from failing. Not all countries issued formal guarantees, but the promise, implicit or explicit, that creditors would be made whole no matter what was universal. (The rating agencies that assess the creditworthiness of bond issuers explicitly recognised this government backing in their ratings of banks.)

The logic behind a guarantee is to tide banks over a temporary market panic. It makes sense when banks' losses are small, and investors' self-fulfilling fears risk unnecessarily forcing them into premature bankruptcy. But this logic turns to madness if there are real concerns about whether the bank will ever be able to honour its debts – and it is hard to see why markets would panic if there was not at least some risk of this. When banks are so deep into the swamp of losses that the government cannot pull them out – which becomes more likely the bigger the banking system – a guarantee will only drag the public finances down with them.

That is what happened in Ireland. Its banks posted mounting losses on real estate loans gone sour. It was becoming clear that few if any Irish banks could avoid insolvency without help – but that would trigger the government's guarantees. The government instead pumped billion upon billion of public funds into what were once private banks in an attempt to keep them standing while collapsing house prices were eating away at their foundations.

It should not have come as surprise, but a guarantee with no credibility was turning out to be worse than no guarantee at all. In its attempt to win back markets' trust in Irish banks, the Irish government found it increasingly hard to retain their trust in itself. As holders of Dublin's sovereign debt worried their money would be thrown into the bottomless pit of the banks' losses, never to be retrieved, a self-reinforcing market panic set in. The rates charged on Irish public debt kept creeping up. In early November, LCH.Clearnet, the main marketplace for Irish bonds, increased the amount of cash that traders needed to deposit for the eventuality of a default. This forced a sell-off by bondholders needing to raise the extra cash, pushing the price even further down.[12] Left to its own devices, Dublin would eventually have to choose between its own creditworthiness and that of Irish banks. Trying to have both would secure neither.

ALTERNATIVES

By mid November, despite the government's protestations, most European observers became convinced that Dublin had no alternative but to turn to the new EFSF, with the Greek-style suspension of sovereignty that this would entail. There was a lot of magical thinking to this consensus, including an almost mystical belief that if government bond yields reached the arbitrary threshold of 7 per cent, the situation became 'unsustainable' and Ireland would be forced into a rescue.

In truth, the government's own finances were not all that precarious. With low original debt, high borrowing costs would be bearable so long as they did not last forever. Moreover, Dublin did not need to borrow for its own spending. As the government was keen to point out, it had cash to cover the deficit for another six months or so. Besides, when the financial aid rescue was later put together, Ireland was made to pour most of its own pension fund into the kitty. That held more than €20 billion, or nearly 15 per cent of GDP. If money was short, Dublin could have raided that reserve on its own; it did not need the eurozone to help it.[13]

In short, Ireland had a choice. On 12 November 2010, a *Financial Times* editorial described the considerations that should guide it:

> Ireland's debt yields, which have reached 8.9 per cent for 10 years, are unsustainable. Fortunately, they do not yet need to be sustained... Dublin should keep its cool. Good cash management means the yields are still largely theoretical: the government does not need funding until the middle of next year. But by then it must secure lower yields. Preparing the ground for liquidity support from the European Financial Stability Facility would be smart. Proving that the Irish state is firmly on the path to solvency would be smarter.
>
> The most imminent test is a new budget and four-year budget plan. Ireland has proved its ability to stomach painful fiscal consolidation. It will have to do more. The pain will be for nothing, however, if the state remains exposed to the banking sector. Anglo Irish, that festering stump of a bank, may at last have been amputated. But the government stands by a megalomaniac commitment to the creditworthiness of all Irish banks – which, it must be remembered, were all private companies once.

> The Irish are a hardy people, but their state is no Atlas. The grow-
> ing residential mortgage crisis could bring another bank to its knees.
> Markets are not crazy to think this is an unbearable contingent
> liability on the Irish taxpayer.[14]

This was the situation when Honohan sprung his fait accompli on the
government.

Despite the amount of money it had already wasted on the banks,
the Irish state was solvent provided it just stopped wasting more. And
with enough time, securing the state's solvency would also fix the
liquidity problem caused by the self-fulfilling mechanisms in the
markets. The question was how much time. If more was needed than
Dublin had ready funds, eurozone liquidity support could buy it. But
with no need to go to the markets for at least half a year, this was less
urgent than it was made out to be – except for the banks.

The funds with which Ireland could try to ride out the crisis would
not allow it to keep carrying the banking sector on its shoulders. The
mounting private losses to which Dublin had foolishly exposed itself
were precisely the reason why its sovereign solvency was now, entirely
unnecessarily, in doubt.

It was looking increasingly possible that Dublin would accept
what it had so long resisted, and restructure the banks' private debt,
including perhaps its own guarantees. Such a volte-face would be
humiliating, given how strongly the government – the same Fianna
Fáil–Green coalition was still in office – had defended the previous
policy. It would also be more expensive and riskier than had it been
done earlier. Some €30 billion, or 20 per cent of annual GDP, had
already been poured into the banks and would be lost in a restructuring. Many bank debts now had government guarantees that would be
hard to unwind without casting doubt on the government's willingness to honour its sovereign debt in full – even as it re-established its
ability to do so.

But Dublin was coming round to reality. In October it flexed its
muscle against bondholders for the first time, making junior bondholders in Anglo Irish Bank – by now completely state owned – an

offer they could not refuse. In a diabolically clever move, the government had junior bondholders vote on a resolution that would reduce the value of the bonds by 80 per cent for those who voted yes, but by 99.999 per cent for those who voted no. Behind this loomed the threat of forcible restructuring, a power Dublin belatedly gave itself by law at the end of 2010. The tough tactics worked: the required 75 per cent supermajority of bondholders in question passed the writedown.[15] The manoeuvre saved the taxpayer more than €1.5 billion. That was far less than the almost €30 billion that had been injected into the zombie bank, but it was not an insignificant amount, and it demonstrated the savings that would have been available by restructuring bonds more widely. The operation was later judged unfair in court,[16] but it illustrates Dublin's belated change of heart about whether taxpayers or bank creditors deserved its protection the most, as well as the savings available to a government determined to use all possible tools to minimise the burden on the public finances.

There was no shortage of such tools. Hardball as they may be, 'liability management exercises' like the one against Anglo's junior bondholders do not even amount to bank resolution, as they involve the consent of bondholders (albeit extracted at gun point). Outright resolution – with legally imposed writedowns of senior unsecured bonds – was always a further option, and even the IMF later admitted it was a mistake not to have used it (it says it advocated creditor writedowns at the time but was overruled by the European members of the troika).[17]

Many misgivings were voiced about such restructuring; none were convincing. The legal framework was not in place to allow for the restructuring of banks, it was said; but nothing stopped the Irish government from introducing it. An off-the-shelf template was available in the United Kingdom's Banking Act, passed the year before. It was also objected that 'haircuts' on bondholders would require the same treatment of ordinary depositors (whose claims were legally ranked the same as, or *pari passu* with, senior unsecured bondholders). But it would have been simple to introduce 'depositor preference' in the pecking order of the banks' capital structure. The United States did this in the early 1990s, and the European Commission would later tell EU states to do the same. It could have been confined to insured deposits, under €100,000.

Finally, there was the even more radical possibility of cancelling or modifying the temporary sovereign guarantee for the banks' liabilities. That guarantee was 'irrevocable' but only because the law said so – and a law can be changed. Selectively cancelling the guarantees (and proceeding to restructure the bank debt) while honouring all actual sovereign bonds was technically possible – what mattered was how markets would react. The received wisdom had it that the guarantee was as sacrosanct as sovereign debt itself, on the grounds that if creditors on guaranteed private bank debt took losses, they would expect the same with Dublin's own borrowing. But this argument ignores that it was precisely the guarantees that were pulling Dublin's creditworthiness down. There is good reason to believe that markets would have understood where Dublin drew the line and that a convincing case could be made that it would honour its sovereign borrowing even (indeed especially) if it cancelled the bank guarantee.[18]

The new fund for fiscal liquidity support, the EFSF, had been set up to offer bridge loans to solvent sovereigns in temporary liquidity trouble – exactly what Dublin could make good use of. But the eurozone set an extraordinary condition: that Dublin must desist from reducing its sovereign exposure to the banking sector. On the insistence of the ECB in particular, liability management exercises, let alone more radical measures, would not be applied more broadly, even though they would buttress Ireland's sovereign solvency. Dublin's belated tentative moves to correct its erroneous bail-out policy were aborted almost as soon as they were begun.

Why did the government not decline this 'rescue' and simply do as it said it would: rely on its own funds for the time being and work to regain market confidence? The significance of human psychology should not be underrated. Ireland's government was close to the end of its days, on the cusp of losing its parliamentary majority and discredited by the economic catastrophe over which it had presided. It had long since been rendered complacent by years in power; its ability to lead stunted by the shock of its own incompetence. The scale of the Irish tiger's humbling made it extraordinarily difficult to act tough in Brussels or Frankfurt, where the begrudging atmosphere was a far cry from the money-fuelled bonhomie of the Galway tents.

Fianna Fáil's excessive machismo at home had emasculated the country abroad. And in addition to an understandable lack of nerve, the eurozone was issuing threats to make the hardiest negotiator blanche.

Quid Pro Quo

By the time the radical idea that capitalism could be applied to banks floated onto the Irish government's intellectual radar, Dublin was deeply dependent on the rest of the eurozone. And for the eurozone, having Irish taxpayers pick up the bill was more convenient than letting banks pay for their own unaffordable mistakes, as it had been in the Greek case. European decision makers would go to great lengths to stop Ireland from trespassing against the dogma that senior creditors to a European bank must never lose money. Dublin's belated and reluctant willingness to look at senior bond haircuts was met, in Honohan's words, with 'no enthusiasm' in the rest of the eurozone.[19] That euphemism hides a breathtaking threat that Honohan himself had a hand in issuing.

To the extent Dublin still wanted to stand by its catastrophic, open-ended bail-out of banks, it would need external aid. To receive that aid there was, as Honohan put it, a 'certain amount of quid pro quo involved'. But the most important 'quid' was not the budget aid from the eurozone rescue fund agreed in the last weeks of 2010 – which the government in Dublin was, if anything, having forced down its throat. It was what Honohan termed the ECB's 'liberal attitude ... in regard to the funding of Irish banks'.

A bank on the cusp of failure needs capital of two kinds. First, injections of new equity to replenish legally required capital cushions that losses may have eaten into. This is the bank's (or its owners') own money at risk, supposed to discourage excessive gambling with the much larger sums the bank borrows from others. Second, it may need to replace those borrowed funds if its usual creditors get cold feet. A bank's assets – its loans to households and businesses – are mostly long term (think of thirty-year mortgage loans) and cannot be quickly liquidated, so it needs constantly available sources of borrowing to refinance short-term debts.

For as long as it lasted, Irish banks could count on the government for new equity. For borrowed funds, however, the backstop was the central bank. Just before the blanket guarantee expired in September 2010, investors redeemed large chunks of Irish bank debt, and they kept drawing down their deposits in the months that followed. To cover this, ECB lending to Ireland reached about €100 billion, and half that again was extended in 'emergency liquidity assistance' by the Central Bank of Ireland.[20] These central bank loans were on the scale of all bank deposits owned by every Irish person and business, or of everything the Irish economy produces in an entire year.

Such central bank dependence is, for sure, a crisis phenomenon. But it was also evidence that the European monetary union worked. Without the eurozone's orderly system to allow the free movement of euros from one country to another, this degree of capital flight would have caused a massive devaluation and a likely collapse of the banking system. Avoiding that is what a central bank is for: it is its job to lend in the last resort when the private market is in distress. And yet this lending, which should have been a point of pride for the ECB, made Frankfurt queasy in the extreme. The central bank plainly feared it might not get its money back. As long as it stepped into the breach in private funding for Irish banks, the ECB behaved as the systemic public safeguard it is set up to be. But its attitude – akin to saving the banking system while pinching its nose – made it look more like a private banking outfit, and an ultra-conservative one at that. Frankfurt disliked doing its job to the point of betraying its mandate as the central public institution for the whole monetary union.

For what Honohan's quid pro quo meant, fully spelt out, was that the ECB was demanding concessions in return for the last liquidity lifeline enjoyed by Irish banks. It would only maintain emergency liquidity assistance, the ECB threatened, if the elected Irish government abdicated its authority over how to allocate the losses from the country's banking bust. And there was nothing indirect about the threats: they were written in black and white in a letter from Trichet to Lenihan – a letter that was secret at the time but that was leaked to the press in November 2014.[21]

The ECB could legitimately warn it would only lend to solvent banks. But it went much further when it demanded that solvency be restored by making taxpayers pay, rather than making creditors face losses. The ECB was quite clearly demanding specific distributive policy decisions as a condition for doing its job as lender of last resort. A policy of 'burning the bondholders', as many in Ireland were now calling for, would mean the end of emergency lending to Irish banks – or so the ECB threatened.[22]

There is no doubt what would have followed from such an act. Ordinary people – wage earners, pensioners and savers – as well as businesses, small and large, would suddenly not be able to pay their bills, withdraw money or rely on their savings being available for anything from retirement to a house purchase. Only emergency lending to Anglo had avoided this in early 2010. Without it, the financial system would cease to function, and the anticipation of this would accelerate the outcome by triggering an immediate run on the banks. If it went that far, the government's only way out of an intolerable scenario would be either to impose capital controls on the banks (bans on taking money out) or provide them with another means of liquidity (that is to say, print its own currency). In effect, the ECB's threat was that it would do its best to force Ireland out of the euro if it did not get its way on a policy decision that was essentially fiscal – about what taxpayers' money should be spent on.

The ECB's strong inflation-fighting mandate means it must be cautious when expanding the money supply, especially if the newly printed money leads to losses on its own account. But it was far-fetched for the ECB to worry about its exposure to Irish banks. The central bank has better protection against losses than most creditors, since its loans are secured against collateral. If a bank fails, the central bank takes possession of the assets pledged as security (which are worth more than the loan itself to leave an extra safety margin) and sells them on as and when it sees fit to get the best return.

The ECB knew this from experience. When Lehman Brothers failed, the Bundesbank, on behalf of the ECB, was stuck with assets from Lehman's eurozone operations.[23] This may have been an inconvenience – it is always simpler just to get one's cash back – but collateral guards against risk. In the case of Lehman, the ECB made its money back after selling off the assets that had backed an €8.5 billion loan for around that amount. The ECB's secured position would have put it ahead of other creditors in any Irish bank restructuring too, limiting its chance of losses.

Moreover, a loss for a central bank is less than meets the eye. Central banks cannot go bankrupt because they can always create money out of thin air. In normal times, this can drive inflation (although Ireland is a tiny share of the eurozone economy, the precedent of printing money to replenish banks' funding could lead to inflation-fuelling expectations of greater liberality elsewhere). But these were not normal times. Because of the broken banking system, the ECB's balance sheet has doubled and trebled since the start of the crisis, but the broad money supply has barely managed to tread water. All the ECB's money printing has at best managed to arrest what would otherwise have been a steep and deflationary monetary contraction.

It is natural to conclude that it was not just its own losses the ECB was concerned about but losses for private banks in other eurozone countries that had put their capital at risk in Ireland.

For the ECB to threaten to go on strike – to stop lending in the last resort – was not an act of financial prudence but one of anti-democratic blackmail against Ireland's hapless government. But if the ECB used illegitimate means, was Frankfurt at least in pursuit of a defensible cause?

LEHMAN SYNDROME

The ECB's transgression was only possible because of Europe's hegemonic consensus that senior claims on banks were untouchable. As with any dogma, this was asserted as self-evident rather than justified by argument. But the professed considerations in its favour crumble under scrutiny. An ideological opposition to restructuring was the fundamental motive behind Europe's actions in the first two years of the crisis.

Cui bono the protection of profit-seeking private investors? The most powerful parties – above all Germany and the ECB, but also the United Kingdom in this case – had a direct interest in Irish banks' creditors being made whole. Those creditors included, to the tune of hundreds of billions of euros, the ECB itself, as well as German and British (and to a lesser extent French) banks. But private gain is not a public justification. The ECB had not been lending to Irish banks to do Ireland a favour; it did so because it was its job. Not all ECB staff grasped this. Klaus Masuch, its head of mission to Ireland, told the BBC that the central bank's lending in the last resort was a 'privilege':

> People in Ireland were not aware of the enormous support that they get from the Eurosystem. This is a privilege, of course. The partners in the Eurozone also expect that every partner ... is doing its own homework.[24]

While Frankfurt would no doubt prefer simply to get its money back without having to deal with the messy process of selling off collateral, convenience does not legitimate the indenture of an entire people. German and British banks, on the other hand, would have incurred real losses if their unsecured loans to Irish ones were restructured. That would have moved Dublin's problem of undercapitalised banks onto the German and British governments' hands. But if that was the problem, the better solution (like with Greece's creditors) would have been to bail those banks out directly. (Even the Bundesbank was not opposed to restructuring Irish bank bonds, according to its later president Jens Weidmann.[25]) Instead, the German and UK treasuries bailed them out on the sly – by lending Dublin the money to pay off private Irish bank debts and handing the bill to Ireland's taxpayers.

One argument heard in the eurozone is that because the Irish government failed to regulate its banks properly, it is right for the Irish government to cover the losses that this made possible. But capitalism is not paternalism, and financial institutions (whether Irish or the foreign ones that lent to them) are not and should not be treated as children whose mistakes are their parents' responsibility.

Another argument is that there was little to gain by restructuring. By November 2010, most of the damage to Ireland's public purse had already been done. Many investors had taken the opportunity to pull their money out, and only a small part of the banks' debt still took the form of senior bonds not backed by collateral or state guarantees. But European pressure did not start only when the rescue package was being negotiated: it had been mounting in step with the increased reliance of Irish banks on central bank support. The right kind of encouragement from Brussels and Frankfurt might have cajoled Dublin into mitigating the mistake of tying its public creditworthiness to the sinking banks. And even after the 'rescue', they could have supported treating the state's own loans differently from guarantees of loans taken up by banks. Instead they insisted that Ireland keep carrying an impossible burden on its shoulders. In any case, to describe the €20 billion of bank debt that was still available for restructuring as 'small' is both misleading and offensive to Irish taxpayers stuck with the burden. It may be small compared with the €10 trillion eurozone economy, or the €750 billion firepower of the EFSF. But it would not have been a small share of the €85 billion rescue programme. Writing off €20 billion, or even less, would have saved Ireland up to a third of the money it eventually pumped into its banks, or some 13 per cent of GDP. Far from being small, that is more than the entire fiscal cost of most banking crises in history.

But most eurozone officials were less interested in how many billion euros Ireland could save than in the damage they feared a bank restructuring might cause. Their official argument was that hurting senior creditors in one bank would trigger a run on banks elsewhere, as no senior creditor would any longer feel safe. 'It would have been a European Lehman', Honohan later said, expressing the view of many ECB colleagues, of the European Commission and of Timothy Geithner, the US Treasury Secretary. It was impossible, at this time, to have a discussion with European officials on the merits of creditor 'haircuts' without quickly butting up against a mention of Lehman. Europe's entire policymaking community was haunted by – and pressured by Washington to give into – the fear that letting investors in a small Irish bank pay the price of its failure would have the same paralysing effect on the international banking system as when Lehman Brothers went bankrupt in October 2008. The same policymaking community refrained from drawing the obvious further conclusion that, if their view of the systemic risk was correct, it was unreasonable to require Irish taxpayers alone to finance the salvation of the pan-European banking system. Irish officials have consistently, correctly and so far unsuccessfully argued that Ireland 'took one for the team', so the 'team' should share the burden, ideally by having the eurozone buy out the Irish government's stake in some of the banks it recapitalised.

In any case, it was a preposterous comparison. Lehman was a global bank, with a balance sheet in the trillions. It was a central hub in the overnight lending market between big banks, and a huge counterpart in the derivatives trade. The bank was at the heart of the world's financial plumbing. Anglo, by contrast, was a small racket on Europe's financial periphery, busily and exuberantly losing its investors' money in the time-honoured way of lending more for houses than they were worth.

Nothing systemic depended on Anglo repaying its creditors in full – unless it was a supposed psychological effect on investors who might think that if it can happen to Anglo, it can happen to any bank. But to think writedowns in one bank, no matter how awfully managed, will sow panic among investors in any bank, no matter how solid, is to slander investors' ability to distinguish between different businesses.

Investors in bank bonds took a much less alarmist view. 'Bailing in' senior bondholders would on average cause banks to pay 0.87 percentage points more to their creditors, studies found at the time.[26] That is considerable – it could amount to hundreds of billions a year across all of Europe – but not the end of the world, especially if it led to a safer financial system.

More fundamentally, the contagion argument is simply wrong. We know this because it has been tried, and in each case investors knew better. Two years earlier, the three Icelandic banks had been wound down leaving senior creditors in the red – and the world did not end. And a month before Honohan asserted that touching senior bank bondholders would cause 'another Lehman', a European bank did just that with the blessing – indeed at the insistence – of its national authorities. The nation in question was Denmark, whose financial regulator, on deeming the small bank Amagerbanken insolvent and unable to recapitalise itself privately, summarily took it over, wrote down shareholders and junior creditors to zero, and cut senior creditors' claims by 41 per cent. It all happened over a weekend, and by Monday a new bank was operating normally, with all its client relationships in place and functioning. Small depositors were made whole by the national deposit insurance scheme, as were some guaranteed bonds, for which the government took the bill. No contagion materialised, beyond a small increase in the funding costs of other Danish banks. Just while most eurozone officials claimed the opposite, Denmark proved that investors react to the removal of a public guarantee by marginally adjusting the price they charge for default risk, not by suddenly seeing default looming everywhere.[27]

Even on self-interested grounds, then, opposing Irish bank restructuring was wasteful; as a policy of general prudence, it set a catastrophically counterproductive precedent of weighing down sovereign finances with private debt burdens. All Europe achieved by its 'rescue' of Ireland was to increase the markets' doubts as to whether sovereign liabilities would be honoured. This policy was rooted not in evidence or principles, but in fear and bias. Like with Greece, a quasi-theological view of debt shaped European decision making, which made a taboo out of restructuring and discouraged any acknowledgement of the fact that debts that cannot be paid, will not.

FIVE
Europe Digs Deeper

DOUBLING DOWN

BY FORSWEARING SOVEREIGN RESTRUCTURING in Greece and bank restructuring in Ireland, the eurozone countries raised the cost of the economic adjustments those two economies had to undergo. Most directly, honouring outstanding external debts in full meant that bigger deficit cuts had to be made elsewhere for a given overall deficit reduction. In addition, banking systems remained paralysingly undercapitalised. The taboo on restructuring meant a bank's solvency was precariously dependent on its government's dubious ability to bail it out. With private sources predictably reluctant to fund Greek and Irish banks until all losses had been purged from the system, and the ECB making clear its distaste for doing its job as lender of last resort, the credit crunch deepened for both countries. The economic damage these policies inflicted, together with the erosion of a democratic and autonomous policymaking process, made the job of economic and budgetary restructuring all the harder. The same procedure – with similar consequences – was followed when Portugal, a few months after Ireland, faced rising refinancing costs in bond markets. Under duress from an ECB threatening to cut liquidity to Portuguese banks, Lisbon resigned itself to financial support conditioned on a similar policy programme: radical austerity, structural reforms, a taxpayer bail-out of banks, and the subjection of elected politicians to the troika technocracy.

These policies would have been painful anywhere and under any circumstances. Many of their detailed prescriptions were misguided. Even so, they might have bought more gain for less pain if growth in the rest of the eurozone had accelerated, boosting financial sector confidence and demand for the programme countries' exports. The eurozone's intervention into these three small, undeniably mismanaged, economies did not, however, bring the broader crisis to an end. Instead it made it worse. Investors shunned the programme countries more than ever, and as 2010 rolled into 2011, Spain and Italy were having an increasingly hard time of it in the bond markets too. Having based its 'rescues' of the first three countries on an erroneous premise, the eurozone was logically committed to doubling down on a strategy that was part of the problem. Rather than admitting mistakes, leaders came to deem the medicine prescribed for Athens, Dublin and Lisbon suitable for the rest of the eurozone too. So long as they held on to their original diagnosis, they could not recognise that the precedents set in the smaller countries were perpetuating the crisis. By letting the same errors govern policy towards the eurozone's bigger members, its leaders turned what had been a grave crisis into an existential one.

Austere Solidarity: All Must Tighten

There was a time, not long ago, when Germany saw the point of fiscal stimulus, though not as something to talk too loudly about. As late as 2008–9, Berlin joined the rest of the world in unleashing the public purse to turn the slumping global economy around. When world leaders agreed to coordinate fiscal stimulus packages, Germany boosted public spending as a share of its economy more than any other EU country.[1]

But even before the sovereign debt crisis broke out, Berlin's selective *sotto voce* tolerance of fiscal stimulus was giving way to an ever more universal *Verbot* in response to the deficits that had opened up like crevasses across Europe and beyond. While Berlin accepted eurozone and US pressure for the Greek rescue and the EFSF 'firewall' in May 2010, it took the fact that they were needed as a vindication of its long campaign against fiscal profligacy. The Greek experience bolstered suspicions, always strong in Germany, that the euro's weaker economies could not be trusted to keep their public finances in order, and that this fiscal irresponsibility was why instability was now rocking the eurozone.

Germany saw itself as leading by example. Only a year earlier it had introduced a *Schuldenbremse,* or 'debt brake', into its constitution, which required the federal government to reduce its structural deficit to a hair's breadth from zero by 2016 and then to keep it there.[2] Now Merkel and Schäuble were determined to make genuine fiscal discipline in fellow euro members – even constitutional *Schuldenbremsen* like their own – the price of German financial support. Recalling (if not quite trumpeting) that Berlin had been one of the first to break the original stability and growth pact with impunity (see Chapter 1), they wanted new rules to be legally ironclad, with financial sanctions automatically imposed on violators, and with the EU's Court of Justice, not politicians, acting as arbiter. In an effort to avoid making a precedent of the 2010 Greek rescue loan, they also insisted on having the option to restructure the debt of any sovereign in need of rescuing after 2013.

The eurozone's sudden turn to universal fiscal tightening was of huge economic significance, but its political importance was even greater. It is a mark of Germany's dominance of Europe that it could prevail over sovereign counterparts who were free to decline the full extent of Berlin's preferred economic policy. This was not just about the desire of others for German money, though it was that as well: a permanent financial commitment was being sought for when the three-year EFSF expired. But it also reflected an inferiority complex towards a Germany that, from 'sick man of Europe' only a decade earlier, was now the region's indisputably strongest economy, and was powering back from the crisis like no other big European country.

This psychological imbalance weighed on the relationship between Germany and France, the traditional dual motor of European integration. At a Franco-German summit in Deauville in October 2010, Merkel and Sarkozy agreed on a policy package mostly along German lines: rooting and circumscribing the sovereign rescue arrangements in the EU treaties rather than ad hoc arrangements – the EFSF would be replaced by a permanent, treaty-based European Stability Mechanism (ESM); backing fiscal rules with harsher legal enforcement; and making it possible to write down the public debt of a rescued government in the future. The only concession to Paris was that sanctions on budget rule breakers would require agreement by EU ministers, not just the say-so of the European Commission.[3]

Deauville caused bad blood for a number of reasons. The rest of Europe, small countries in particular, resented having the privately agreed Franco-German pact foisted on them as a fait accompli. The substance, too, was badly received. Most countries thought Germany was crazy to demand treaty change after a string of traumatic episodes where EU constitutional reforms had suffered humiliating referendum defeats in some countries and barely scraped by in others.

The talk of restructuring infuriated states desperate not to spook restive markets whose demand for their own bonds was in doubt. Trichet, in one of the ECB's many trespasses onto the ground of national fiscal policy, was livid at the softening of sanctions for fiscal indiscipline.[4] And – though this is largely forgotten today – many were angry at the whole idea of a permanent rescue fund. Olli Rehn, the commissioner for economic and monetary affairs, railed against the 'moral hazard' the existence of such a fund would create, since countries reluctant to reform their economies and fix their finances would now feel the pressure was off.[5]

As always, European policy was born from compromise, and the Deauville decisions were marginally adjusted to take account of everyone's main priorities. But for many eurozone countries, and for much of the ECB, the overriding aim was to secure the German financial underwriting of the euro that they perceived as absolutely necessary. That required accommodating the imperative for Berlin and its allies, including the European Commission, to limit the indebtedness that generated this demand. It also required as much control as possible over the money that creditor countries would lend to prop up debtors. The final agreement, moreover, hollowed out the minor French victory at Deauville. Rather than requiring the express support of a majority of ministers, sanctions would now go ahead automatically unless a majority opposed them.

This pattern asserted itself repeatedly over the next eighteen months. In sum, Merkel overwhelmingly got her way not just with Sarkozy but with the rest of the eurozone too. Her quick march through the European institutions – which soon spawned new powers for the Commission to inspect and reject national budgets as well as tougher sanctions for straying from the straight and narrow budget path – culminated in the 'fiscal compact', the full name of which is the 'Treaty on Stability, Coordination and Governance in the Economic and Monetary Union'. It obliges not just eurozone states but almost every EU government, as a matter of international law, to run a structurally balanced budget, and, if its debt is above the Maastricht limit, a big enough surplus to reduce it by 5 per cent every year.

THE EUROZONE'S SELF-INFLICTED SECOND DOWNTURN

These institutional innovations, all favouring tighter fiscal policy, were matched by policy actions. In the first three months of 2009, the eurozone economy had shrunk at a speed corresponding to 10 per cent per year. But even as Europe was joining the rest of the world in a coordinated fiscal stimulus to arrest the economic collapse, it was busily preparing to reverse course. A crisis-fighting summit of the G20 (the world's twenty most powerful economies) took place in London in April 2009. Only months later, the EU enthusiastically wielded the 'excessive deficit procedure' (EDP), that cease-and-desist procedure of the stability and growth pact by which a government is told it is breaking the fiscal deficit rule and must stop doing so. A full twelve eurozone countries (as well as the United Kingdom and most of central Europe) were put into the EDP, with more to follow in 2010. The requirement to cut deficits was, it seemed, universal.

Compliance was more or less universal as well, if measured by how much governments reduced their structural primary deficit – the underlying gap between revenue and spending net of interest expenses, adjusted for the effect of the economic cycle and one-off embellishments. From 2009 to 2010 all EU countries except Greece, Ireland, the United Kingdom and Belgium had let their structural primary balances worsen or at least remain unchanged. But from 2010 to 2012, almost all were implementing severe cuts – most notably every large eurozone economy. (See Figure 5.1.) Germany, France, Italy and the Netherlands all tightened their structural primary balance by 2–3 per cent of GDP; Spain cut its structural primary deficit by more

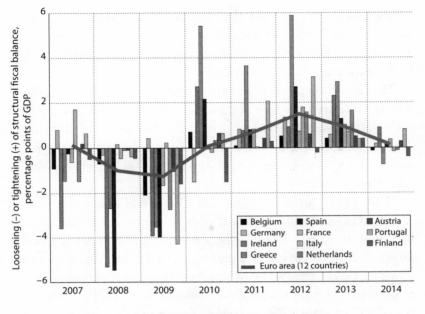

Figure 5.1. From stimulus to austerity.
Source: EC Annual Macroeconomic Database.

than 4 per cent of GDP. For the eurozone as a whole, the structural tightening was 2.4 per cent of GDP over those two years.[6]

The misguided generalisation of local austerity programmes in countries that had little other choice into a policy of universal belt tightening undermined the recovery and shrank the revenue base from which the public debt was supposed to be serviced. Academic research has estimated that the eurozone's GDP in 2013 was 7.7 per cent lower than it would have been without the fiscal consolidation; other studies suggest output losses two or even three times as large. As a result of the big impact on economic activity, the actual budgetary savings from fiscal consolidation were small. Even in terms of their ostensible purpose – making public finances more sustainable – deficit cuts in a barely recovering economy were exactly the wrong thing to do.[7]

But blame also falls on the ECB, whose monetary policy exacerbated the fall in economic activity. Like other central banks, Frankfurt's monetary loosening since the global financial storm made landfall went far beyond what central banks ever thought it was conceivable for them to do. In particular, the ECB had vastly expanded the size of its operations to flood eurozone banks with as much cheap funding as they asked for. But compared with the scale of the challenge, the ECB's measures, while extraordinary, were also too timid.

The decision to raise interest rates in April 2011, and then again in July, is the clearest instance of the ECB's tight-fistedness. It coincided with the growing political impetus for universal fiscal tightening. Where monetary policy could have softened the blow of the fiscal backtracking – itself misguided in its eurozone-wide scope – the ECB added weight to the punch.

There was no justification for this. One would have had to squint very hard to catch sight of any inflation on the horizon. Price growth had accelerated into the mid-2 per cent range, a bit above the ECB's target of 'close to but below 2 per cent'. But Trichet himself put this down to a short-term spike in commodity prices that was expected to pass. Private forecasters agreed. Indeed, in the ECB's regular survey of independent forecasters, the average inflation prediction did not exceed 2 per cent for any period beyond the same year.[8] What was more, this had been true since the start of 2009 – and has remained true since. The ECB was fighting a danger nobody else could see.

In doing so, it aggravated the real dangers that threatened. Since the start of the crisis, banks had been telling the ECB that they were making it harder for businesses and households to borrow. They were just beginning to stop tightening lending standards when Trichet and his colleagues saw fit to raise the cost of credit to the banking system. Predictably enough, the combined fiscal and monetary squeeze made banks even more unwilling to lend. (See Figure 5.2.) Moreover, the factors that banks most blamed for the hardening credit squeeze were their own funding costs and poor prospects for economic growth – both of which would be hurt by the ECB's rate hike.[9]

The credit crunch was evident from the figures on lending growth, or rather the lack thereof. (See Figure 5.3.) Lending to households was barely keeping up with inflation; lending to businesses had completely stagnated, so adjusted for inflation, real credit to Europe's employers was shrinking.[10] The broad money supply (known as M3)

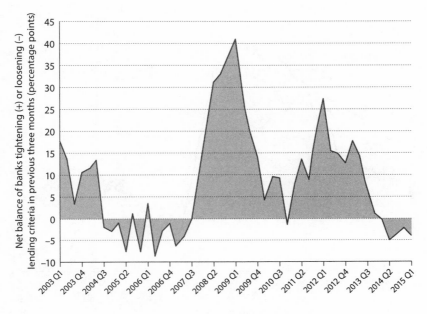

Figure 5.2. The six-year credit crunch.
Source: ECB.

had peaked just before Greece lost access to financial markets and was treading water in early 2011. In inflation-adjusted terms, a shrinking volume of money was supporting what was hoped to be a growing pace of economic activity. This was because the relationship between the expanding monetary base – money directly created by the central bank – and the volume of money for transactions circulating through the accounts of households and businesses was being compressed by the paralysis of the banking system. Despite Frankfurt's relative monetary activism and low interest rate, monetary conditions in the economy were getting tighter, not looser.

The results were entirely predictable. In the first quarter of 2011, the eurozone grew at a respectable annualised rate around 3.2 per cent. But by the end of the year, the bloc was back in recession. (See Figure 5.4.) From mid 2011 on, the French and Austrian economies ground to a halt; Italy, Spain, the Netherlands and Finland went into reverse for the next two years. Even Germany's economy ended 2012 the same size as it had been at the start of the year.

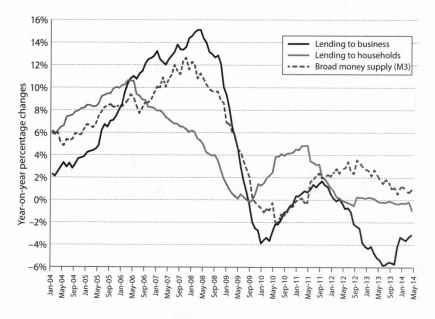

Figure 5.3. Money and credit conditions.
Source: ECB.

The countries with the biggest deficits or largest debts were also those whose GDP suffered the most from fiscal and monetary tightening at the eurozone level, which eroded the external demand that could have offset the damage to domestic demand from national belt tightening and credit crunches. The Spanish and Italian economies had both shrunk by almost 10 per cent by the end of 2013; the smaller rescue victims by much more. This made debt burdens heavier: to reduce the debt of a state whose economy is shrinking, it must run just to stand still – and that running makes things even worse.

Unsurprisingly, bond markets, which had stabilised after the Greek and Irish dramas, again began to shed Spanish and Italian bonds in response to the bad economic news. In February 2011 the additional interest investors demanded to lend to Madrid and Rome, rather than Berlin, had fallen back to about 2 and 1.5 percentage points, respectively. By July, after Trichet's two interest rate hikes, they had risen to 3 and 2; by November, to 4 and 5. (See Figure 5.5.) Universal austerity and monetary tightening, both justified as necessary for debt

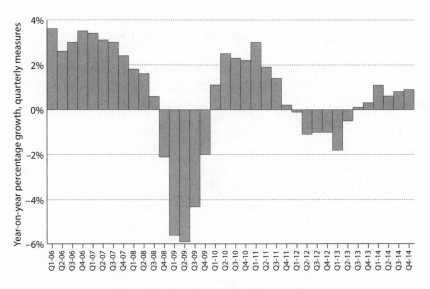

Figure 5.4. Eurozone economic growth.
Source: Eurostat.

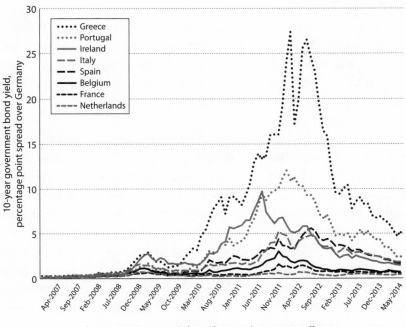

Figure 5.5. Euro periphery borrowing costs spike.
Source: ECB.

reduction and to win back the confidence of creditors, had made debt burdens worse and market confidence more elusive than ever.

Letting Zombie Banks Roam

The credit crunch was exacerbated by the ECB not taking more aggressive action to boost money and loan growth, but its root cause was in the sorry state of Europe's banks. It was clear that they were vastly undercapitalised: in 2009 the IMF had estimated that the euro-zone banking system was some €550 billion short of required capital once unrealised but likely losses were taken into account.[11]

Keeping badly run and loss-ridden banks alive clogs the pipes through which credit flows. Europe's heavy reliance on banks made the crisis worse – bank-intermediated finance tends to amplify the damage of a given financial disruption more than other types of financial flows.[12] Because damaged banks know that their capital is likely to be eaten up by losses yet to come, they try to retrench rather than expand, reducing their lending – 'deleveraging' in the jargon – to meet capital adequacy requirements more easily. That holds the real economy back, which in turn increases the losses of banks. Zombie banks stalking Europe's credit market – too damaged to live but kept from dying by the black magic of public backstops and regulatory forbearance – were by 2010–11 starving the economy of credit and blunting the effect of monetary stimulus. That is why the ECB needed to do more, not less.

There are three ways one can address this sort of problem, aside from a long-term imperative to shift the financial system away from banks as the main providers of finance to business (discussed in Chapter 8). In the short term, the fixes all involve getting enough capital into the sickly banks to absorb any conceivable losses, so that they are free to expand lending again.

One solution is to buy newly issued shares from the banks with public funds. This is what the Irish did. Aside from being a public subsidy of private profits, such funds are hard to divert from other uses at a time of fiscal stress. *In extremis*, doing so can sink the sovereign's finances.

Second, banks could be forced by regulators to raise more equity from private investors. But private money managers had little reason to put their money at risk in European banks whose true state of health remained obscure after unconvincing capital adequacy tests. More transparency – and it would have had to be much more – would have allowed investors to separate the wheat from the chaff, robust balance sheets from threadbare ones. But that would quickly have made the situation worse for the most rotten specimens, which was something European governments, with their misguided tribal attachment to 'their' banks, went to great lengths to avoid. Until late 2014, the EU's stress tests of its banks were tragicomically ill-suited to inspiring investor confidence, unlike the US ones, which started righting the banking sector from early 2009.

The third option, and the natural course to take with zombies, would have been to let them die, using special resolution regimes to carve out good banks that would carry on with the essential banking business and leave the loss-making parts in the remaining shells of the old. By earmarking enough assets for the good bank, wiping out shareholders and subordinated bondholders in the process and turning creditors into shareholders in the new bank, almost any needed amount of recapitalisation can be achieved. Europe's taboo against losses for senior creditors to banks, however, ruled this option out. The banking system was left to rot.

The situation was especially bad in the peripheral countries. Here were the banks that had overreached the most in their attempt to recycle the enormous current account deficits coming their way – often courtesy of German and French lenders – into dubious investments. They were also the most exposed to the troubled sovereigns. As the bonds of the governments in Madrid and Rome sank in market value, so did the balance sheets of Spanish and Italian banks, which made it harder for them, too, to borrow at reasonable rates. Since governments were expected to backstop ailing banks, this in turn added to the potential debt burden of the government, adding to the fright of sovereign bond buyers. Now the danger of Europe's entanglement between states and banks became clear. The desire to maintain a national banking system inside a currency union – a system where banks are primarily a national responsibility and in return buy a lot of their own government's debt – leads to a situation where banks and state can drag one another down in a mutually lethal embrace. A sovereign debt crisis affects banks because of the doubt it casts on fiscal support; bank insolvency affects the sovereign because the cost has traditionally been taken on the government budget.

This should not be seen as a flaw in the euro's design. Nothing about the euro itself forced governments to maintain such incestuous relationships with banks. No technical barriers stopped them from following Denmark's lead of recapitalising failing banks by forcing losses on bondholders. But as Ireland showed, any government ready to contemplate this was met with intense peer pressure to refrain. It was only when a collective commitment was struck to share some costs of bank bail-outs that the eurozone's sovereigns began to give up their special relationships with banks (on which more in Chapter 6) – and even that only happened after things had first got much worse. Blaming the euro for this political foot-dragging misses the point.

In all these ways the eurozone's early crisis policies made things worse. The doctrine of bailing out bank creditors added to public debt; excessive fiscal and monetary tightening squeezed the output from which that debt service could be paid; and the taboo on restructuring ensured that if debt problems emerged in either the public or the private sector, one would infect the other. Predictably enough, these policies hurt confidence in debtor economies' creditworthiness rather than boosted it. Lenders and investors began withdrawing their money from debtor Europe en masse, with little discrimination between the private and public sectors.

The euro's creators had thought the single currency would protect a country's private sector from public irresponsibility. By adopting policies that actively chipped away at that protection, their successors were unpicking the monetary union's seams.

DEATH BY ACCOUNTING

In 2011 an obscure accounting convention, from which the public had been mercifully shielded by the shroud of boredom that usually envelops such things, suddenly morphed into a powerful propaganda tool against the monetary union. The credit for this belongs to Hans-Werner Sinn, the president of the Munich-based Ifo Institute for Economic Research. Through his denunciations of Target2, the euro's settlement system for cross-country bank transactions, the single currency was nearly destroyed by the implications of double-entry book-keeping.

When the European monetary union was created, it retained vestigial traces of the pre-euro era by delegating monetary operations to the national central banks. Money transferred between bank accounts in two different countries passes through the two national central banks on the way. If a euro is sent from an Irish bank account to a German one, for example, the Central Bank of Ireland deducts a euro from the central bank reserves of the bank where the sender's account is held, while the Bundesbank issues one euro to the reserves of the German recipient's bank. In the accounts of the eurozone monetary system (the 'eurosystem'), this shows up as a debt owed by the Central Bank of Ireland to the eurosystem as a whole, and as a claim held against the eurosystem by the Bundesbank. As the example shows, this does not mean the Bundesbank has lent a euro to Ireland; it simply reflects that a euro has been electronically withdrawn from circulation in Ireland and 'printed' in Germany to accommodate the transfer. If the operational implementation of the euro had left commercial banks to deal directly with the ECB, only changes in their account balances with the ECB would have been visible, with no effect on national central banks' balance sheets. But as an artefact of the eurosystem's operational procedures and of double-entry book-keeping, any euro crossing a national border shows up in notional claims and liabilities between the eurosystem's constituent national banks.[13]

In earlier times, balance-of-payments crises meant outflows of gold or foreign exchange reserves, and, if the problem was big enough, devaluations – sometimes drastic ones – when the reserves ran out or humiliated governments gave up the fight. With monetary unification, this was history. A euro travels from one EMU country to another with no movement of reserves or gold necessary to back the parity of the exchange, just like a dollar between US states. Still,

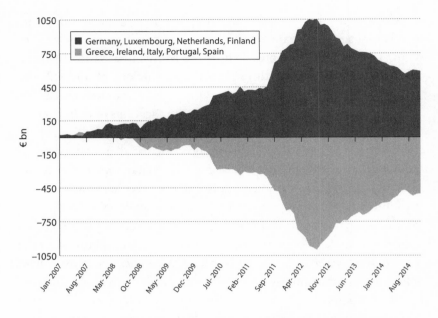

Figure 5.6. Target2 balances. *Source*: Euro Crisis Monitor, Institute
of Empirical Economic Research, Osnabrück University.

as if in a virtual monument to Europe's history of currency crises,
every border-hopping euro is accounted for in Target2. When money
started leaving debtor economies for the perceived safety of creditor ones, the notional liabilities of the former and the corresponding
claims of the latter – the virtual gold flows of Target2 – ballooned.[14]
(See Figure 5.6.)

In the spring of 2011, Sinn launched a series of articles and lec-
tures[15] arguing that the Bundesbank's Target2 claims should be considered German money at risk, just like the loans and guarantees in the
eurozone rescue funds. He caused a furore in German public opinion,
where those already feeling betrayed by what they saw as a bail-out of
the profligates (although it really was a bail-out of German and other
banks with investments in Greece and Ireland) were shocked at what
Sinn and others told them was the true scale of Germany's credits to
weaker euro economies. If Sinn was right, these amounted to several
hundred billions of euros more than was officially stated. The bulk, he

implied, had been put at risk through technocratic stealth and evaded the democratic controls of the Bundestag budget committee.

Sinn's accusation was wrong for reasons ranging from technical misunderstanding to a neglect of context. Target2 imbalances are not actual loans from the 'creditors' to the 'debtors'. If they reflect a transfer of money it is in the opposite direction: from the debtor country to the creditor country, in the course of which the accounting imbalance appears.[16] The ultimate owner of the euro in question, of course, does not change: it is the person who orders the transfer from his Irish bank account to his German one.

The official answer to Sinn from the central banking establishment was that these claims and liabilities would only ever come into force should the euro fall apart. That answer, of course, heightened both anxiety about the euro's future and frustration in Germany and other creditor countries. It was easy for their publics to feel like they were being blackmailed into keeping the show on the road. In addition, this answer conceded too much. What would happen to Germany if a debtor country left the euro? In accounting terms, perhaps the Bundesbank would have to write off its share of the leaver's Target2 liability. But in no sense would it entail a loss, let alone a fiscal expense or transfer, for Germany.[17] Target2 claims are not loans or bonds that have to be repaid on a certain maturity date. The way they are wound down in practice is the opposite situation from the one in which they arise: when euros flow back from accounts in creditor countries to debtor countries. If the debtor country in question had left the euro in the meantime, the last thing German account holders would need to worry about would be getting their euro's worth. After the certain plunge of a debtor country's new currency upon exit from the eurozone, the return transfer would buy a lot more in its now devalued destination than before the round trip started.

Propaganda need not be correct to be effective. Sinn's campaign hardened the determination to keep both the amount of German largesse and the behaviour of its beneficiaries firmly under control. But it also helped to reinforce the broader misconception that the single currency could only survive if underwritten by German resources. That is, after all, the logical thing to conclude if Target2 balances, which simply record central bank mechanics to facilitate capital flows, constitute credits from Germany to the rest of the currency zone.

Sinn's focus on Target2 is in fact enlightening in what it gets wrong. Sinn has called Target2 liabilities a stealth bail-out of the debtor countries; in reality, they reflect the bail-outs of investors belatedly getting out of unwise investments – and these investors were disproportionately based in Germany and other creditor economies. That is, after all, a creditor economy's defining trait: it has more savings to invest than (domestic) projects to fund. In fact, the sum of German banks' exposure to the eurozone periphery and the Bundesbank's Target2 surplus has been roughly constant since the onset of the crisis: the rise in Target2 claims almost exactly matches the banks' repatriation of capital from these markets.

Nor is the system a demonstration of the euro's flawed design. Quite the opposite, the Target2 imbalances are the record of the euro's robustness, of its ability to accommodate capital swings between different parts of the union so massive that in earlier times they would have broken the exchange rate pegs of the most determined central bank. Target2 proved that a euro in any member country was indeed a euro in every country. That made it part of the solution to eurozone instability, not part of the problem.

IRREVERSIBILITY REVERSED

The essence of monetary union is that it allows money to flow freely and costlessly across national boundaries, as the huge sums lent and invested by creditor Europe in the eurozone's debtor economies during the boom duly did. When the crisis came, however, investors pulled their funds home. That this great repatriation of funds was possible without tearing the eurozone apart is testament to the strength of the euro's structural design in general and Target2 in particular. (See Figure 5.7.)

That does not mean the flows themselves were not destabilising. The notionally single financial market began to fragment into its national constituents. That, of course, was much worse for debtor economies, who by definition had relied on foreign capital inflows before the

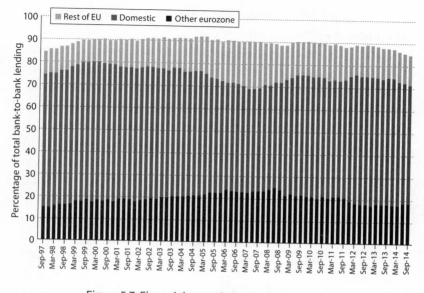

Figure 5.7. Financial repatriation in the eurozone.
Source: ECB.

crash, than for creditor economies, who now found themselves flush with the credit they had earlier exported. It bears noting that such financial fragmentation was not just a eurozone phenomenon: the eastern EU states, whose banking systems were predominantly made up of local outposts of big western European banks, were also suffering from a repatriation of funds to the creditor core. Here, however, a successful political effort was made to limit the capital flight (see note 14 from Chapter 2).

The result of the financial market fragmenting along national lines was that not just the sovereigns but all debtors in the periphery faced higher borrowing costs. A Spanish export company and a German one, serving the same markets and with the same fundamental economic creditworthiness, were treated differently by their banks – and this would be so even if they had the same bank. Indeed it was said that some regulators strongly discouraged their banking groups from supplying capital to their own subsidiaries in the periphery. From Greece to Spain the same complaints could be heard: that there were companies wishing to hire, expand and export, but they could not borrow at reasonable rates, and certainly not at the rates prevailing in the creditor core. (See Figure 5.8.)

The 2011–12 panic in the financial markets cannot be reduced to fears that the Spanish or Italian government might default. Italy, after all, posted the eurozone's biggest primary surplus in 2012 (its growth, however, went into reverse as a result of its ill-timed structural fiscal tightening). The sell-off of these countries' sovereign bonds was part of a broader evacuation from Spanish and Italian investments generally, and in particular from their banking systems. There was a self-reinforcing mechanism at work, with sovereign debt risk and banking debt risk fuelling each other. This created what came to be known as a bank–sovereign 'doom loop' as long as the taboo on restructuring remained in force. But the giant homebound rush by cross-border investors was not just a self-fulfilling prophecy. It was exacerbated by policy choices.

It is commonly thought that the capital flight from peripheral banks and sovereigns was triggered by the speculation that these

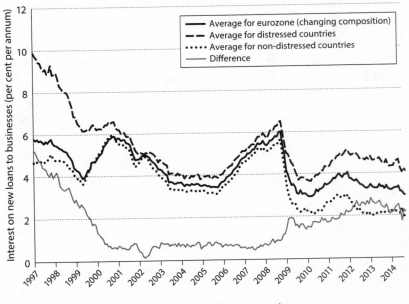

Figure 5.8. Financial fragmentation.
Source: ECB.

countries would leave the euro, and that probably had indeed been the case with Greece and Ireland at the beginning. But by 2012, this had been turned on its head. It was now the speculation of break-up – fuelled by eurozone leaders' evident willingness to entertain it – that drove financial fragmentation, not the other way around.

Leaders had once vowed with one voice that the euro was irreversible. By 2011, however, the genie was out of the bottle. A myriad impressions conveyed the sense that an exit from the single currency was no longer unthinkable. In domestic political debates governments found themselves on the back foot against those arguing that it would be better for some country or other to leave the euro. By insisting on the payment of unpayable debts, eurozone policymakers essentially invented a new and potentially impossible-to-fulfil condition for continued euro membership. Behind it all lurked the ECB's seeming willingness to expel members from a currency of which it was meant to be the common guardian, proved by its threats to cut off the blood supply to the banking systems of Greece, Ireland and Portugal (it would later threaten Cyprus with the same). In 2015 the previously veiled threat was bared for all to see when the ECB explicitly capped emergency liquidity to Greek banks until the government in Athens accepted its creditors' conditions for a third loan programme.

In the case of the small rescued countries, a fistful of euros in the guise of a helping hand at least made capital flight more manageable. But when the same blinkered diagnosis and counterproductive policy demands were applied to the much larger economies of Spain and Italy, it was impossible for money managers not to plan for a possible break-up of the euro. Through 2011, both private financial companies and eventually governments and the main European institutions developed plans for how to deal with monetary disintegration – even the ECB had a top-secret 'plan Z' to manage a euro exit.[18] But once break-up was an acknowledged possibility, all investors with a financial stake in the eurozone periphery had reason to pull their money out, regardless of whether it was with the government or a private company and, crucially, regardless of the fundamental solvency of their debtor. For a reassurance of repayment in full is no reassurance at all against the fear that the repayment might be redenominated in a new and plunging currency.

By their apparent willingness to contemplate freezing a country out from the single currency, the ECB and the creditor countries' leaders managed to commit the spectacular unforced error of rendering all debts in the euro periphery suspect – whether public or private, whether owed by weak borrowers or strong ones. Angela Merkel repeatedly said, 'If the euro fails, Europe fails' – implying that an inherently fragile euro had to be supported to safeguard Europe's post-war achievements. The reverse was closer to the truth: if Europe fails, the euro fails. The currency's integrity was weakened by policy choices and threats that actively impaired its stabilising mechanisms.

By late 2011, such actions had made the unthinkable possible. For the politicians who achieved this to say that the euro was inherently unstable from the start is self-serving in the extreme.

The Mutualisation Fix

When Spanish and Italian borrowing costs rose in the summer of 2011, the increasingly nervous reactions of European policymakers centred on the idea that a scaled-up version of the 'rescues' of Greece, Ireland and Portugal was needed. The debate on the euro's future became obsessed with the question of whether this could be done.

Three types of intervention were hotly debated. One was the EFS-F/ESM model: the explicit pooling of funds from each member state's government budget to make loans to distressed states, or purchase their bonds. Another was 'eurobonds': the idea that states would mutually and jointly guarantee one another's sovereign borrowing. And third, the monetary 'big bazooka': central bank intervention to keep down the yields of sovereign bonds that were under attack. What all three had in common was an acceptance of the idea that in a monetary union, stability requires a form of risk-sharing, in which common resources, whether fiscal or monetary, would backstop the resources of any individual member. All are forms of a proto-fiscal union; the first step on a road that logically ends, implicitly or explicitly, with common budgets. (This is true, too, of central bank intervention to reduce sovereign borrowing costs, since the ECB is backed by the fiscal resources of all the member states.) In 2011 and 2012, a lot of creative solutions were proposed along these lines, such as the clever idea of giving the EFSF/ESM a banking licence so that it could refinance any bond purchases with the ECB, thereby multipling its capacity for fiscal support.

But there was something puzzling about the assumption that resource pooling was necessary to keep the euro together, and perhaps sufficient to stop the run on peripheral public debt. The three first rescue programmes all involved fiscal support, and the EFSF was clearly big enough to cover Ireland and Portugal's fiscal needs. But none of these rescues had succeeded in bringing down the bond yields of the supposedly salvaged countries. On the contrary, in 2011–12 they were far higher than before (though Ireland's, it would turn out, had by now peaked). The same holds for central bank monetisation. For the ECB did in fact buy outright the bonds of troubled sovereigns on two occasions: in May 2010 for Greece, Ireland and Portugal, and in July 2011 for Italy and Spain. Neither intervention had the desired effect of making it easier for the countries in question to borrow.[19]

There were shortcomings of both policies that partly explain why they did not prevent the problem they were meant to address from worsening. The official loans were granted on conditions that made the recipients' debt burdens worse: proscribing writedowns and welding the financial sectors' debts irreversibly to the governments' liabilities. And in practice, the monetary interventions were also conditional on these policies. For monetary support to be credible, meanwhile, it needs to be able in principle to buy up the entire public debt stock – otherwise markets might still stay away through fear that the ECB's willingness to buy government debt was not infinite.[20] This fear was entirely reasonable, as unlimited asset purchases run up against the ECB's circumscribed legal authority[21] and its even narrower political limits. The bond buying that did occur was draining the ECB's legitimacy in German public opinion. By the summer of 2011, two German members of the ECB Governing Council had resigned because of irreconcilable differences with the institution's policy.

If the main risk preoccupying investors had remained just (just!) that borrowers might default on their debts, better-designed fiscal or monetary mutualisation of debt (politics permitting) would have been a workable alternative to restructuring. The much-talked-of comparison with the United States – whose currency is said to work better than the euro because of its fiscal union – is, however, misguided. That is partly because the individual US state governments are not in fact bailed out by one another or by the federal government, so that in this respect the United States is no different from Europe. But it is also because fiscal risk-sharing between individual US state economies is much smaller than commonly thought.[22] In any case, by 2011 markets feared something worse than defaults. European leaders had needlessly planted and nourished the worry that the single currency might break up and that the countries under pressure would have to return to their national currencies. The ECB's own research has attributed nearly half of the widening difference in borrowing costs between crisis-hit countries and Germany to 'redenomination risk', or the market's fear that the countries in question would leave the euro for restored national currencies.[23] No amount of mutualisation of debts would bring investors back so long as their fear of 'redenomination risk' was left unattended. For in a situation where a country did leave the euro, let alone was expelled from it, any mutualisation agreement would probably break down. It is hard to imagine a guarantee of a country's debts in euros being honoured (in full, at least) if that country had just returned to a national currency plunging in value. Mutualisation alone cannot fully dispel the risk of fragmentation, since fragmentation itself makes mutualisation hard to sustain.

Another problem with mutualisation is that it requires sufficient trust that it will not be abused. This is the problem of 'moral hazard' – risk-sharing can encourage riskier behaviour. The fear in Germany above all was that help for the victims of an emergency would be perverted into a 'transfer union', where rich economies permanently subsidise poorer, weaker and more unruly ones. The rhetoric that permanent fiscal transfers were necessary to solve the eurozone's problem have only exacerbated that fear. (Here, too, it should be noted that the fiscal transfer union in the United States has not stopped its constituent sovereign entities from getting into deep fiscal trouble.[24])

For mutualisation to end the euro crisis once and for all, a strong substitute for trust would therefore be needed. The substitute that was proposed was centralised control over national policy – a degree of control strong enough to reassure those who stood to be net contributors to any common pool of resources that they would not be taken advantage of. The political push for less national autonomy was a necessary consequence of leaders' flirtation with eurozone exit. By suggesting, even implicitly, that some countries ought to leave the euro, let alone by actively creating reasons for them to do so, Europe's most senior policymakers proved beyond any doubt the screaming absence of trust, and the degree of control necessary to make up for that shortfall.

To see the importance of trust, consider why there was no sovereign debt crisis in Belgium. Its fiscal situation was very similar to Italy's but it never suffered a speculative attack in the markets. The argument here suggests that a profound reason was a sense of political belonging. Belgium was incontrovertibly 'part of the club'. Whereas investors could imagine a scenario in which the eurozone's top leaders might sever their monetary ties with the southern periphery, any smaller eurozone would always include the Benelux countries.

So the politics that tore the monetary union to breaking point in 2011–12 concerned the difficulty of finding policy constraints to substitute for trust that could satisfy both the creditors and the debtors. This question remains the key orientation of European politics today, and returned explosively in the Greek loan negotiations in the summer of 2015. Although the governments of all the vulnerable countries except Greece have largely accepted their loss of autonomy, they struggle to keep their people behind them. The challenges from the populist flanks on the right and left have proved that a large part of the European electorate chafes under the cash-for-control consensus.

The Tyranny of Technocracy

When control serves as a substitute for trust, the less trust there is between creditor and debtor the greater will be the loss of self-determination of a debtor financially at the creditor's mercy.

The loss was glaring in the pioneer 'programme countries' Greece, Ireland and Portugal, even if each case came in a different shade of subservience to the troika – itself effectively an overlord. In Greece, the list of policies the government must implement as a condition for financial aid was set out in extraordinary detail (with the generous technical assistance of the IMF and the European Commission's Task Force for Greece). This infantilised the Greek body politic, which was already weak. As we saw in Chapter 3, the eurozone's most powerful leaders twice clamped down on attempts to bring popular deliberation back through the side door of a plebiscite – the first time successfully, and the second with just enough force to alienate swaths of the Greek public. In contrast, the Irish budget consolidation and structural reform policies were in the main homegrown, indeed many were formulated before the rescue loan was agreed. But the fiscal 'rescue' and the attached prohibition on mitigating the bank bail-outs were something Ireland's elected leaders were strong-armed into by the ECB and the rest of the eurozone establishment. One way or another, the rescue loans suspended democratic decision making in economic policy – or constrained it so much as to amount to the same thing. While the economies of all three countries were 'patients' in the medical sense of suffering and needing a cure, their polities were 'patients' in the term's original, literal meaning: passive subjects submitting to actions operated by others, rather than agents actively choosing their own course.

Apart from Cyprus, no further country has had rule by troika inflicted on it, but in many more countries democratic deliberation has had to cower before technocratic diktat, and concern for the people's will has been muscled aside by perceptions of what was necessary to end the crisis. In only one country, for instance, was the population more than summarily consulted over the fiscal compact, and that country – Ireland – was in no position to rock the boat.

Albeit in weaker form, the Commission's and the ECB's empire over the programme countries has been generalised to debtor Europe as a whole. This has been done on the pain of censure and fines in the Commission's case. In the case of the ECB, it was done by threats not to extend a helping hand – or even to close a fist that should, by rights, be open.

While Brussels was at least empowered to act in this way, Frankfurt took the responsibility upon itself. In the first three programme countries, the ECB overstepped its authority by blocking bank restructuring, but at least it had a mandate of sorts to meddle with fiscal and economic policies as a member of the troika. It did not, however, have a mandate to impose the huge distributive policies in favour of Irish banks' foreign creditors that the bank bail-outs implied. The European Court of Justice (ECJ) has come close to suggesting that even its mere participation in the troika was illegal.[25] And elsewhere, Frankfurt had no justification for dictating fiscal and economic policy at all.

Yet on 5 August 2011, Trichet wrote two stern letters to the prime ministers of Spain and Italy, José Luis Zapatero and Silvio Berlusconi, each co-signed by the country's central bank governor (in Italy this was Mario Draghi, who would a year later succeed Trichet at the helm of the ECB). Both letters started with an identical admonishment for urgent action to support the credibility of their 'sovereign signature' in capital markets. They followed on with lists of policies to implement, including not just additional and immediate fiscal consolidation measures but changes to wage bargaining traditions and reforms of labour and product markets. Without any apparent appreciation of the irony in dictating the outcome of a democratic process, the central bankers magnanimously gave Spain's authorities until the end of the month to implement the ECB's preferred labour reforms, while for Italy they indicated that the actions be taken 'as soon as possible with decree-laws, followed by Parliamentary ratification by end September 2011'.[26]

Though the letters were hidden from the public, it was widely understood that these were the central bank's conditions for intervening in the two governments' debt markets to arrest the run on their bonds. Within days, both governments had announced measures along the lines of the ECB's demands, and, satisfied its words had been heeded, Frankfurt cranked its Securities Markets Programme back into gear, buying close to €100 billion of Spanish and Italian bonds over the next two months.

There is no question that both Zapatero's and Berlusconi's responses to the crisis had left much to be desired. Berlusconi, in particular, deserves a special mention for reneging on reform commitments once the ECB had started buying Italian bonds. But Europe's history should make it wary of letting decisiveness trump democratic deliberation, even of the highly imperfect sort. There was a time in much of Europe when generals (or worse) took it upon themselves to protect the national interest from dithering politicians. It is less bloody when central bankers do it, but nearly as noxious to democracy.

The climax of technocracy's triumph over democracy came with the engineered demise of Silvio Berlusconi. Italy's showman prime minister had rattled counterparts by raving that Italy would leave the euro if the ECB did not intervene more forcefully in its debt markets. His loss of international standing was complete when, in a joint press conference, Merkel and Sarkozy could not stop themselves from smirking when asked about their trust in Berlusconi's ability to bring public finances under control. His domestic standing, too, was dwindling with the active help of European leaders and officials. President Giorgio Napolitano, it is now known, was warming up Italy's former European Commissioner Mario Monti to take over from Berlusconi as early as the summer of 2011.[27] Merkel called Napolitano to pressure him to engineer this switch of Italy's prime minister.[28] Italian parliamentary party leaders have told of ECB teams visiting to probe the economy insisting on their desire for a Monti government. And then-US Treasury Secretary Timothy Geithner has said European officials wanted him to veto any IMF aid to Italy unless Berlusconi left office.[29]

By early November this extraordinary pressure had done its work. In a budget vote, Berlusconi could no longer muster a majority of parliamentarians. Italian bond yields broke through the 7 per cent threshold revered by those prone to magical thinking. Less than a week after Papandreou had resigned from the premiership of Greece,

Italy's prime minister did the same. That Greece would become the stage of a palace revolution in which European powers substituted their preferred technocratic government for an elected one was merely tragic, not surprising. That it would happen to Italy was astounding.

Germany's Conditions

These violations of the EU's many separations of powers (a European invention: Montesquieu was the first to explore it in depth) were at once a political offence and an intellectual one. They were political in their execution and in their substance, but they were intellectual in their origin. The villain in this story is Europe's pathological conflation of safeguarding prosperity with sanctifying debt contracts. For as long as Europe recoiled from restructuring debts that could only be repaid at the cost of enormous economic damage, if at all, it automatically put itself in the position of *demandeur* vis-à-vis its biggest creditor.

The dynamic is most visible with the fiscal compact, which is even more extraordinary for the fact of its existence than for the wrong-headedness of its substance. Signing up to international treaty obligations is a concession of sovereignty, which states by definition cannot be legally compelled to do. They can of course be coerced in other ways, and the countries already in the troika's clutches no doubt felt they had no choice. But the fact is that most of Europe's governments voluntarily agreed to amend their constitutions and clip their budgetary wings at Berlin's request. Even most non-euro countries went along willingly. Only the United Kingdom and Slovakia, whose *soi-disant* vetoes of the fiscal compact treaty were nothing of the sort, declined to sign up, although George Osborne's austerity programme at home meant that the United Kingdom was enthusiastically complying with the spirit of the compact anyway. If Europe's newly institutionalised fiscal hawkishness is a subjection to German preferences, it is an entirely voluntary servitude.

Similar points can be made about the other elements of the EU's new fiscal regime, and about the ECB. The same balancing act between calls for German largesse and deference to German policy demands that has consumed decision making at the European Council has also indirectly framed the debate on the ECB's Governing Council. Here it was less a question of creditor countries contributing to pooled financial resources than of their acquiescence to unleashing the powers already pooled in a common central bank. But the quid pro quo was the same: control over how the beneficiaries of the common funds made use of them. If anything, the pressure coming from the ECB – which had an institutional interest in expanding its influence – was stronger than that from Germany, which only reluctantly let itself be dragged into being the eurozone's director.

Given the conviction that Germany must financially underwrite the monetary union, then, it is no mystery that Berlin could and did set conditions. The deeper question is why Berlin's demands were what they were?

German policymaking is accused, with some justification, of treating the economy as the stage of a morality play where virtue and vice must get their due desert.[30] The temptation to moralise against the countries locked out of the market was too strong for much of creditor Europe to resist. Countries had transgressed doubly by living beyond their means and breaking the common rules; being forced to tighten their belts was both a necessary correction and an appropriate punishment. That, at least, was the view among many of the German government's Bundestag members, both among Merkel's own Christian Democrats and within the Free Democratic Party, the junior partner in the 2009–13 centre-right coalition government. Merkel's foot dragging, so often the target of criticism from outside Germany, was caused by her being shackled at the ankle to an iron ball of Bundestag scepticism.

Influential though the moralising was in creditor states' domestic politics, it is easy to make too much of it. Had retribution really been Berlin's primary motivation, the purse strings would have been kept tighter for longer, and Europe would, one might say by default, have had to go through the restructurings it resisted. As this book argues, that would have been the better outcome.

So it is important to recognise the more pragmatic arguments for Berlin's stance. For countries that ran out of market financing, there was a straightforward case for fiscal retrenchment: they had no other choice. If anything, rescue loans allowed them to adjust their budgets more slowly than they might otherwise have had to do until markets opened their doors again (but of course the associated taboo on debt restructuring increased the overall amount of fiscal austerity to be undertaken). For all the complaints against 'austerians' – policymakers emphasising fiscal consolidation – they financed a Keynesian palliative to the inevitably contractionary process of cutting deficits that the private sector was no longer willing to fund.

This did not, however, justify greater fiscal discipline across the board, including in countries – such as Germany itself – that had ample fiscal space. That insistence flowed instead from a particularly German analysis of markets, which appealed to confidence, credibility and consistency. Unlike the Keynesians, who saw economic growth as a prerequisite for returned market confidence, the *Ordnungspolitik* in which the German policy elite is steeped saw things the other way round.[31] Growth could only result from re-establishing markets' confidence that euro member states would honour their debts. This gave pride of place to the credibility of politicians' intentions to make painful choices to improve public finances – a view shared, incidentally, by the government of Keynes's homeland. And credibility – as German politicians told exasperated Keynesians ad nauseam in 2010 and 2011 – requires a consistent approach across the eurozone. If the more comfortably situated states cannot bring themselves to improve their finances, how could anyone expect the squeezed eurozone periphery to do the right thing? Or so the argument went.

The debate between (often Anglo-American) Keynesianism and (German) *Ordnungspolitik* is too often a dialogue of the deaf. But in this particular case, the ordo-liberals are on shaky ground, for even in their own terms, their argument fails. The short-term effect of universal austerity is to slow down the economy, since one person's spending is another's income. That may be fine when other forces can keep demand buoyant. When all those other forces are weak, however, it only debilitates them further. This directly increases government deficits but, more importantly, it shrinks the revenues from which the debt can be serviced. For markets with narrow time horizons, the credibility of governments' *willingness* to honour their debts pales in importance compared with their *ability* to do so. And the higher the initial debt, the more a given contraction in economic output increases the debt burden.[32] So the more unsustainable a country's public finances are to begin with, the greater is the further damage done to sustainability by a given amount of fiscal consolidation. As Figure 5.9 shows, a considerable portion of the increase in crisis-hit eurozone members' public debt burden has been caused by economic contraction rather than by actual borrowing. The norm is that GDP growth reduces the debt-to-GDP ratio. In the eurozone periphery, negative growth has instead raised it, even when no new borrowing has taken place.

There are, further, economic limits on how much can be extracted out of an economy for the purpose of servicing external debts. Beyond a certain point, the extraction itself puts such a burden on production

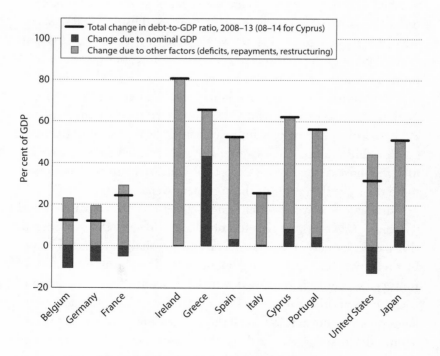

Figure 5.9. Economic slumps and debt burdens.
Source: EC Annual Macroeconomic Database.

that either the economy collapses or the population rebels. This is related to the old 'transfer problem' (discussed by Keynes among others) of whether Weimar Germany could realistically pay the war reparations bill it was presented with at Versailles. It is tragic that of all people, Germany's ordo-liberals should be the ones to have forgotten this lesson.

While the credibility view was most forcefully pushed by Berlin, it was not alone in promoting it. The European Commission supported the German line with gusto – perhaps a not entirely unsurprising response from an institution for which Berlin's diagnosis entailed more power over national policymaking. Spain was another partner in crime. Like Ireland, it was coming into the crisis with negligible debt and low deficits. Its commitment to 'credibility' was so strong, however, that it vowed early on to exceed the deficit cuts asked of it by the Commission.

The Logical Extreme

At the root of all this lies the refusal to accept that debts that cannot be paid, will not, and that it is worse to pretend they will – even from the point of view of collecting as much as can be had – than it is to try to manage their restructuring in an orderly manner. From that error flowed the colossal mistakes that the eurozone would go on to make, ranging from Greece and Ireland early on to the damaging stand-off with Athens in the spring of 2015. Once the early mistakes had been committed, the euro's leaders had either to remain consistent with the analytical framework that produced them or change course, thereby admitting they had been wrong. They should, of course, have changed course. The next chapter discusses how they eventually began to do so – but not before pressing on with the logical implications of the original anti-writedown thinking. That meant applying their prescription for the programme countries to the currency union at large. For too long, the eurozone swept the banks' problems under the carpet, pushed for universal belt tightening and deleveraging, and entrenched itself in the reciprocal blackmail between creditors and debtors that reduces politics to negotiations over how much autonomy to trade away for how much financial aid. This produced a second recession, the near unravelling of the single currency, and huge damage to the currency union's democratic fabric. The eurozone only turned when it was almost too late, and it turned too little while pretending not to. But turn it did.

SIX

Righting the Course: From Bail-Out to Bail-In

Learning from Failure

As 2011 turned into 2012, economic reality increasingly intruded into eurozone policymakers' world view. The countries that had been 'rescued' from writing down their debt were further from economic salvation than ever, even by the narrow measure of regaining market confidence, let alone in terms of the growth needed to make debt burdens more manageable and arrest the decline in living standards.

The macroeconomic mistakes that flowed from the taboo on restructuring – universal fiscal austerity, tightening monetary conditions and a failure to unclog a credit system paralysed by retrenching banks – were taking their toll on the stronger eurozone economies as well. In the spring of 2011, the time of Trichet's first interest rate rise, economic confidence plunged in the eurozone core (see Figure 6.1). Half a year later the eurozone sank into a second recession that would last for eighteen months (see Figure 5.4). By mid 2012, the implosion of the single currency itself loomed as a greater threat than it had before its leaders had put in place their measures ostensibly to save it.

Europe had failed the Hippocratic test of first doing no harm. But to its credit, it eventually responded to reality. While one is hard-pressed to find any admission of mistakes by the leaders that oversaw the eurozone's crisis response, they slowly began to stop scoring own goals.

A change of the guard at the ECB helped. Mario Draghi, Italy's central bank governor, replaced Trichet in November 2011 and quickly laid the political groundwork for better monetary policy. The sheer cost of the economic policy mistakes also helped to persuade those leaders with their ear to the political ground to modify the fiscal course even as they preached steadfastness.

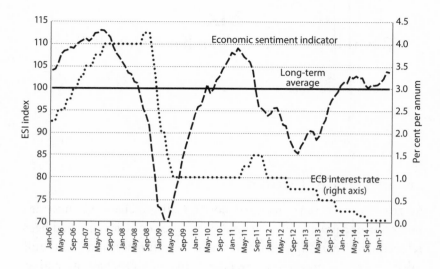

Figure 6.1. Economic confidence in the eurozone.
Source: European Commission.

Starting in the second half of 2011, Europe's policy errors were slowly, divisively and incompletely righted. Within less than two years, the early taboo on debt writedowns had given way to Europe's first sovereign restructuring in generations and to an agreement that failing banks should write down creditors' claims before receiving any government aid. On both the sovereign and banking sides, the eurozone was moving from bail-out to bail-in.

Accepting Default

For almost a year, the Greek policy programme seemed to bear fruit. The government narrowed the deficit by 5 per cent of GDP in 2010, an impressive feat given that its efforts were undermined by a 3 per cent contraction of the economy (to achieve this, Athens improved its structural primary balance by an astounding 7.2 per cent of GDP in one year). That scale of downturn was manageable, however, and compatible with the creditors' prediction that growth would soon resume.

But instead the economic and political crises worsened. The more the government cut, the worse the economy suffered; the IMF was later forced to conclude that the damage to economic activity from deficit cuts had been badly underestimated. With no recovery for sovereign debt, and with the downturn eroding private borrowers' ability to service their loans, Greek banks sat on growing unrealised losses. They were unable to channel credit to those private sector companies that might have expanded, so a credit crunch compounded the fiscal austerity to depress the economy further. And on the streets of Athens and in workplaces around the country, ugly confrontations and costly strikes became commonplace, hurting both production and the tourism industry even more, not to speak of Greece's social cohesion.

By spring 2011, it became obvious that the rescue programme would not restore Athens's ability to service its debt by the time the credit line was exhausted. The IMF's presence meant the issue could not be easily fudged: its rules prohibit it from lending unless it judges that the debtor's full financing needs are met twelve months ahead. The need for a second rescue package shifted the eurozone political balance in Berlin's favour. Germany had gone along with the proponents of 'solidarity' in May 2010; since then, its increasingly restive parliamentarians had had to approve funding for two more rescues. This time Berlin would insist on what was euphemistically called 'private sector involvement' in the financial aid package: a sovereign restructuring in all but name.

Even as the eurozone belatedly confronted its phobia of debt writedowns, it was tying itself in knots. Leaders were desperate to keep the restructuring – which would involve swapping new, less onerous bonds for the outstanding ones – formally voluntary for private sector creditors. This particular piece of hypocrisy (one European bank chief said his participation was 'as voluntary as a confession during the Spanish inquisition'[1]) had to do with the market for credit default swaps (CDSs), a form of insurance policies that would pay out if Greece was deemed to default unilaterally. Why European leaders should want to avoid triggering these securities – which were small in number, and designed precisely to protect financial institutions against the consequences that had ostensibly been the eurozone's reason to resist a sovereign writedown in the first place – is a paradox best explained by their dim understanding of financial markets.[2]

Another problem was that the ECB, which in support of the first rescue loan had spent tens of billions of euros on Greek sovereign bonds to prop up the market, with ephemeral success, was not in a mood to accept losses 'voluntarily', or indeed at all. Trichet sounded increasingly shrill as Europe turned against the no-writedown policy he had pushed more than anyone in the first Greek rescue. The disagreement he consistently voiced from the pulpit of his monthly Frankfurt press conference shone a garish light on his last few months as ECB president, after the agreement on the writedown laid bare that the majority of policymakers had left him behind.[3]

It took nine months to work out the details of the restructuring of outstanding bonds in private hands. Much of it came down to coaxing banks into accepting an amount that would make a noticeable difference to Athens's debt burden. The banks had come out with an offer early on: a risibly light restructuring, whose purpose was to pre-empt the eurozone's political leadership from settling on harsher terms. There is a lesson here: no matter what they may say, private creditors will collaborate on an orderly writedown if they believe that governments are otherwise prepared to choose a course that will cause them even bigger losses.

In the end, a steep 'voluntary' debt exchange took place in March 2012, with the agreement of investors holding about 60 per cent of the eligible debt. The roughly €200 billion face value of their bonds was cut by just over half, the length of the loans stretched out for decades, and the interest rates kept low. The ECB was made whole through a separate debt exchange for its benefit only, just weeks before the private creditors were written down. This should have been the time instead to relieve the ECB of its exposure. Replacing the bonds it held with an EFSF loan before the restructuring would have permanently addressed worries about monetary financing of governments. Instead, the missed opportunity guaranteed that the ECB's continued holding of Greek bonds would later come back to haunt the eurozone. The stand-off between Athens and its creditors in the first half of 2015 took place under the shadow of €7 billion of ECB-held bonds falling due in July and August. Despite having run a primary surplus for two years and needing no loans to cover spending, Athens was at the mercy of its creditors if it was to meet these payment deadlines.

Two facts about the 2012 debt exchange are especially noteworthy. The first is that it went without a hitch.[4] Greek long-term bond yields would not reach their February 2012 high again, and no wave of bank failures followed. Even the dreaded CDSs – which were triggered in the end, despite the eurozone's uselessly complicated manoeuvres to achieve a 'voluntary' writedown – were settled in an orderly fashion. In other words, the CDS market worked; and that market and others showed they could take a managed sovereign default in their stride.

The second point of note is that the recipe for restructuring had been available for years – both in the form of other countries' experience and, for Greece in particular, in the form of a paper by the world's most seasoned restructuring lawyers aptly entitled 'How to restructure Greek debt'.[5] The main procedural step, for example, of using 'collective action clauses' (by which a majority of bondholders can bind them all to accept a writedown), which Greece could unilaterally introduce into bonds issued under Greek law, was set out in the guide.

The depressing economic and political damage wrought by the failure to restructure Greece's debt at the outset had finally broken Europe's taboo on sovereign default. The eurozone's policymaking class quickly reinstated it, however, by insisting that Greece was a unique case and smothering talk of restructuring any other eurozone sovereign's debt. But a fundamental shift had occurred.

The shift was partly in the power of precedent: what has been done once can be done again. The instruments for replicating a Greek-style writedown exist, even if the political will does not. Collective action clauses are now mandatory for all new eurozone sovereign debt issues; within a decade, they will cover the bulk of that debt. The rules of the ESM open up the way for making any future loan from the rescue fund conditional on a prior restructuring. The IMF, too, is mulling a wider scope for asking creditors to moderate their claims before a debtor state obtains its support[6] and, as already mentioned, has acknowledged it was a mistake not to restructure Greece's sovereign debt and Ireland's bank debt. So both the tools and the know-how are at hand, should markets again turn their backs on sovereigns – which are more indebted today than at the height of the crisis. In this sense, progress towards an orderly restructuring mechanism is more advanced than that towards a fiscal union, although the eurozone has (at least officially) foresworn the former in favour of the latter as their preferred ultimate destination.

Learning the Irish Lesson

Unlike the Bourbons, the eurozone's governing elite learns from its mistakes. The devastation wrought on Ireland sowed doubts about the wisdom of making bank creditors whole at the expense of tax-payers. The growing consciousness that Ireland was ill treated was also partly due to the altogether higher calibre of diplomacy displayed by the Fine Gael–Labour government than by the decimated Fianna Fáil–Green coalition it replaced shortly after the rescue deal had been signed. The new prime minister and finance minister, Enda Kenny and Michael Noonan, quickly impressed eurozone counterparts by hunkering down to structural reforms and fiscal consolidation, competently managing an Irish EU presidency without undue emphasis on Irish interests, and discreetly but insistently reminding them that Ireland had 'taken one for the team' by making reckless private investors whole (many of them German) as European doctrine had demanded.

The sour experience of the Irish case also meant European policymaking sensibilities were more attuned to the danger of conflating sovereign and bank indebtedness when the same story seemed to be playing out in Spain. That country's pre-crisis growth was cut from the same cloth as Ireland's. Like Dublin, Madrid went into the downturn with low public debt and a balanced budget. But it was riding high only on the back of a private sector wave of housebuilding, financed by a politically connected banking sector that was almost as big as Ireland's (in proportion to the economy; much bigger in absolute terms), and a current deficit that was even worse. In 2007, Spaniards collectively lived beyond their means by 10 per cent of GDP.

Ireland's small size had made it affordable, if unwise, for the euro-zone to finance the perpetuation of its mistakes. Spain's banking problems were not quite as abysmal as Ireland's. But the European authorities' tendency to underestimate the hidden losses in their banks had by 2012 been revealed too many times to ignore. With a GDP of €1 trillion and a banking sector balance sheet of €4 trillion, everyone knew that Spain was too big to save, if 'salvation' was again going to put taxpayers on the hook for bank losses. An Irish scenario for Spain would risk the wildfire in sovereign bond markets leaping from small countries to big ones; 'Italy is next in line' was a common observation. That is why, in the spring of 2012, markets and governments were obsessing as much about Spanish banks as about the electoral shenanigans in Greece.

One bank in particular was in the spotlight. Bankia consisted of the merged loan books of seven regional savings banks. The idea behind the reforms that had produced Bankia was that its scale would bolster the ability to absorb the losses ineluctably inflicted by a collapsing housing market, and that management would be improved by including private shareholders in the governance of institutions previously controlled by local politicians. But true to European form, things were a lot worse under the hood of the flagship new bank than was suggested by its polished surface. Bankia was headed by Rodrigo Rato, a former finance minister and the managing director of the IMF between 2004 and 2007 (when the organisation signally failed to sound the alarm about financial trouble ahead). On Rato's watch Bankia rushed to list on the stock market with provisional accounts, supposedly put on stable footing by several billion euros of taxpayer money. But in May 2012, less than a year after the shares went on sale, the bank admitted it was bust and applied for and received another €19 billion from Madrid's bank bail-out fund. The shareholders, many of whom were Bankia retail customers whom the bank had convinced to buy its securities when sophisticated investors stayed away, lost billions. The stock market offering is under criminal investigation for fraud. During all this, Rato and his colleagues were using company credit cards to fund personal expenses to the tune of tens of thousands of euros (he was briefly arrested on suspicion of tax evasion in April 2015).[7] One would be hard pressed to invent a more telling illustration of how incestuous the relationship between the political class and the banking sector can become.

The fear was that, as in Ireland, the debacle marked the start of a worsening banking crisis in Spain. While a fully fledged fiscal financing programme for Madrid was difficult to contemplate for all sides, the Spanish government came under growing pressure to sign up for a limited loan confined to recapitalising banks. At the same time, the dread of an Irish outcome writ large – in Spain, but potentially in other countries as well, including Italy or France – nourished the realisation that the lethal embrace between banks and sovereigns had to be prised loose. So long as governments were expected to recapitalise failing banks, while banks disproportionately invested in their own governments' debt, problems in either would pull down the other. The 'doom loop' had to be disabled.

Severing the banks' umbilical cord to nation states was always a matter of political will, not technical feasibility. A piece of legislation can allow the authorities to split up a bank in a hurry so that they can safeguard its systemic functions. Ireland belatedly proved that such laws could be passed in a single late-night legislative session in an emergency. The obstacle has always been that weak-willed governments fear the humiliation of national champions, the defenestration of politically well-connected bankers, and the wrath of the failed banks' creditors – and of other governments if those creditors are foreign. Whatever the reason was, bank failures were seen as the worst possible outcome. When the crisis entered a new convulsion in the spring of 2012 it finally became clear beyond doubt that this was not the case.

Prising Loose a Deadly Embrace

Logically, there are two ways to quarantine a nation's banking system and prevent the debt woes of private banks and those of governments from contaminating one another. One is to let banks' losses fall where they may, or rather, to allocate them (via special resolution regimes) in such a way that the vital functions of the bankrupt institutions are safeguarded and the most vulnerable creditors, such as ordinary small depositors, are protected. That is to say, when a bank is overwhelmed by losses, its remaining assets should be earmarked to service the most important claims and functions in a carved-out good bank. Other claims should be curtailed according to how the relevant bankruptcy legislation ranks creditors and how much money is left over. Those with secured claims will seize and sell their collateral; unsecured creditors will stand in line for any remaining assets according to the priority specified by contract and law.

The other way is to get another country to bail out one's banks when they get in trouble.

European states had never had to choose between these options before. Until 2008, it had always been affordable – though neither wise nor fair – for national governments to bail out the banks incorporated in their own territory. It took Ireland's fall and Spain's teetering for Europe to understand that this was no longer true. Even then, Europe could not quite bring itself to embrace either alternative wholeheartedly. The countries for whom unaffordable bank losses loomed largest – the credit-addicted peripheral economies as well as Italy and France – were understandably keen to maintain the practice of taxpayer bail-outs but share the costs at the international level, where they would be the likely beneficiaries at the expense of Germany and other surplus countries. Equally understandably, creditor Europe insisted on limiting the exposure of taxpayers – their taxpayers – to reckless banks that had been badly regulated by someone else.

In June 2012 Europe followed its hallowed tradition of can-kicking compromise by setting out on both routes at once.

One route was the European Commission's Bank Recovery and Resolution Directive (BRRD). This requires member states to restructure failing banks with a compulsory policy of 'bail-in': that is, imposing losses on creditors.[8] Key to the directive is a prohibition on taxpayer rescues before at least 8 per cent of a bank's liabilities have been written down.

Then, at a dramatic summit in the last days of June 2012, the monetary union's governments vowed to break the lethal embrace between banks and sovereigns by creating a 'banking union', which would lift supervision and resolution powers from national regulators up to the ECB and a new resolution board. This 'single supervisory mechanism' and 'single resolution mechanism' would be backed, eventually, by a 'single resolution fund' – a mutualised pot of money to finance banks restructured under the new rules, financed by levies on eurozone banks.

With these two moves, Europe's governing elite for the first time addressed the root of both the eurozone's financial fragmentation and the credit crunch that was stifling growth. This would soon help turn the tide of economic confidence and be followed by an upswing in economic performance.

But the conjunction of bail-in rules and a common bail-out fund (a 'fiscal backstop', as the jargon goes) defied economic logic. If the point of bail-in is to end taxpayer subsidies of mismanaged banks, why reproduce such subsidies at the pan-European level? There is a good argument for supranational supervisory and resolution powers: experience shows that national authorities tend to favour the banks they are supposed to rein in over the citizens they are supposed to protect (just look at Bankia). The supervisory and restructuring aspects of banking union were necessary to make sure that national politics did not spare well-connected banks from being wound down; in other words, to enforce the recovery and resolution directive. But why a common bail-out fund?

The logic behind this combination of policies was political rather than economic. Europe's politicians were unwilling to let go of their old habit of treating the banking system as a branch of the state, so a provision for state support of banks was retained for cases of urgent importance. Berlin saw the bail-in option and common supervision as useful tools to protect itself against the cost of bank collapses in other countries, rather than in Germany itself. It consequently fought hard to keep smaller German banks outside the new system's jurisdiction. But Germany needed to grant something in return. That something was the common bail-out fund, which German banks expect to pay more into than they will ever take out. They may well be proved wrong about this. But most other countries shared this expectation and wanted a slice of German money. Partly this was sheer greed, partly a sense of entitlement given the concession of national control over banks, and partly because they were told by most experts that the monetary union could only hold together if money flowed from stronger to weaker states. A mutualised bank bail-out fund was a surreptitious way to establish such transfers. (The ESM rescue fund can in principle inject capital directly into restructured banks, too. But this is conditional on unanimous approval and is therefore subject to veto by any eurozone government. It also has a self-imposed limit of €60 billion for direct bank recapitalisation.)

The result of the compromise was too little of everything. Rather than taking Europe's banking system completely off taxpayers' shoulders, the obligation to write down creditors was limited to 8 per cent of liabilities (with gaping loopholes), despite well-known cases of banks having racked up significantly greater losses. Many small banks were kept outside the new rules – even though just a few years earlier a provincial Irish real estate lender had been treated as if it was as important as Lehman. And if one really does want to continue bailing out banks, the single resolution fund is laughably inadequate for a pan-European recapitalisation reserve. It will amount to €55 billion when fully funded, which could not even have covered little Ireland's bank bail-outs in full. National governments may still end up footing the bill.[9]

TESTING THE WATERS

Because the June 2012 decisions (the BRRD and the commitment to banking union) preserved the ambivalence over whether banks would be bailed out or in, their ability to free Europe of its bail-out addiction depends on the politics of how they are implemented. So far, European policymakers have not distinguished themselves much from other recovering addicts. Their determination to stay clear of taxpayer bail-outs has swung between spells of fortitude and lapses into old habits.

The most promising early signs of sobriety came from the heaviest addict of them all. As Chapter 4 mentioned, shortly before Dublin was strong-armed into the eurozone 'rescue', the Irish authorities began displaying a previously unseen cleverness in making some creditors share in banks' losses. Next, Ireland's political confidence vis-à-vis the ECB also began to recover from its bruising. It came into its own when the government – not before time – liquidated the bank that became a byname for excess: Anglo Irish. By 2012 this was a shell containing little more than a single asset: a €30.6 billion promissory note (a non-tradable bond) from the government that the bank pledged as security for a loan from the Irish central bank. The loan had been used to repay Anglo's bondholders. That money was gone forever, but there was still room for reducing the damage. The promissory note had a steep repayment schedule, matching that of the central bank loan. The government had to pay more than €3 billion out of its budget every year to Anglo, requiring tighter fiscal policy than without the promissory note, all else being equal. But to compound the pain, the payment would mostly serve to redeem portions of the central bank loan, which would be money withdrawn from circulation (a small share would constitute interest, which would revolve to the government as central bank profits). This was perverse: a significant amount of not just fiscal but also monetary contraction in the midst of an economic depression.

After two years of patient planning, Irish persistence paid off. During the night of 6 February 2013, the Irish government hurriedly put the rump Anglo into bankruptcy proceedings and swapped the promissory note for a government bond with a lower interest rate and a longer repayment period. This brought significant relief both for the budget and for monetary conditions. But the political significance was even bigger. Ireland did not secure the permission of the ECB (which oversees loans by national central banks) before going ahead. For the first time, after years of threats to cut off bank lifelines if countries did not behave, a small euro country called the ECB's bluff – and won. The next morning the ECB simply stated it 'took note' of the Irish swap, even though it had the monetary policy effect of slowing a programmed tightening.

Plunging In

The ECB, by now alone in its anti-restructuring fundamentalism, had itself begun to move. The influence of Jörg Asmussen, a former high official at the German finance ministry and now Merkel and Schäuble's man on the ECB executive board, reflected the shifting priorities of his masters. These included limiting the size of the next eurozone rescue – destined for Cyprus, a country decried in the German press as a haven for Russian money laundering.

Whatever else it was, Cyprus was certainly a mismanaged financial system. Another island-state-turned-hedge fund, its banking system, consisting largely of two big banks, owed seven times the country's annual GDP. They were in a threadbare state. One had made huge losses in the writedown of Greek sovereign bonds and both were suffering from a recession and housing market slump. As elsewhere, the national leaders showed a touching solicitude for the clients of banks – far greater than for their citizens at large. The state had run out of market credit, and only a bridge loan from Russia tided the government over a nine-month negotiation with the troika.

A large proportion of these clients were indeed Russian individuals and companies. The politically awful prospect of eurozone financial 'solidarity' seemingly benefitting tax evaders and oligarchs strengthened those among Cyprus's putative creditors who were willing to see restructuring happen. With a German election looming, Berlin demanded that private creditors would this time have to share the burden. On Asmussen's direction, the ECB did the same. This was a stunning trajectory for the eurozone's central bank. Two years on from the Irish affair, Frankfurt was engaging in the same dark arts as before, though now in the pursuit of the diametrically opposite course. The ECB threatened to cut off liquidity to Cypriot banks if the government did not do what Frankfurt wanted. But whereas the ECB had threatened Dublin in order to *stop* it from restructuring its banks, it was now forcing Nicosia to do precisely that.

Who were the creditors lined up to take losses? Since Cypriot banks had issued very few bonds, the bulk of their funding came from depositors. During the winter of 2012–13, this was the nub of the negotiations between the eurozone paymasters, unwilling to bankroll a rescue of unsavoury bank clients, and the Cypriot government, running out of cash but desperately protective of its offshore banking industry. Nicosia wanted a loan of €17 billion: €10 billion to keep the government going and the rest to bail out the banks. Germany drew the line at the €10 billion: the banks would have to come up with the needed capital themselves.

Things came to a head late into the night of Friday 15 March, when Asmussen gave the Cypriot negotiators an ultimatum: if they did not conclude a deal, the ECB would veto the continuing liquidity provision to the two big Cypriot banks. As with the 'rescues' of Ireland and Portugal, it was a choice between obedience and possible expulsion from the euro. The Cypriot government finally buckled, but it gained one concession that betrayed how closely it aligned itself with the interests of its banks. Rather than a resolution of the two banks in which the few unsecured bonds they had issued and deposits over €100,000 would be written down (smaller deposits are insured by the government under EU rules), the same money would be raised by a special tax on all depositors (but not on bondholders). The idea was to keep the losses incurred by big depositors – the mainstay of the island's offshore banking business – in single percentage figures, at 9.9 per cent in fact. But the consequence would have been to leave the banks themselves unreformed and to charge a 6.75 per cent one-off levy on the supposedly insured deposits of small savers and businesses.

That all the other eurozone countries, the ECB, the Commission and the IMF agreed to this is as puzzling as it is shameful. Perhaps it was the all-night meeting that blunted everyone's common sense. Perhaps it was deference to a member country's head of state: president Nicos Anastasiades was personally present at the finance minister's meeting where the decision had to be made. Whatever the reason, all other parties seemed happy to let Cyprus decide how to raise the money.[10]

The decision they tolerated, however, undermined the credibility of deposit insurance across the eurozone. A government guarantee that you can safely put up to €100,000 in a bank without a risk of loss must be just that; it means little if the government sees fit to raid the same deposits through a back door, even if the guarantee is not technically violated. The deal unforgivably betrayed those with the most to lose and the least to answer for in the crisis.

Of equal significance was the fact that, while the eurozone's leading decision makers had finally come around to the need to save taxpayers from the losses of banks, they were content to leave the loss-making banks otherwise untouched. They had got half the need for bank resolution right – protecting public finances from those of banks – but remained oblivious to the other half: ending impunity for poor and politicised bank governance, which state support without restructuring only serves to perpetuate.

This scandal was greeted with the outrage it deserved. Cypriot depositors were furious, financial professionals globally were shocked, and Cypriot parliamentarians rejected the plan. All bank branches in the country were closed on government orders and ATMs limited withdrawals. Within ten days a new plan had been drafted, and this time the eurozone got it right. Insured depositors would remain insured; uninsured deposits would take a bigger loss to make up the difference. And crucially, this would be done not through a levy but through a restructuring of the two banks' balance sheets. To prevent a bank run, capital controls were imposed in the eurozone for the first time. Even insured deposits, which in the end did remain insured, could only be withdrawn in drips.

Much nonsense was spouted at the time that this meant Cyprus had effectively left the euro, since a euro in Cyprus was no longer equivalent to a euro in other countries. This claim conflates a country with its banks. It is the case everywhere that depositors in a failed bank may see their accounts frozen until deposit guarantees kick in. It so happened that in Cyprus, the country's banking system was virtually coextensive with just two banks, both of which were in massive failure. It was not so much that a euro in Cyprus was 'worth less' than in other countries (strictly speaking it was less liquid), but a euro held in those particular banks was worth less than a euro in other banks. After all, customers of the Cypriot branches of foreign banks retained unfettered access to their euros. That being said, the controls were stricter and lasted longer than necessary (they were gradually relaxed and were finally terminated in the spring of 2015). They should not have been applied to banks other than the main two. Once the latter had been put through resolution, the ECB should again freely have issued liquidity to the whole banking system, and enough to replace any quantity of deposit outflows. The best way to stop fleeing depositors in their tracks is to give them all the cash they want without delay.

Be that as it may. The most significant reactions to the Cyprus solution were those that did not materialise. For three years eurozone leaders had wrung their hands worrying about contagion. But when they finally adopted the policies they had until so recently abjured – senior creditor and depositor writedowns, even capital controls – there was no contagion in sight. Deposits in Spanish and Italian banks, whose flight it was thought would signal the endgame for monetary union, stayed resolutely put. The unruffled market reaction to the Cyprus restructuring (the political uproar notwithstanding) proved just how unfounded Europe's Lehman Syndrome had been. The eurozone had finally got it.

Or had it? After the revised Cyprus agreement, the head of the eurogroup of eurozone finance ministers, Jeroen Dijsselbloem, suggested resolution and writedowns would be the norm for future problem cases.[11] It was always a bit rich coming from him: as the Dutch finance minister he had protected the senior creditors to the failed SNS Reaal with taxpayer money just a month before the Cyprus catharsis. But to the extent he meant it, he deserved to be liberally praised. Instead he was rapped over the knuckles by eurozone colleagues, who demanded, and got, a 'clarification' that Cyprus was a special case.

The ambivalence with which European leaders have continued to view bank resolution and restructuring is clear in other bank failures since 2012. Spain's agreement on a credit line with the ESM for bank bail-outs explicitly required creditor writedowns – but only for subordinated and hybrid debt.[12] When Franco-Belgian Dexia was bailed out for the third time in December 2012, senior bondholders were protected in full, as they were when Dijsselbloem nationalised SNS Reaal two months later. In the summer of 2014, Portugal split up the loss-ridden carcass of Banco Espírito Santo in such a way that subordinated debt holders would carry much of the cost, but senior bondholders were again protected. In Greece, there has been no pressure to save public money by imposing losses on creditors of Greek banks, which in 2012 were all bailed out in full by the government with funds borrowed from the eurozone. Even in 2015, when the threadbare state of Greek bank assets was used to justify limits on liquidity in the middle of a bank run, Greek authorities resisted a restructuring, and the ECB in its capacity as regulator did not force their hands by revoking the banks' operating licences.[13]

In short, European leaders have equipped themselves with powerful tools for swift and safe bank resolution, but not yet with the courage to use them consistently.

Fiscal and Monetary Let-Up

Europe had embraced fiscal austerity with unseemly enthusiasm in the crisis. The motivation had been the fear of public debt stocks rising from already high levels. The turn to austerity was the logical twin of the taboo on default: an obsession with squeezing the flow of new debt rather than cutting the stock of outstanding debt. The result was, as we have seen, to kill off the recovery, worsening debt burdens further and straining the financial integrity of the eurozone as a result.

The more enlightened view of debt restructuring that came to the fore in 2012 was matched by a realisation that consolidation was not working. The eurozone's second recession undid much of what the fiscal consolidations underway had been expected to achieve, and emboldened calls to relax the belt tightening.

Thus in the course of the same few months that the eurozone made a decisive turn from bail-out to bail-in, Europe's leadership also eased up on austerity. Most governments looked sure to miss the deadlines set in 2009–10 for bringing their deficits under the 3 per cent of GDP limit. After first doubling down on its mistaken policies, Europe had mellowed, and the deadlines were extended and extended again.

The biggest eurozone economies – Germany, France, Italy, Spain and the Netherlands – had all originally been told to get to 3 per cent by 2013 (2012 for Italy, whose deficit was not enormous but whose debt stock was the biggest by far). In the summer of 2012, Spain and France's target dates were pushed back two years. In June 2013, Spain's was extended further to 2016; the Netherlands, too, was given an extra year; France's deadline would be shifted back several more times. Only Germany achieved its goal ahead of time, largely on the back of better-than-expected growth. With capital gushing in, looking for a safe haven, the German economy had thrived on the credit crunch elsewhere. This is one benefit that Germany has reaped from the crisis of others without fully appreciating it. Record-cheap credit was no doubt an important, and entirely undeserved, contributor to its decent growth performance from 2010 on.

Italy met its target on time – but at the cost of stagnating, whereas the target had been based on solid growth from 2011 on. The Netherlands did in the end get under 3 per cent during 2013, but its drive for premature consolidation pushed it into recession.

Monetary policy, too, was revised in the face of the economic deterioration it had helped cause. Mario Draghi wasted no time on becoming ECB president in November 2011: his first two Governing Council meetings reversed Trichet's interest rate rises earlier in the year. A further cut came seven months later, hot on the heels of the momentous about-turns on banks and austerity in June. Within months of his arrival at the helm, moreover, Draghi's ECB for the first time offered three-year loans to banks, injecting more than half a trillion euros of fresh liquidity into the financial system. It also allowed banks to pledge a broader set of assets as security for central bank loans and halved the amount of cash reserves banks must hold against their deposits. In just the first six months of Draghi's tenure, the euro monetary base grew by almost 50 per cent. (Figure 5.1 on page 111 and Figure 5.3 on page 114 show how austerity eased and monetary growth resumed around 2012.)

The fiscal and monetary let-up came not a moment too soon. For the worst-hit countries, Europe-wide austerity had compounded the damage to demand caused by their own rushed budget cuts. It had failed on its own terms to rein in debt, let alone on the criterion of political harmony and popular support for reforms. Monetary tightening, meanwhile, had sent recovering economic confidence indicators sliding back down in spring 2011. They only began to improve again in the second half of 2012, once fiscal and monetary policymakers had stopped tightening the vice. (See Figure 6.1.)

Whatever It Takes

But Draghi was not yet done.

A central bank's power lies not just in what it *can* do with its money-printing press but in what it can make markets believe it *will* do. Mervyn King, who led the Bank of England for a decade until 2013, once explained this by pointing to Diego Maradona's goal against England in the 1986 World Cup:

> The truly remarkable thing is that Maradona ran virtually in a straight line ... the English defenders reacted to what they expected Maradona to do. Because they expected Maradona to move either left or right, he was able to go straight on.[14]

Similarly, by managing markets' expectations of what the central bank will do, it can make them do its work for it.

Draghi has an acute understanding of the power of expectations. Shortly after the European Council and the Commission's break-through on banking policy, he deployed it to great effect. Addressing investors in the City of London in July 2012, the former Goldman Sachs banker had pencilled in a few extra words in the margin of his speech at the last minute: 'Within our mandate, the ECB is ready to do whatever it takes to preserve the euro.' After pausing for effect, he looked up – staring the financial market in the eye – and added: 'And believe me, it will be enough.'[15] A few months later, the ECB followed up with the details of a new policy – Outright Monetary Transactions (OMT) – by which it would, under specific conditions, be ready to buy unlimited amounts of sovereign bonds of countries that had been granted rescue loans from the ESM.

This was widely welcomed by economists, who had long complained that the ECB was refusing to play a role as lender of last resort to governments. This failure was first diagnosed by Paul De Grauwe, who in 2011 quite rightly pointed out that a central bank responsibility to prevent self-fulfilling runs on the debt of a solvent government is as imperative as the long-recognised responsibility to prevent self-fulfilling bank runs.[16] The lender of last resort analogy, if rhetorically justified, is somewhat misleading. De Grauwe did not say that the ECB should lend money to governments, but that it should intervene in publicly traded sovereign bond markets (what are called open-market operations, which central banks everywhere undertake all the time for other securities). A technically correct term would be a bond buyer of last resort. By buying the bonds of governments who are solvent, but which investors worry will run out of cash because of the bond market panic itself, the central bank can end the run. The difference is important, for De Grauwe's argument is sometimes taken to prove a design flaw in the euro, as discussed in Chapter 2. The ECB is legally prohibited from lending to governments; but its authority to buy and sell securities in any publicly traded market it sees fit is explicitly stated in the EU treaties. The sovereign debt crisis was not caused by the eurozone's lack of a bond buyer of last resort but by the central bank's long fumbling of the powers at its disposal.

Understanding that fumbling is crucial for understanding the following events. There is no doubt that Draghi changed the psychology of the markets, and thereby played an important role in turning the fortunes of the euro. But the importance of his 'whatever it takes' speech has been misinterpreted. It should not be given sole credit for ending the sovereign debt crisis, as is often done. Draghi's speech was not the only big turning point in eurozone policy in the summer of 2012. And it was less the policy content of the OMT programme than the changes it reflected in eurozone high politics that helped the sovereign debt panic to finally abate.

The lionisation of Draghi is typically based on how the borrowing costs of the euro's crisis-hit states fell after his speech – not just a drop in the days immediately afterwards but a steady decline in the months and years that followed. But there is a problem with this narrative: in almost every country, borrowing costs had already been falling for some time. Dublin's borrowing costs had peaked a year earlier; by the time Draghi dared the markets, its risk premium was half what it had been in July 2011. Greece's spread had peaked in February 2012, just before the restructuring, and although it rose again between the two elections in May and June, it was already coming down once Samaras had won. Italy's spread had been at its highest around Berlusconi's ousting in November 2011; Portugal's had been falling since January. It was only for Spain that the risk spread's highest point coincided with Draghi's speech. Besides, the fragmentation of credit conditions, while it did not intensify further, remained high for the following years (see Figure 5.8).

True, the fall in sovereign yields in the months after the 'whatever it takes' speech was rapid and proved to be sustained, with measurable drops on days when details of the new policy were published. But to give Draghi all the credit is to forget about the other momentous events that took place in June and July. These included a new Greek government bowing to troika demands; a clear political commitment to limit governments' liability for loss-making banks through both bail-ins and common funds; a moderation of universal austerity; and the end of the recession. As for Spain, Draghi's speech came within days of the stand-off over Spanish banks ending with an agreement on a limited rescue loan, devoted solely to financing Madrid's expenses on bank recapitalisation – which, for the first time, included a minimum requirement that at least some creditors would bear a share of losses.

As for the OMT programme, it is problematic to credit it directly for the change in market sentiment. Not only has the ECB always had the power to buy government bonds, it had already used that power on two occasions: in May 2010 (for Greece, Ireland and Portugal) and August 2011 (for Spain and Italy). These interventions, however, had little effect except on the particular bond issues that were bought.[17] Announcements about OMT did, however, have a discernable impact on Italian and Spanish bond prices, which fell sharply relative to French and German ones.[18]

Yet what Draghi proposed was a remarkably circumscribed programme. OMT would see the ECB buy short-dated government bonds of a crisis country – but only if the government still enjoyed or had regained access to private markets, and only if it had entered a rescue programme with the ESM and subjected itself to the attached conditions. An ESM programme would have to be agreed unanimously among euro members; in other words, Berlin had an effective veto on OMT. This is quite a limitation, especially as De Grauwe himself cited the German veto right as a reason why the EFSF/ESM fiscal rescue funds could not substitute for the ECB as lender of last resort.[19] Even with this constraint, a group of professors asked the German constitutional court in Karlsruhe to rule the policy illegal. The testimony of Bundesbank president Jens Weidmann to the court displayed such an antipathy to the policy – and indeed to the ECB's responsibility for keeping the euro together – that it caused bad blood in Frankfurt and raised eyebrows across Europe. To all this, markets merely shrugged. They shrugged again when Karlsruhe issued an unexpectedly tough ruling, asking the ECJ to deem the policy illegal unless it was delimited in ways that would defeat its purpose. In 2015 the ECJ put doubts about OMT's legality to rest, though it reiterated that there were limits on how far the ECB could go.

The fact that market confidence turned before the ECB had actually presented its policy, and was unruffled by the prospective setbacks to its ability to actually buy government bonds, means that the real importance of Draghi's speech did not lie in the prospective bond purchases themselves. What mattered most was the politics behind his vow to do 'whatever it takes'. The fact that he could make such a sweeping statement suggested that, of the two central bankers in Frankfurt, Merkel was now putting her support behind Draghi and not the Bundesbank's Weidmann. This was reinforced by how closely the other German Governing Council member, Jörg Asmussen (Schäuble's former advisor), worked with Draghi on developing the policy. It all signalled that Merkel had made up her mind no longer to entertain the expulsion from the euro of countries the German public might see as financial miscreants.

The greatest threat to the single currency had been not its design, but the willingness of (especially) German and ECB leaders, as well as leading opinion makers, to countenance its break-up. They demonstrated that willingness by throwing doubt on the political legitimacy of how the design did its job (e.g. emergency liquidity assistance and Target2 transfers), questioning Greece's suitability for the currency union, and treating a specific direction of economic policy as a de facto requirement of euro membership. The crisis abated when leaders backed away from their flirtation with break-up. Draghi's speech was above all a signal that they had.

LASTING INJURY

The partial ability of the eurozone's governing elite to revisit its wrong-headed principles – manifest above all in the shift from bail-out to bail-in, incomplete as it is – reversed the course of the crisis and belatedly allowed better policies to take the place of counterproductive ones. That still leaves a lot to be desired, and the bad instincts remain strong. In addition, some of the steps the eurozone has taken in the belief that they are needed to make monetary union work are actually putting the best policies out of reach. In its attempt to 'fix' illusory structural flaws in the single currency, the eurozone has introduced real ones.

One of these flaws that we have already discussed is the tightened stability and growth pact. By requiring surpluses over time, it complicates fiscal demand management and blocks debt-financed investment programmes of a certain scale. (Had Norway been a member of the EU and found oil today instead of forty-five years ago, it would have struggled under current EU rules to make the investments necessary to build up its oil industry – investments that in the 1970s made for double-digit current account deficits.) This reduces a fiscal flexibility that a single currency makes more necessary, not less.

The eurozone has also undermined national governments' ability to manage the domestic credit cycle through bank regulation. True, the long-overdue tightening of bank capital requirements (in the form of the directive known as CRD IV) will make banking much safer, by limiting banks' ability to gamble with borrowed funds. Regulatory competence has improved, as has the understanding of 'macro-prudential' rules (which guard against threats to the financial system as a whole and not just failures in individual financial entities). And Europe-wide regulation is being vastly improved by the banking union. But the EU has not contented itself with setting minimum standards that member states must impose on banks to stop regulation from being too lax. It has also legislated for 'maximum harmonisation', which is to say that it prohibits national governments from regulating banks more strictly than the rest of the union – except in special cases with the permission of Brussels. This means a country wanting to rein in a domestic credit bubble – as Ireland could have done had it wanted to – depends on the Commission not being swayed by other countries whose banks may be profiting handsomely from such a bubble.

Nor has the ECB shed all its old habits. At the time of writing, it is keeping a very tight rein on liquidity to Greek banks even as depositors are withdrawing their money at a fast pace. Again, it is using the liquidity lifeline as a tool to make policy demands from a national government, in this case to push Athens towards renewing its rescue programme with the eurozone. This is no more legitimate than in past instances. The ECB itself deems Greek banks solvent in its new capacity as the banking union's bank supervisor. As long as it stands by that recent conclusion, it cannot refuse to facilitate deposit transfers out of Greece if that is what depositors want. The drip feed of liquidity administered by the ECB in the months after Syriza's election victory softly but undeniably pushed Greece further apart from the rest of the eurozone. If, on the contrary, the ECB harbours doubts about the banks' solvency, it should demand their immediate restructuring to carve out new banks with access to as much liquidity as they may need. This neither–nor attitude is what necessitated the imposition of capital controls on Greek banks in June 2015, with the economic havoc these will have caused.

These relapses are problems for economic policy: they curtail the ability that countries previously possessed (but failed to use) to help their economies weather volatile capital flows within the currency union. But they are also problems for democracy. This is because they shrink the space within which the citizenries of Europe's nations may choose what policy course to take.

The trend in European politics is towards shrinking the 'policy free space' further. The eurozone's tendency to arrogate democratic power in favour of technocratic rule – manifest in the troika system and the unseating of Papandreou and Berlusconi – was unchained again in its dealings with the left-wing radicals in power in Greece from January 2015. Eurozone leaders did not even bother to hide their 'advice' that they would like to see a different government in Athens. When Alexis Tsipras called for a referendum on the proposed terms of a third loan programme, his counterparts attempted a replay of November 2011, denouncing the plebiscite and impressing on Greek voters the claim that they were voting on Greece's euro membership rather than the actual question asked. These efforts to enforce the cash-for-control paradigm were backed by the ECB's reckless limiting of liquidity to Greek banks just as a bank run was underway. If Athens didn't behave, the ECB looked ready to act as the other euro members' bouncer and throw Greece out of the club.

The stand-off with Athens is still playing out. Beyond Greece, the most egregious example of technocratic imperialism is the proposal of legally binding bilateral contracts between national governments and the Commission (tellingly, this was first promoted by Mario Monti, whose premiership was no paragon of democratic propriety, together with Merkel). These would bind a country to pursuing specific structural reforms in return for greater funding from some mutual source. It is hard to see this as anything other than an attempt to prevent governments from having second thoughts (perhaps in response to popular protest) over policies they accepted under economic duress. This attitude has been clear since the winter of 2014–15, when European leaders first interfered in the Greek election campaign, heavily hinting that Greeks should not elect Syriza, then let it be known that prime minister Tsipras ought to reshuffle his cabinet to make it less radical and finally reacted aggressively to Tsipras's call for a referendum, in a repeat of November 2011 (see Chapter 3).

Other initiatives echo the push for greater centralisation. They have included Schäuble's proposal for an EU budget commissioner with the authority to overrule national budgets and Draghi's call for the Commission to be given similar monitoring and sanctioning power over structural economic policies as it has over fiscal policy.

All these decisions have a common origin and a common consequence. The origin is the intellectual premise that a well-functioning monetary union requires transfers from the stronger economies – for which read Germany – to the weaker ones. This forces political questions into the one-dimensional track of bargaining over how much policy autonomy to give up for what amount of German subsidy. The peripheral countries, including Greece's ostensibly radical Syriza government, are as guilty of indulging this premise as the core – they just disagree how much subsidy can realistically be extracted. The consequence is to narrow the scope for governments to reflect their electorates' views of how they want to live their economic lives. Those views may differ between countries and over time – and indeed within countries, which is why the national political process must be able to offer genuine alternatives to voters.

The elite is alert to this democratic problem. The European Parliament has criticised the intrusive nature of the troika surveillance of the crisis countries. The ECJ has objected to the ECB's role in the troika. And before Syriza's election, Brussels was reported to be considering handing control of Greece's adjustment programme back to Athens. Doing so would have recognised what should have been clear from the start: that policies chosen and motivated by those they affect are more likely to succeed – and are more palatable – than externally imposed ones.

Similarly, there is a push – from Germany and Schäuble in particular – to strengthen the democratic legitimacy of eurozone policies by more voter engagement at the European level, e.g. through a eurozone parliament or a directly elected president of the European Commission. The same thinking lay behind picking European Parliament party group candidates for Commission president in 2014, in the hope that a more personalised campaign would engage voters and strengthen the parliament's democratic heft.

We should be suspicious about these efforts. Not just because citizens are unexcited by them. Nor because some of them come so late as to seem an afterthought. It would be a good thing if voters felt better represented and saw their preferences more strongly reflected at the European level (and indeed at national level). But there is no guarantee that if this were the case, they would support the policies the technocrats deem necessary – such as the allegedly incontrovertible centralisation of both resources and policymaking power. If voters make the 'wrong' choices, recent experience gives every reason to fear that even if their voices were better heard, they would not be more heeded.

SEVEN
If Europe Dared to Write Down Debt

Renouncing 'There Is No Alternative'

This book started with Spinelli's call for the abolition of the nation state and observed that the euro constituted the ultimate test of his belief that only a federal Europe could secure progress, peace and prosperity throughout the continent. Confusingly, two conflicting lessons have been drawn from the sovereign debt crisis that nearly tore apart Europe's economic and political fabric. One is that the euro has proved Spinelli fatally wrong: abolishing national sovereignty in monetary affairs has caused political disintegration instead of unity. The other is that it has proved him ineluctably right: monetary integration makes full national sovereignty untenable in other domains of policy. The common premise is that the euro as designed was deeply flawed and a prime cause of its economic troubles and, therefore, its political ones.

According to the revisionist history I have told in the previous chapters, both sides are wrong, and the premise they share is a mistake. Monetary integration is not the source of the crisis. The blame for the economic stagnation and political morass which submerged Europe after 2009 should be pinned largely on eurozone policymakers' unforced policy errors – their free choice to pursue some actions rather than others, such as bail-out instead of bail-in; delay instead of resolution. The euro's design is erroneously blamed for ruling out any alternatives to the toxic bargain of financial transfers traded for contractionary policies. What really constrained policymakers' freedom of manoeuvre was not the euro but their reluctance to be honest with electorates about the inevitability of losses once the credit bubble burst, and to settle politically where those losses were going to fall. Because of this neglect, serious losses grew into devastating ones. Because the euro was scapegoated for it, the single currency is at risk of unravelling, which would make things worse still.

To say that not the euro but bad policy choices were responsible for Europe's predicament is to assert that other choices would have led to better outcomes. This chapter aims to justify that assertion with an argument about what those outcomes could have been.

A Stroll through Counterfactual History

Suppose that, when the crisis washed over them in early 2010, Europe's governing elites had navigated by a different principle than the abhorrence of debt writedowns. In this counterfactual history, they would have applied capitalism to capital. That would have meant making private investors bear the burden of their bad loans. It would have meant facilitating a Greek sovereign debt restructuring and an Irish bank resolution without delay. It would, too, have meant honouring the principle behind these choices when making policy for the monetary union as a whole.

Uncowed by a taboo on restructuring, the eurozone's leaders would have seen that the potential fallout from a Greek default was outweighed by the advantages. These were numerous: they included respecting the promise not to bail out governments; putting the interests of citizens and taxpayers over those of private investors; and averting the politically noxious state of reciprocal blackmail in which successive bail-outs ensnared both Athens and its rescuers. Europe's leaders would have addressed any reasonable worry about contagion with measures to make a default as orderly as possible, like they eventually did when writing down Greece's debt in March 2012. As for hurt pride over a eurozone government being toppled by markets, they would just get over it.

Greek authorities, while perhaps redoubling their early reform efforts in a last-ditch attempt to regain the confidence of bond markets, would also have been preparing the ground for a debt restructuring, seeking a voluntary debt exchange if possible, and a forcible writedown if necessary. The substance of the restructuring could have looked something like what was achieved two years later – a 53 per cent nominal haircut, more than 70 per cent when accounting for the stretched-out repayment schedule – but it could usefully have been tougher still.[20]

In Ireland, the eurozone would have shown greater solicitude for Dublin's creditworthiness than the government itself did in the early crisis. Ireland's counterparts would at a minimum have encouraged and supported the Irish government's attempt to make up for its earlier mistakes and put banks through special resolution procedures. These would have moved insured deposits and secured debts to new, good banks, whose funding by the ECB for as long as necessary would be put beyond doubt. Non-guaranteed creditors would be left to hold the pieces of the old assets.

Stretching our imagination to breaking point, Europe could even have leaned on Ireland to stop treating the blanket bank guarantees from 2008 as if they were the same as ordinary sovereign debt, with the goal of unwinding them or at least mitigating their cost. After all, the guarantees required, and obtained, repeated approval from the European Commission. Withdrawing that approval would have given Dublin an excuse to go back on the guarantees while honouring actual sovereign borrowing in full.

Finally, in our parallel universe, the restructuring paths taken in Greece and Ireland would inform a generalised policy for the eurozone. Any aid to sovereigns would only be considered after halting all outstanding debt service (if not writing the sovereign debt down outright, then postponing payment and formally subordinating it to any rescue loans). Any taxpayer aid to banks, beyond the standard guarantee of deposits up to €100,000, would be ruled out, and harmonised special resolution regimes for undercapitalised banks would be swiftly introduced in every EU country. We can think of this as having passed a stricter version of the Bank Recovery and Resolution Directive as soon as 2009 (the United Kingdom passed its special resolution regime for banks in February of that year), and as having adopted the supervision and resolution elements of banking union (but not the common bail-out element: the 'fiscal backstop') as early as possible.

There would, moreover, have been the political will to actually use restructuring vigorously as a way to revive undercapitalised banks. This presupposes a willingness, an eagerness even, on the part of eurozone authorities to shine a light into the deepest recesses of banks' balance sheets – probing their vulnerability to sovereign debt writedowns in particular – and to require losses to be fully realised and equity to be amply replenished. It was not until the ECB's 'comprehensive assessment' of banks newly under its supervision in October 2014 that Europe began to evince such a willingness, and even that exercise was far from perfect.[21]

All these would-haves carry a tinge of the absurd, of course. But counterfactual history is perforce an exercise in imagination. Given that in two years the eurozone elite came round (albeit partially and grudgingly) to the need to write down the debts of at least one sovereign, and of banks, and given that the head of the eurogroup, Jeroen Dijsselbloem, once vowed to make Cyprus a model for future eurozone rescues,[22] it is not so far-fetched to consider a world in which leaders had made those better choices to begin with. Moreover, many of these policy options were well understood by the international economic policy community because they had been actively considered or even implemented in other cases.[23]

We have to imagine, too, what the results of such a different approach would have been. The only thing we can be confident of is how the financial industry would have responded to a policy of broad restructuring: with howls of protest. All else is speculation. But not all speculation is equal, and we can make ours as informed as possible by taking into consideration how markets and politics work.

FAIL EARLY, FAIL OFTEN

How would the eurozone economy have fared if these policy principles had guided the policy response to the crisis from the outset?

Start with applying market forces to banks. Financial supervisors unafraid of bank resolution would not tolerate the embellishment of ugly balance sheets. They would instead force banks to value their assets conservatively and require them to replenish their capital accordingly. In the absence of private investors willing to pick up the bill, this would be done through resolution and forced debt-for-equity swaps. With this prospect in place, any regulatory agency slow to put banks' feet to the fire would quickly find that investors would do its job for it. For with a credible resolution regime in place, bondholders would cut their exposure to any bank they perceived to be on the course to eventual restructuring. Secured loans from the central bank might replace some of this fleeing capital, but since insolvent banks by definition lack enough assets to put up as security for all their funding needs, a sustained creditor flight would force them into resolution. The result would be that as soon as a bank lost the confidence of either regulators or markets, its investors would go to bed as bondholders and wake up as shareholders in a newly restructured bank.

This is not an outlandish proposal – with the Bank Recovery and Resolution Directive, it is now official policy – and it should not have seemed outlandish in 2009–10. A precedent existed in the United States, where the Federal Deposit Insurance Corporation has regularly resolved failing banks for decades (at a rate of 150 a year in 2009–10, and about two a month as the crisis has abated).[24] Its rule has been to compensate insured depositors in full and let other creditors take a share of the failed bank's losses according to their rank. Only a few weeks after Lehman's bankruptcy, the Federal Deposit Insurance Corporation unceremoniously seized Washington Mutual from its parent company to arrest a run on the bank. The process, which saw the restructuring of some $300 billion in assets and liabilities, did not bail out unsecured senior creditors. There was no practical obstacle to adopting similar procedures in Europe, as Denmark demonstrated in 2011. The failure to do so flowed from a mix of a cultural aversion to debt writedowns and a misguided fear of the consequences.

What would these consequences have been if, from the start of the crisis, the eurozone had ushered its failing banks into resolution? There is little reason to think they would have been any less manageable than in the United States and in Denmark. There would of course be big practical challenges to address. Many institutional investors such as pension funds, for example, may have investment mandates that require them to invest only in certain bonds, and might not be allowed to hold newly converted shares in a resolved bank. But this just means they would have to sell to investors who could. Given that the new banks would be thoroughly cleansed of risk, it should be possible to eventually find willing owners. The original investors in the resolved banks (again, often pension funds or insurance companies) would of course endure losses, and more importantly a transformation of their fixed income claims (bonds with a promised regular coupon and repayment schedule) for equity claims (a right to the uncertain residual profits of the business). But that is no objection: it would be the point of the exercise (recall Figure 5.8).

In April 2009, the IMF estimated that European banks needed some €550 billion in fresh equity just to get back to the capital cushions that had prevailed before the 2000s boom.[25] We can consider this a conservative estimate of the scale of the losses faced by eurozone bank bondholders if restructuring had been the norm (new equity would have been hard to raise in such a policy regime until the expected bail-ins had actually been carried out).

Would the economy have suffered under this practice – worse than under the actually prevailing one of resisting debt writedowns? The figure of €550 billion should be seen in proportion: it amounted to about one-tenth of total eurozone bank bonds outstanding at the time[26] and therefore a much smaller part of total bank liabilities. While the impact would vary across banks, the overall impact would not have been devastating. The loss in paper wealth might have caused a drop in consumption demand from the losers, but it would also have mitigated a larger drop in spending by cash-strapped governments landed with the bill.[27]

The macroeconomic effect would also depend on what happened to bank lending as a result of widespread bond restructuring. The long failure to resolve zombie banks in the eurozone contributed to a credit crunch that made the recession worse. Conversely, recapitalising the banking system through speedy resolution would have much more quickly led banks to a position of wanting to lend rather than shrink their loan books (as it was, eurozone banks did not stop tightening their lending standards until 2014, as Figure 5.2 showed). This in turn would have better allowed them to feed low ECB rates through to businesses in crisis-hit countries. Moreover, the proper scrutiny of banks' balance sheets, with weak ones put into resolution, would lift the fog of uncertainty from banks that were in fact in good shape. Rather than being tarred with the same brush as the zombies, solid banks would find it easier to fund themselves cheaply, and thus to expand their business. What is more, the good banks emerging from the resolution regimes would by design be strongly capitalised and rid of problem assets. They, too, ought to have no difficulty attracting funding in private markets. Neither group would need to deleverage (that is, shrink their lending) since their assets would already have been robustly written down by the regulators. All these factors would have contributed to more and cheaper credit.

Some may question the merit of returning to fast credit growth. If this was a crisis of overindebtedness, did not banks and their debtors need to pay down their debts before one could safely expect credit, borrowing and spending to drive growth again? This aversion to having more of what brought us into the crisis in the first place is understandable. But it is also harmful. It has served as an excuse for neglecting the eurozone's supply of money and credit, which the ECB allowed to remain stagnant and even shrink in inflation-adjusted terms until 2014. Moreover, in a eurozone liberated from the taboo on debt restructuring, leverage would automatically and immediately have been cut when the debts of sovereigns and banks were written down. Having their liabilities written down would, in turn, make banks more willing to restructure their own unrecoverable claims on borrowers, rather than 'pretend and extend' lending to overindebted businesses and households.

So a renewed expansion of credit would not come on top of already unsustainable debt mountains, but start from a freshly levelled base. Real productive resources, and the credit to invest in them, could be allocated to new or growing companies rather than hoarded to keep the boom year's failures on life support. The US experience, where indebtedness fell faster than in Europe through bankruptcies and restructuring, suggests this is much less damaging to economic activity than the slow grind of deleveraging through reduced spending and debt repayments.[28] Policies that restructure debt improve not just the degree of credit growth, but the quality of its composition.

What about the greatest fear voiced by eurozone policymakers: that letting a weak bank fail would threaten other, fundamentally healthy banks; that any Anglo Irish could prove as dangerous as a Lehman Brothers? It is true that once investors come to fear widespread resolution operations, they may withdraw even from strong banks to avoid any risk of being written down. But there are two reasons why this need not be something to fear in a world where orderly resolution is the norm for insolvent banks.

The first admittedly requires optimism. One may hope that if resolution-minded regulators enforced greater transparency of bank balance sheets, this would help good banks flaunt their strengths. The light that exposes weak banks, hastening their passage into resolution, also helps to show investors in strong banks that they have no reason to flee. This should make self-fulfilling panics in bank funding markets less, not more, likely for genuinely solvent banks. The US experience with Washington Mutual shows that the optimism is warranted.

The possibility of panic cannot, however, be ruled out. If investors in our imagined resolution-friendly world worry that a bank may be forced into resolution because of a run – even if there were no objective reasons for one – this might discourage them from lending to it. But even in the worst-case scenario, indisputably solvent banks should always be able to rely on the ECB for sufficient emergency liquidity. This is the second reason not to fear our hypothetical world: a more enlightened ECB would have been proud rather than embarrassed about lending in the last resort to banks and letting Target2 accommodate capital movements across borders. By putting strong banks' access to liquidity beyond any doubt, the ECB would minimise the likelihood of runs and eliminate the dangers of those that happened anyway. As for banks on the vague borderline between solvency and insolvency, resolution (if investors panicked and fled) would come as a relief rather than as further agony. It would draw a line under the run and see to it that the bank re-emerged cleansed of all doubts about its solvency. Creditors would at worst suffer very small losses, which they would in any case stand a good chance of recovering through future profits if the bank really was just a borderline case all along.

In short, with resolution being an orderly, well-understood process leading to better banks and more efficient credit flows, periodic waves of contagion should not keep anyone up at night. Even if one bank's resolution did trigger others, this would at most amount to a spring cleaning of the banking system, with some changes to management and an overnight uplift to the banks' capital cushions. If experience shows anything, it is that we should count ourselves lucky to have such renewals occur frequently.

Ending the Cult of the Sovereign Signature

Let us now turn to how the sovereign debt crisis itself would have unfolded in our hypothetical eurozone unafraid of debt restructuring.

If 'solidarity' in the form of rescue loans had only been forthcoming on the condition of halting payments to private investors, Greece would have been forced to restructure in May 2010. Other sovereigns could have tried to ride out the market storm for longer than they did – the popular notion that rescue loans were inescapable as soon as interest rates hit 7 per cent was just a piece of magical thinking. But of course, a liquidity squeeze that lasts long enough can deliver even the most solvent borrower into bankruptcy.

Chapter 3 showed the vast amounts of money that Greece could have saved by restructuring in April 2010, up to arguably some 90 per cent of the total rescue loans it was granted. The question is whether the repercussions on the wider economy, and on other sovereign borrowers that were under pressure, would have been costly enough to outweigh the direct savings to the treasury in Athens.

With the benefit of hindsight, the actual writedown in 2012 demonstrates that it is perfectly possible to manage a sovereign restructuring without the sky falling down. But that writedown was anchored in an ongoing rescue programme with official loans to fund deficits in Athens. The effects of restructuring in April 2010 would have depended on the attitude of the rest of the eurozone. It would have made a big difference if other governments had helped to make the writedown go smoothly (in particular by leaning on their banks to accept a debt exchange, like they had leaned on banks not to pull out of central and eastern Europe) and offered financial aid, post-restructuring, to fund an agreed fiscal deficit path (but no debt service) until markets again considered Athens worthy of their credit.

Even a perfectly executed writedown would inevitably have felled Greek banks. In the 2012 restructuring, their losses were made good to the tune of €40 billion, paid for by Greek taxpayers instructed to take on additional troika loans in that amount.[29] An April 2010 writedown would have rendered them immediately insolvent instead. But this insolvency could have been managed through the type of bank resolution we have just discussed. There was enough equity and bond debt in Greek banks at the end of 2009 to absorb a 100 per cent writedown of their sovereign bond holdings.[30] A significant part of the Greek state's past excesses could thus have been redeemed by an effective expropriation of its own citizens, and the rest by the annulment of claims held by foreigners (both directly and through foreign claims on the banks). But the important point is that they would have been immediately redeemed. This would have brought certainty that lending to Athens and to Greek banks from then on did not mean throwing good money after bad.

With no credit available to it after an April 2010 restructuring, the Greek government would immediately have had to eliminate a 10 per cent primary deficit. That is twice the deficit reduction that Athens actually achieved in 2010 (from a headline figure of 15 per cent, including interest payments, to 10 per cent). In addition, private demand would be cut back somewhat following the losses of restructured bondholders. The economy would have been knocked off its feet. But even under these conditions it may have fared much better than what actually transpired.

The first reason is that credit would probably have begun to flow again quickly – even to the government. As I will argue in a moment, the political situation would have favoured official assistance to Greece after a restructuring. But even without it, Athens would not have been completely deprived of credit. Freshly recapitalised Greek banks, strong enough to raise funding abroad, would have been eager to put their capital to work. That would have encouraged them to loosen the purse strings for the strongest parts of the private sector, which would have mitigated the inevitably severe downturn. The banks would have faced little risk buying at least some new government paper, too, once the government's debt overhang was gone. The lesson of history is that the finality offered by proper debt writedowns quickly draws investors back in.[31] Even foreign private lenders may have returned to Athens sooner (as they eventually did for a short while in 2014), especially if Greece's eurozone partners had been willing to offer at least a small amount of help.

In other words, we should reject the misguided fear that bankruptcy – whether that of a sovereign or of banks – increases the cost of credit in the future. Investors do not care about past failures except insofar as they indicate a risk of similar failures in the future. In Greece, the opposite was true: a large enough restructuring would improve the sovereign's ability to pay, and investors would reward this with lower borrowing costs. Resolution of bankrupt banks has the same function. By recapitalising them at a stroke, enforced debt-for-equity swaps turn the walking dead into safe investments and, equally importantly, into eager lenders. A sovereign restructuring with bank resolution would have made Greece look more like Cyprus after its 2013 rescue: not pretty, but a lot healthier than the depression that eventually engulfed Greece after 2010; and with strong banks under new, private sector management rather than the heavy hand of the Hellenic Republic.

The second reason why post-default economic growth would have been stronger is that the uncertainty that weighed on Greek business for years after 2010 would have been resolved much faster. In the best-case scenario, the country's clientilism would have crumbled once the state was no longer able to bankroll it. The economy would have been radically disrupted, but the balance of that disruption may well have hit the old privileged sectors worse than the competitive parts of the private sector (whereas the policies actually agreed between the government and the troika had the opposite effect). A properly designed and sufficiently deep sovereign writedown would have made for a predictable future. The prospects of any further losses for those exposed to the state would have been small, and the fear of 'Grexit' from the euro would have receded rather than intensified. All this would have benefited the best-run segments of the private sector, in particular the parts of the economy least entangled with the state and most connected to international trade: precisely the sectors Greece needs to grow.

All of this, of course, assumes that the ECB would not have put the single currency at risk by cutting off liquidity upon a restructuring, as it threatened to do both in Greece and in Ireland – and eventually did when Athens was unable to pay the IMF in June 2015. The ECB cannot legally lend to insolvent borrowers against defaulted collateral; but it should have recognised at the outset that a restructuring of Greece's sovereign and bank debt would have ensured solvency, not jeopardised it. Being a secured creditor, the ECB would have seen its claims protected throughout the restructuring process, and it should have been willing to freely offer any amount of liquidity the newly recapitalised banks might need. Had this enlightened perspective been firmly in place, it is likely that Greece and its banks would fairly quickly have been able to attract new private financing. Sovereign yields would have fallen like they did after the 2012 restructuring, and so would the borrowing costs of the private sector. That would have allowed for a more gradual adjustment of both fiscal and current account deficits, and in turn less of a stranglehold on the Greek economy. The brief recovery Greece glimpsed when it paused austerity in 2014 could have been secured years earlier, and been made to last.

There was, admittedly, genuine uncertainty at the time about whether Greece was insolvent or merely having liquidity problems in a dysfunctional market. If it was actually able to pay its debts if only given enough time, it was legitimate to ask whether a restructuring would not give other solvent countries an unfortunate incentive to write off their debts, too. But this uncertainty could have been accommodated in the details of the writedown. The compensation given to restructured creditors could be explicitly tied to measures of debt sustainability. The terms of the restructured obligations could, for example, be tied to future economic growth (there were precedents for this in Iceland, and it also constituted a minor feature of the Greek restructuring that did eventually take place). If the debt really could be paid, Greece would have to pay it; if not, debt service would be kept within predetermined levels and subordinated to any new borrowing. Either way, new lenders would not need to fear being crushed by an overhang of existing debt, and old ones would not have felt cheated if Greece's problems had turned out to be temporary. Bank of England research has shown that GDP-linked debt can bring huge benefits for the country that issues it, too.[32] When Syriza came to power in Athens in January 2015, its first proposal to its official creditors was to convert the debt into GDP-linked obligations. The total refusal to engage with this idea was yet another missed opportunity.

SOVEREIGN CONTAGION

An early Greek default, then, was more likely to bring Athens's bond yields down than drive them further up. What about the borrowing costs of other sovereigns? Those who stood in the line of contagion – Ireland and Portugal, but also Italy and Spain – rightly worried that investors might think that what happened in Greece could happen in other high-debt or high-deficit states. Would investors expect writedowns there, too, and force states into undeserved defaults as they tried to move their investments out of harm's way all at once?

It is of course possible that the markets would have seized up for other debt-laden states if Greece had defaulted in 2010. This is the conventional assessment of Merkel and Sarkozy's Deauville agreement to condition future sovereign rescues on first restructuring outstanding debt. Most commentators and policymakers take it for granted that this sent such fear into the hearts of investors that it triggered the wider sovereign debt crisis. That view, however, does not quite stand up to scrutiny. The moves in distressed governments' bond yields in the days after Deauville were largely in line with how they had developed in the week before the surprise announcement: no shock can be discerned in the market movements.[33] A broader academic analysis of market movements in the sovereign debt crisis generalises this finding: if there was any contagion, it was vanishingly small.[34] In any case, it is not as if 'saving' Greece from default kept the markets' doors open for Ireland, Portugal and Cyprus in the years that followed. It is a mystery why we should think that contagion from managing an orderly restructuring would have been worse than the one actually caused by the failure to do so.

Suppose, however, that it had been. In this counterfactual history, where no rescue money would be offered without a debt restructuring, what could the eurozone periphery governments have done?

One option would have been simply to pay the usurious interest rates demanded by investors while gradually reining in the deficit. That was possible for some of the periphery countries. Ireland could clearly have afforded to sit out higher interest rates for much longer in the hope that market sentiment would turn (it had a cash pile and a pension fund to draw on), and Spain actually did so.[35] If those two countries had swiftly restructured their banks – which the eurozone could have demanded as a condition for financial aid, like it did in Cyprus – the market would have had good reason to think the danger to public sector finances had been contained (remember that the two states entered the crisis with low public debt). Their sovereign borrowing costs would have come down accordingly.

Italy was in a more difficult situation. It was only paying for old sins: its current deficits were small, and it successfully set about cutting even them. But it had to refinance a big stock of debt falling due, and thus needed a revolving supply of credit that no realistic amount of austerity could do much to limit. Portugal faced a mix of the Italian and Spanish/Irish predicaments. Still, the fact that none of these others shared Greece's uniquely awful combination of enormous outstanding debt with yawning deficits has two important implications. The first is that the scale of the required borrowing was significantly smaller than for Athens, and so buying time was more affordable. Given how badly markets reacted to the 'rescues' of Ireland and Portugal, buying time to carry out reforms (in particular bank restructurings) of their own accord rather than on troika orders would probably have done more to restore investor confidence than what actually transpired.

The second implication is that even if investors had continued to stay away, a writedown of Greek dimensions would not have been necessary. What might have been needed *in extremis* for Italy would have been to use Greek tactics (that is to say, bond swaps encouraged by existing or retrofitted collective action clauses) to achieve an automatic refinancing or temporary debt standstill. It would only have needed what in the jargon is called a 'reprofiling': extending the maturity of outstanding bonds beyond their original due dates while respecting both the interest rate and the principal amount originally agreed.

Would this have been something to fear? Anticipation of even just a reprofiling in a large eurozone economy such as Italy could have worsened the capital rout. But it could also have made it easier to handle. Enforced extensions of existing bonds on unchanged terms would have spared official rescues the need to pay off creditors who would have taken the money and run. Funding peripheral Europe's primary deficits (the difference between governments' tax revenue and non-interest spending) required much more modest sums than servicing old debt. Italy, in fact, recorded primary surpluses for most of the crisis, and would have needed minimal fiscal financing even if a reprofiling had caused a steeper downturn than the one actually experienced. The financing needs of Italy and Spain together would have been well within the reach of the €500 billion of rescue fund that the eurozone set aside. It is only because outstanding debt service was being treated as sacrosanct that Spain and Italy could be said to be 'too big to save'.

And like in Greece, a debt standstill or reprofiling for any of the other crisis-hit countries would have permitted less severe austerity, and bank resolutions would have lessened the credit crunch. The better growth performance that would have resulted might well have boosted market confidence, thus halting capital flight rather than exacerbating it. Italy's market attractiveness in particular suffers more from its poor growth record than from current profligacy.

There is one more reason to think capital would not have fled Spain and Italy if debt payments had been extended. The financial fragmentation of the eurozone was caused not by insufficient austerity but by the taboo on restructuring combined with resistance to letting Target2 and emergency liquidity provision do their intended job to maintain a seamless currency union. Conversely, it is likely that in our hypothetical restructuring-friendly world, where losses would be tolerated but the integrity of the euro put beyond any doubt, both the fragmentation and the funding crisis it inflicted on sovereigns and banks would have been less severe.

Banks – the largest holders of government debt – would of course have complained about any sovereign reprofiling. It is in their nature to protect their own interests, and it is their prerogative to do so. But the harm to them would be largely notional, at least from the point of view of the economy as a whole. The banks' principal need for government debt is to hold and use it for liquidity purposes; there is no social benefit in banks' placing temporary speculative bets. Accounting conventions – or our *ex hypothesi* diligent regulators – could usefully have forced banks to recognise losses as market prices for sovereign bonds fell. If that made some banks formally insolvent, the bank resolution procedures could have handled it by immediately converting the banks' bonds into shares, thus restoring well-capitalised lenders. The combination of bank and sovereign restructuring is important: the ability to quickly create good banks out of bad ones both makes a government less likely to default (since it is no longer on the hook for failed banks) and reduces the disruption to the real economy should a sovereign debt writedown or standstill nonetheless be needed. The existence of bank special resolution regimes, in other words, drains much of the terror from the prospect of sovereign restructuring as well.

The lesson from the Greek thought experiment, in other words, is a general one. The worry that a restructuring scares away investors is overdone: investors look to the future, not to the past. This is borne out by historical experience. In general, debt restructurings are followed by a rapid return to financial markets access and reignited economic growth.[36] Only gratuitous expropriations of claims that states could easily service make investors worry more about a state's willingness to pay than its ability to do so. They distinguish between overburdened and frivolous debtors. The eurozone periphery – even Greece – is not Argentina, and markets know the difference. Therefore a clean slate, which ensures the ability to service new debts, is an invitation to invest; an overhang of debts still to be serviced is a sign telling the smart money to stay away. Even Greece's too-little-too-late writedown in March 2012 quickly set interest rates on a downward path: Athens's borrowing costs peaked in February of that year. Restructuring other heavy debt burdens would have had the same result.

RESTRUCTURING POLITICS: DEALING WITH GREECE

Allowing banks and sovereigns to restructure matters in terms of euros and cents. Europe's reverence for debt contracts imposed unnecessary material suffering on millions of European citizens. But the deeper benefit would have been political. The cost of the taboo on restructuring must be counted not just in cash but also in terms of how it drained Europe's reservoir of political fellow feeling.

This is most obvious in the Greek saga. By clearing away the government debt overhang, Europe could have avoided a trap that entangled Greece's 'rescuers' even more comprehensively than the Greeks themselves.

The failure of the first rescue – due to the mismatch between the scale of aid and the size of the debt left in place – fed the German feeling that Greece was being helped not out of European solidarity but at the point of a gun. The spectre of default was constantly hovering over the Greek programme, and having foresworn a debt writedown the eurozone creditors could not easily threaten to pull the plug on Athens. The arguments by which the rescuers had justified the initial rescue logically committed them to put as much money on the line as might be needed to stave off a sovereign bankruptcy.

This meant Greek leaders could afford brinksmanship. They dragged their feet over many of the painful policy choices their lenders demanded of them, reasoning that the loans would come in the end. The German public in turn could be forgiven for increasingly thinking it was being blackmailed into helping. Against that backdrop it was politically impossible for Berlin not to try to control as tightly as possible what the Greeks (and then the Irish, the Portuguese and the Cypriots) did with their money – even though the bulk was not spent by the recipient countries at all but promptly recycled back to pre-existing (private) creditors. In other words, the suspension of domestic policy autonomy – and the extreme fiscal consolidation and radical structural reforms that were imposed in its stead – were a direct consequence of the large transfers that recipient countries accepted. This political logic was only exacerbated by the more strident government that took power in Greece in January 2015.

By restructuring Greek debt at the outset, the eurozone could have avoided this political morass. A much smaller rescue loan would have come as less of a shock to a German public that had been told it would never have to bail out another state. More importantly, a post-writedown loan would have been much less prone to the upward revisions that gnawed away at Germans' solidarity with the Greeks and eroded Merkel's repository of trust in the more eurosceptic quarters of the public.

Recall from Chapter 3 that an early Greek restructuring would have significantly cut the amount of financial aid Athens required from the rest of the eurozone, and from Germany in particular – potentially by as much as nine-tenths. Just as importantly, by demanding a restructuring before any money was lent, Germany (and any other contributor to the rescue loan) would have been in a position to credibly veto further disbursements if Athens failed to make good on its promises. A premature cutoff of the rescue loan would have been a huge problem for Greece – but it would have been Greece's huge problem. The wider fear of sovereign default with all its horror-inspiring repercussions would have been defused, because that gun would already have been fired.

Such an ability to end the programme would have removed the rationale for the troika's intrusive micromanagement of Greek policy-making. The rescue would no longer aim – ostensibly or objectively – at saving the euro from a sovereign default, since one would already have taken place. Instead it would have been squarely about temporarily relieving the pain of a fellow European country while it began to sort out problems of its own. Insisting on control over policy might make sense for someone bailing out a debtor whose ability to repay was in serious doubt. But a properly designed restructuring would have lifted those doubts. If it had not written down liabilities outright, it could have subordinated them to any new loans. As Chapter 3 showed, the loans in question may have amounted to 10–20 per cent of Greece's 2009 GDP – something it would never have been a problem to service. Indeed private markets may have welcomed Greece back much sooner, once investors were reassured they would not have to foot the bill for earlier lenders' unpayable claims. The need for official loans would then have been smaller still.

In short, an early restructuring would have required eurozone creditors to lend much less money, on terms leaving no doubt about repayment, and without any feeling of being taken advantage of by the Greeks. The politics of extending such a rescue (one worthy of the name, in contrast with the policy that was actually pursued) would have been immeasurably healthier than how things turned out.

RESTRUCTURING POLITICS: A LESS CONFLICTED EUROPE

Every debt crisis lays waste to the economic predictions upon which people have borrowed and lent. The moment it becomes clear that losses are unavoidable, the political imperative is to remove doubt about where losses will fall – whether predominantly on lenders (who cannot get back what they expect), on borrowers (who find themselves poorer, and their debt burdens heavier, than they had thought) or on society at large (including those who, having heeded Polonius's advice to 'neither a borrower nor a lender be', can rightly claim to have no responsibility for the debt crisis). The eurozone's political haplessness since 2008 can be put down to its inability to settle this question, instead leaving every group to fight as hard as it could to protect its own interests. With all sides trying to minimise the cost to themselves – in part by pushing losses onto others – no one was working to minimise the total losses for all. That was bound to create conflict; conflict that turned an economic opposition between economic interest groups – debtors and creditors – into a political opposition between nations.

The polarised politics of Greece versus Germany in particular, especially in 2011–12 and again in 2015, have been the low points of ill feeling between Europeans. But the equivalent political stand-off writ large has taken hold of the monetary union as a whole, if not in quite as virulent a form. Someone with no knowledge of the personalities and peculiarities of European politics could nonethe-less easily have predicted the fault lines after the crisis from a simple ranking of countries by their accumulated current account balances. The euro is split into two camps of debtor and creditor economies: the victims of capital flight aligned against the havens to which that flighty capital has fled. The obvious imbalance in the relative power of these two camps led the eurozone periphery almost without exception to bow to the demands of creditor countries. Those unsure to which camp markets may assign them – above all France – have wobbled uncertainly in the middle, lacking both the desperation of the most distressed countries to undertake radical change and the courage to challenge Germany for the leadership of eurozone policymaking.

The rescue loans put under lock and key the national self-determi-nation of the 'rescued' states. But they were not the only ones forced into a policy straitjacket. Spain and Italy may have avoided full-fledged rescue programmes, but they were nonetheless compelled to adopt a similar orthodoxy to the 'programme countries'. As Chapter 5 described, the discipline was inflicted not just by market pressure but at the hands of other eurozone policymakers – most explicitly the ECB under Jean-Claude Trichet, who made policy demands far beyond the central bank's remit a condition for buying government bonds. The effective veto power of the German Bundestag's finance committee over any fiscal rescue packages (and therefore over the ECB's 'whatever it takes' bond-buying programme, too) implicitly pressured other countries into complying with German preferences in the hope that Berlin would bankroll the single currency.

Much is said, and much of it correctly, about the misguided eco-nomic policies Germany demands from the rest of the currency union. Angela Merkel has been criticised as a recalcitrant European. In truth, she is constrained by domestic politics like every other leader; if she is different, it is that the domestic political work she has to do is harder. Much of that work has involved addressing Germany's grow-ing national nervousness about the (frequently exaggerated) amounts of money put at risk in propping up other sovereigns. A feeling of solidarity with fellow Europeans and an unwillingness to throw them to the wolves of global finance were shared by many Germans when the sovereign debt crisis first struck. They still are. But they have been undermined by the growing suspicion that the rescues weren't working, that good money was being thrown after bad, and that German solidarity was being taken advantage of. These suspicions have been eagerly fuelled by a vocal minority opposed to the euro from the start.

More fundamentally, complaints about Germany fail to take into account the fact that Berlin's power to impose its policy preferences on others is the power they granted it by making themselves dependent on Teutonic alms. All the euro's members – not just the ones under direct threat from markets – subordinated their decision making to the conventional wisdom that only German money (and money from other surplus states) can save the single currency.

This shared understanding has made Europe's political elites, in their traditional tribes of centre-right and centre-left, coalesce into an extraordinarily collusive consensus. A grand coalition rules in Germany; another ruled in Greece from 2012 to 2015 in the form of a New Democracy–Pasok coalition. Other countries sport governments that are grand coalitions in all but name. In Italy, social democratic prime minister Matteo Renzi set out to reform the country in 2014 in collaboration with Silvio Berlusconi. Elsewhere, mainstream parties that nominally compete for power differ so little on what they actually want to do in office that voters can be forgiven for thinking they are all the same. And in Brussels, of course, power is clubbily divided among the main political families, which favours backroom consensus rather than a publicly fought contest between clearly opposed alternatives.

The outsiders in European politics use this collusion to their advantage. Pablo Iglesias, the leader of Podemos, the political party that grew out of Spain's *indignados* protests, explicitly makes the point that the old centre-right and centre-left pursue the same agenda. Groups like his and Greece's Syriza, which at least ostensibly want alternative policies within the euro, have benefited from voters' feeling of powerlessness against the discredited elite. But so have the xenophobes, neo-fascists and eurosceptics. It is in response to the establishment's pretense that there is no alternative that Marine Le Pen and the *Front National* can expect to attract French voters by exclaiming:

We have to account for everything to the EU, ask permission for everything, as if we were an infantile people... France does not control anything, not its budget, not its currency, not its frontiers. It is time to say 'stop' to the EU.[37]

In light of this, Berlin deserves less blame for resisting its partners' demands than for not resisting them enough. If the German government had denied Greece a rescue loan unless its debts were first restructured, and if it had taken the same stance towards Ireland as it did towards Cyprus two and a half years later, writedowns would swiftly have followed: there would truly have been no alternative. This would have done away with the need for German money on a large scale and, therefore, with Berlin's (and, by delegation, Brussels's) ability to dictate the terms of its financial support.

As with Greece, the economic and political consequences for the eurozone as a whole would have been healthier in every way. Unable to stave off the unavoidable writedowns, governments would – almost despite themselves – have cut through the fog of uncertainty about where losses would fall. The banks on their watch would have been resolved and rebooted with less debt than before, as described earlier. Both outcomes would have ended the credit crunch that in the event was allowed to go on for six years. On economic policy, Germany's counterparts would no longer be compelled to go along with Berlin's fiscal compact or the revamped stability and growth pact. Space would have freed up for more diverse policy proposals of how to adjust public finances and reform crisis-hit economies. More modest fiscal austerity, a lesser squeeze on aggregate demand, and more growth-friendly structural reforms would have been within the ken of acceptable policy choices.

Politically, one might expect one of two dangers from letting debt restructurings rip through the eurozone. One is that it would irreparably damage the legitimacy of the existing political order – not just monetary union, but conventional national politics. The policy establishments that had presided over the accumulation of unpayable debt would no doubt be discredited, to the advantage of the populist fringes on both the right and the left. That would be a risk both in debtor Europe, where elites would be blamed for the disgrace of default, or at least for the economic disruption associated with it; and in creditor Europe, where the establishment would be seen as guilty for allowing banks and savers to expose themselves to losses. But as the populist insurrections across Europe show, this loss of legitimacy has taken place anyway. How much more discredited could policy elites have become than they actually are? Ending the resistance to restructuring would have unleashed a countervailing political force. By allowing a greater diversity of policy ideas, it would strengthen the political centre against the populist fringe by allowing it to renew itself. If policymakers no longer swore by 'there is no alternative', then alternatives are what they would have to propose. No longer could it be claimed of the old elites that 'they are all the same' – and *¡que se vayan todos!* Relative to what has actually happened, cleaning out the debts would have been less likely to undermine the legitimacy of governing elites than to have buttressed them.

That, however, could also have posed a danger: one of complacency. The southern eurozone members, as well as France, undoubtedly need to limber up their labour markets and pry open local monopolies. The view in surplus Europe has been that southern politicians could only be trusted to do the right thing if they were forced to, by market or political pressure. Hence Berlin's insistence on strict conditions for any financial support. From this perspective, one might think that since Berlin's hold on other eurozone governments would have been much weaker in the restructuring-friendly world we are imagining, all motivation to reform would be lost. Greece would remain in its inveterate clientilism; Berlusconi would still be mismanaging Italy.

This view ignores the serious shortcomings of the creditors' own policy demands, discussed elsewhere in the book. But more profoundly, it misjudges just how counterproductive outside pressure can be for domestic motivation – and, therefore, what other political incentives could have emerged for reform had the eurozone gone with writedowns instead of bail-outs. Duress spawns resistance: hence the support for populist fringes from Beppe Grillo to Marine Le Pen. Without an external scapegoat, national policymakers would shoulder the blame for national economic failure alone. What is more, without the punishing policy enforced from Brussels as a result of grovelling for German money, a more benign economic climate would make it easier to win voters over to national reforms, and national economic performance would to a greater degree reflect whether those reforms were good or bad ones. Mainstream political parties would have both the opportunity and the incentive to up their game rather than, as now, to stick their heads in the sand, and like the unexceptional investors once described by Keynes, fail conventionally rather than succeed unconventionally.

Across national borders, too, the politics would be more constructive without the debt overhang and its looming shadow of zero-sum. It would hardly have been lambs lying down with lions: surplus and deficit countries would still have divergent (though more compatible) interests, and the dependence of each member state on the economic policies of every other would continue. Therefore, so would the struggle over what those policies should be. But two things would have been very different. First, the custodians of the single currency would not have been faced with temptations to put the euro's integrity in doubt. That would have avoided a lot of the eurozone's self-inflicted economic and political damage. Second, greater national autonomy would have encouraged better collective solutions – both because the negotiations over what those solutions should be would have been more balanced, and because the greater room for policy manoeuvre by national governments would have produced a wider range of policy proposals. Just what form those better policies might have taken, and still could take, is the subject of the next chapter.

EIGHT
Europe's Real Economic Challenges

Three Tasks

The members of the single currency face three economic challenges. The first is to deal better with balance-of-payments crises – both finish the job of fixing the financial fragmentation from 2010–11 and safeguard against future ones. This is a financial and monetary task, one of ensuring that capital flows across national borders in an orderly and efficient way. The second challenge is a 'real economy' task of ensuring that each economy's resources are fully employed: the classic macroeconomic problem of aggregate demand management. Both of these tasks are largely about undoing self-inflicted errors. Finally, the long-run challenge is to make labour and capital as productive as they can be, which is what sustains long-term improvement in living standards.

Europe is not doomed to fail in the face of these challenges. In the glory days of post-war social democracy, Europe delivered on all three – but in a world that remained fragmented, had relatively little movement across borders of either goods or capital, and where growth was easier to come by. Needs were greater but expectations lower. There were more young people, while those needing care were fewer and lived less long. Governments were emerging from the war economy enjoying enormous control over people's economic affairs. And growth could be sparked by simply getting on with rebuilding what had been destroyed.

Today's circumstances are less propitious for strong growth even if Europeans enjoy vastly higher living standards. But the current inability to prosper, which jars so sharply with still-living memories of the post-war era, is not the fault of monetary unification. The advent of the euro changed but did not eliminate the tools to safeguard against balance-of-payments disruptions. The recent double-dip recession and the deflationary stagnation that succeeded it, meanwhile, were inflicted by unnecessary policy errors. And the productivity slow-down long predates the euro.[1]

The upshot is that nothing in the nature of Europe's monetary union condemns its members to stagnation or perennial instability. That means the eurozone's economic prospects are better than pessimists allow, and in particular better than its governments managed after the aborted recovery of 2010. In 2015, significant improvements are already making themselves seen in many eurozone countries.

The following pages set out some important policy steps needed to realise the eurozone's potential more fully – gingerly setting the politics aside until Chapter 9.

MAKING THE EUROZONE SAFE FROM SUDDEN STOPS

The lesson from Chapter 2 was that national governments had simple and rather obvious tools at their disposal to tame current account deficits throughout the boom years. The fiscal deficit should have been tighter than it was in Greece and Portugal, and Spain and Ireland should have run significant surpluses. Italy, uniquely among countries punished by the markets, was not running large external or fiscal deficits. But Silvio Berlusconi frittered away a fiscal surplus that could have reduced the huge public sector debt left over from the 1990s.

The domestic banks that channelled most of the enormous private credit flows could have been required to hold much more capital against their loans. Bankruptcy rules should have been changed to favour borrowers so as to make lenders confront more of the risk they were generating (and later restructure private debts faster). And regulatory and tax policy should have favoured equity flows rather than debt flows. All these measures would have made the reliance on foreign funding lesser and safer; as the Bulgaria case shows (see Chapter 2), a drought in equity financing is much less damaging than a reversal in debt flows. On top of this, governments could have acted to steer whatever capital did flow in into productive investments rather than consumption (as in Greece and Portugal) or misplaced housebuilding (Spain and Ireland). Planning and tax policy could have favoured sustainable, useful infrastructure that would increase the productivity of goods and service providers, especially tradable ones.

Most of these risk-prevention tools remain available to national governments, and the experience of the crisis should encourage their use in the future. (The most important exception is the 'maximum harmonisation' rule on setting capital requirements for banks, described in Chapter 6.) The eurozone has passed some specific reforms which add to that encouragement. For example, Brussels's new monitoring and sanctioning powers include a responsibility to watch over current account imbalances. That means private debt will at least be noticed, even if the greatest focus remains on public debt. Surpluses and not just deficits on the current account are scrutinised from now on, even though the eurozone has chosen to treat one side of the coin more leniently than the other. The warning threshold for deficits is at 4 per cent of GDP, that for surpluses at 6 per cent. This was at the behest of Germany, whose current account surplus in the year these thresholds were agreed was … 5.9 per cent of GDP.

The moves towards banking union and the new Commission's focus on improving capital markets both help to make capital movements safe. Banking union makes it easier to restructure banks; 'capital markets union' aims to encourage the growth of equity financing. In the future, all this should help eurozone governments avoid taking the blind risks of the last fifteen years.

Although most of the crisis-afflicted countries have seen capital returning since 2012, they have to live with the risk of a new sudden stop until the eurozone is back on its feet, and debt burdens are visibly lower. But the main point of this book has been that a sudden stop in capital inflows, though never a pretty sight, is more manageable than the eurozone's leaders have seemed to think. The option to restructure debt, public or private, has always been on the table, and as Chapter 6 showed, it is no longer dismissed out of hand. What has been lacking is the willingness to see that definitively writing down debt does not scare capital away but invites new capital in. Even if the external debt obligations of peripheral Europe are greater than ever, the risk that a creditor panic will throw the monetary union off track as badly as it did in 2011–12 has diminished, provided, at least, that the political will to write down debt is found when it is needed. If that will is lacking, especially after everything that has happened, the euro is hardly to blame.

The Case for Restructuring Now

In fact a strong case can be made for expediting debt restructurings today without waiting for markets to force the issue. The real or suspected insolvency of governments, banks and private sector companies and households still spreads uncertainty, blunts monetary stimulus and the credit growth it should produce, and depresses spending and investment. In Greece, the weakness of banks became the pretext for the ECB to force capital controls into place in the run-up to the July 2015 referendum. Elsewhere, bond purchases by the ECB are currently keeping credit conditions under control. But removing the debt overhang is the quickest and most definitive way to forestall any renewed capital flight at a later point and relax the brake on growth. Some of Europe's most prominent independent economists argue convincingly for a large-scale sovereign debt swap operation now.[2]

Take each type of debtor in turn. For sovereigns, debt could be restructured without reigniting any panic through negotiated maturity extensions, or even unilateral debt maturity management. At the time of writing, it is cheap to borrow for all eurozone governments except Greece, and they can easily issue very long-term debt to replace current, shorter-term, debt issues, reducing the risk of any future refinancing crisis. Indeed it is a perfect time to introduce perpetual bonds at a large scale, on the model of the United Kingdom's consols. These are bonds that pay interest in perpetuity, so the government can choose never to pay down the original loan amount. This would eliminate refinancing crises for good.

For Greece and Ireland in particular, the eurozone should help to lighten the load. Greece's debt burden has already been significantly reduced by pushing redemption dates into the future, but more needs to be done, as the Syriza government requested from the moment it took office, and as the IMF has explicitly acknowledged. Athens's creditors – largely other eurozone governments – should at a minimum replace all debt falling due in the next five years with loans whose repayment is tied to sufficient economic growth and that extends maturities even further from the current average of 17–18 years. Better would be to write down eurozone loans explicitly in the degree that they were used to repay financial institutions in the creditors' own countries. The principle should be to retroactively mimic the restructuring that should have taken place at the outset, and that other eurozone countries resisted for fear of their own banks. That would fairly share the burden across the eurozone rather than put the entire burden on the Greek taxpayers.

The same principle applies to Ireland. Ireland's debt burden is as large as it is in part because Dublin 'took one for the team' by bailing out Irish banks' bondholders on the order of the ECB. The least the rest of the eurozone owes Ireland is to let the ESM take over the debt Dublin had to issue to finance these bail-outs (some 40 per cent of annual GDP), in return for ownership of the banks the Irish government thereby nationalised. The amounts spent on bank bail-outs in Portugal and Spain were much smaller as a share of GDP. But to the extent the rescue loans they were pressured to take up were spent on bailing out banks for the sake of eurozone financial stability, there too the cost should be assumed by the eurozone as a whole. In each case the ESM could take over the relevant government ownership in bailed-out banks.

As for bank debt, the 2014 stress tests were a huge missed opportunity to convert more of it into equity. The tests purported to show that most of Europe's large banks have enough capital to weather very challenging economic circumstances (though they neglected to test for the impact of the deflation that was then threatening the eurozone). But the measures used make-believe estimates of how safe bank assets were. Independent tests, which used investors' valuation of bank equity rather than the banks' own, found that not only were the banks hugely undercapitalised, but that the most vulnerable banks were in Germany and France. That should not be surprising: these are the countries in which banks most heavily discount their exposure to possible losses with aggressive 'risk weighting'.[3] If markets are right and bankers (and the regulators who trust them) are wrong, much more capital is needed. The quickest way to provide it is to write down the debt of the weakest banks, as the new banking union rules now make it easier to do.

Finally, many of the banks' loans to households and companies need to be written down too. Private non-bank debt is over 100 per cent of GDP in a number of eurozone countries, including France, Spain and Portugal. If banks fear some of this will never be repaid, they have an incentive to 'extend and pretend'. But that reduces their ability to issue new loans to healthy businesses and solvent households. For the sake of the economy, it is better to wipe the slate clean. In the case of already thinly capitalised banks (which are the most probable offenders), this should be done in conjunction with bank restructuring. Such writedowns would help the borrower tied to a house worth less than her mortgage, or the entrepreneur forced to maintain a barely profitable business activity just to pay interest on his company loan. Rather than indefinitely paying for a debt they will never redeem in full, they can move on, relocate to a place with better jobs, or free up workers, capital and entrepreneurial skill for more productive activities. But for this to happen, bankruptcy procedures must be orderly and swift. In many countries they are the opposite. For example, before the crisis forced reform, Irish law did not discharge bankrupted individuals from their debts for twelve years. Europe may no longer have debtors' prisons, but in too many countries the unwillingness to let borrowers put debts behind them has much the same deadening effect on human activity.

The Dispensability of Fiscal Union

The conventional view, pushed by the euro's critics and resignedly accepted by its friends, is that a monetary union without a fiscal union is doomed to fail. The most common reason given is some version of optimum currency area theory: that in the absence of independent monetary or exchange rate policy, countries must have a mechanism for sharing the risk of 'asymmetric shocks' (the risk of events that affect the prospects of one economy while leaving others unscathed) that they can no longer offset on their own. A fiscal union, at least in theory, would redistribute resources from those hitting a lucky streak to those struck down by misfortune, stepping in when private capital flows suddenly reverse.

There is certainly a good economic case for risk-sharing: it is the principle behind insurance. But that principle is not limited to currency unions. Nor does risk-sharing typically have to be done through fiscal means.

Having its own currency does not by itself insulate an economy from disruptions and shocks. Events such as the collapse of an export market, the discovery of a new resource, or increased international competition will make a country poorer or richer regardless of the currency regime. The best that a flexible exchange rate can do is to make the adjustment to the new situation less costly (but currency volatility can also amplify instability). It is nonetheless frequently taken for granted that risk-sharing is particularly badly needed within a monetary union.[4] But as Nobel prizewinner Jean Tirole has recently underlined, it is 'puzzling' to think that the benefit of risk-sharing is limited to participants in a common currency.[5] The general principle is that the more uncorrelated the fluctuations of different economies are, the more such economies would benefit from sharing their risks with one another. And if anything, economies that share a currency tend to be more closely correlated with one another than those with separate currencies.[6] If risk-sharing requires fiscal transfer mechanisms, one might just as well argue that the United Kingdom should enter a fiscal union with the rest of Europe, euro or not.

Besides, it is a misconception that strong monetary unions do a lot of fiscal risk-sharing. It is often said that the dollar 'works' better than the euro because the United States is a fiscal union. But this was not the case for the first 150 years of the dollar's existence – as late as 1936, the federal government's revenues were barely 5 per cent of GDP. Today, the federal tax system does redistribute from richer to poorer states – but it does not do much to cushion individual states against idiosyncratic economic swings. Only 15 per cent of state-level GDP fluctuations is smoothed out through federal fiscal transfers. Fiscal risk-sharing is just as modest between Germany's *Länder*. A similar degree of fiscal union between eurozone countries would have mitigated the economic collapses in the periphery only marginally. In both the United States and Germany, a much larger share of risk-sharing (more than half of local GDP swings) takes place through integrated private capital and credit markets.[7] This does not mean a eurozone fiscal union is undesirable, but that there is no auto-matic implication from the existence, let alone the composition, of a monetary union to a *sine qua non* of fiscal union between its members. A system of international fiscal insurance may be worthwhile for a larger group of countries than those in the euro; or for merely a subset of the euro's members. The desired insurance can also be pursued through financial markets rather than fiscal union – as is the norm within federal states.[8] And any hope that fiscal union can somehow overcome other forces of economic divergence must come to terms with how 150 years of Italian fiscal union has still left the Mezzo-giorno relatively underdeveloped, or how US fiscal union did not pre-vent chronic underperformance and unsustainable government debt in Puerto Rico.[9] One should be cautious about expecting better from a Europe-wide fiscal union.

Having said all this, even if it is not necessary it is of course *possible* to design a fiscal risk-sharing mechanism to neutralise runs on sov-ereign debt. The most discussed option is for sovereigns to issue debt jointly, with collective responsibility for payment. Blueprints for such 'eurobonds' are well developed, the most influential proposal being the Bruegel think-tank's work on 'blue bonds'.[10] These would be jointly issued debt for up to the Maastricht 60 per cent limit of countries' GDP only, so as to avoid encouraging excessive debt accumulation. Any debt over this limit would remain the national government's sole responsibility (in the form of 'red bonds').

The reason why such 'eurobonds' can end the vulnerability of sovereign debtors is often misunderstood. It is not because it would involve creditor countries subsidising debtor countries (this could be an additional effect, but one that the bond could be designed to exclude). Rather, eurobonds can prevent runs on sovereign debt because they limit where investors can run to. In the 2011–12 crisis, creditors fled from peripheral state debt (and private debts too) to move their money into German and other core country debt – it was a flight to safety necessitated by policymakers' willingness to consider a euro break-up. With eurobonds, where would investors run? The eurobond, properly designed, would be the benchmark safe asset: the safe haven that investors see in German securities today. If all eurozone public debt was mutualised, the market would be bigger than the US Treasuries market and much bigger than the Japanese market. Investors would to some extent be trapped: there would simply not be much else to invest in if a significant share were to be pulled out. No doubt investors could demand higher yields, but the self-fulfilling panics of 2011–12 could not have occurred.

Eurobonds of course constitute a rudimentary fiscal union. That is why this route to ending the sovereign debt crisis was vetoed by Berlin. Why Berlin should have been granted the ability to hold back others from mutualising their debt, however, is a question that is too seldom asked. In the next chapter I explain that other eurozone countries missed a trick by not going ahead without German participation. If they really want eurobonds, the current structure of the euro does not stop them.

Idling Europe's Economic Engine

The eurozone has been too slow to deal with its aggregate demand problem. The reasons are understandable. Fully acknowledging the demand destruction would discredit the authors of the policies that caused it. Also, any frank discussion of aggregate demand risks intensifying the existing political polarisation between Germany/creditor Europe and debtor Europe. Those who say the eurozone has a demand problem – for too long mostly independent observers – tend to blame Germany because the country has forced austerity on others and runs an unnecessarily tight budget for itself. It is also the biggest brake on looser monetary policy. Berlin and its defenders, for their part, see demand stimulus as a form of moral hazard: it would blunt the incentives for what they think is really needed, namely supply-side reform in both France and the periphery.

There are problems with both views. The excessive fiscal contractions cannot be blamed only on Germany, since every member state willingly tightened the fiscal rules, subjected itself to a Commission that made austerity a point of pride, and signed an international treaty codifying bad fiscal policy. Some countries were strong-armed into this, as often by the ECB as by Berlin. Some – notably Spain and the Netherlands – chose to tighten even more than they were being forced to because they were true believers, and in Spain's case also because a fiscal policy machismo designed to align the country incontrovertibly with Berlin. Meanwhile, everyone bought into the idea that German money was needed to save the euro, so German policy preferences must be heeded whether one agreed with them or not.

The monetary policy mistakes, too, can hardly be blamed on Germany alone. The ECB was, after all, run by Trichet when it stifled the recovery by raising rates. Overly tight monetary policy continued after his tenure, and after the resignation of two German members of the bank's Governing Council – hardly a sign that Germany was ruling the roost. The credit crunch worsened until 2013, and longer than that in many countries. The ECB's excuse is that the recession meant companies did not want to borrow. But this is wrong: European banks themselves reported that it was they who were tightening lending standards well into 2013 (recall Figure 5.2). A better excuse for the ECB might have been that the weakness of the demand stimulus its monetary policy managed to generate was caused by supply-side, structural problems, namely undercapitalised banks with no desire to spread cheap credit through the economy. The weakness of monetary stimulus, in other words, was driven by the idea that bank restructuring must be avoided at all costs. But of course the ECB was a strong proponent of that idea until 2013.

Even if the caricature of Germany as the eurozone's demand-destroying monster is just that, there nevertheless cannot be serious doubts that aggregate demand in the eurozone falls far short of supply. That is the obvious cause of the eurozone's unique combination of a sharp slowdown in inflation and a big share of economic resources lying idle, with millions of people out of work and billions of capital placed in liquid positions with negative real return rather than funding physical investment. Getting out of stagnation depends on finding uses for these human skills and financial resources currently wasting away. That requires boosting demand for them. There are ways to do this at both the national and the collective eurozone level. Both should be pursued without delay.

Needed: Aggregate Demand Policy for the Whole Union

The euro members' hapless approach to domestic aggregate demand might just about have been tolerable had they at least had a collective aggregate demand policy for the eurozone as a whole. The absence of one in the middle of a drawn-out stagnation, let alone depression-like conditions in many parts of the currency zone, has been an abdication of responsibility. Remedying this situation requires better policy on both the monetary and fiscal sides.

Monetary policy. The ECB's long monetary policy inertia manifested itself in the contraction of the eurozone money supply and tightening credit conditions. These were caused by Frankfurt's resistance to loosening policy in two important ways. First, the eurozone's central bank pulled its punches on interest rates throughout the crisis. The ECB has consistently behaved and talked as if interest rates at record lows meant interest rates were at sufficient lows. While the ECB quickly reversed Trichet's rate rises once Draghi took over in late 2011, it then took a full year and a half to reduce it further, from 1 per cent to 0.5 per cent. The central bank then waited for more than another year to bring the main policy rate down to almost zero (0.05 per cent) in September 2014, where it has stalled (see Figure 6.1). All the language emanating from the ECB's leadership shows they accept the idea that a 'zero lower bound' means a central bank cannot impose negative rates.[11] But this is a bound imposed by the conventional thinking of central bankers – according to which negative interest rates are not the done thing – rather than any economic law. The Swiss National Bank proved as much when it started targeting a negative range for the interbank lending rates in December 2014; the central banks of Sweden and Denmark took their rates negative around the same time. At the time of writing, policy rates of −0.75 per cent have been realised, with no flight from bank deposits into cash, which is what supposedly makes negative rates impossible. There is all reason to think the ECB could lower its main rate by another percentage point. And it is well known how to overcome the technical difficulties that create a lower bound when one is finally encountered.[12] In any case, rates can clearly be somewhat lower than zero, and if there is one monetary jurisdiction that has needed this recently, it is the eurozone. Instead, the ECB has contributed to Europe's stagnation with an unjustified and self-imposed floor on interest rates.

The other brake on ECB action was, until January 2015, its difficulty in coming to terms with using its balance sheet as a policy instrument. All the other major central banks had resorted to balance sheet expansion – buying up assets – as an alternative form of monetary stimulus years earlier. Besides directly lowering the cost of borrowing through short-term interest rates, they expanded the money supply by buying securities in the financial market, paying for them with newly created central bank reserves. The effect was a significant easing of credit conditions.[13]

Since its inception, the ECB has operated mainly through banks, which dominate credit allocation in the eurozone. It traditionally controls the cost of credit by the price it sets on secured loans to banks, but a side effect of this practice is to contract out the size of the money supply to the private banking sector. Targeting a rate and waiting for banks to turn up lets the monetary base depend on the loan offers banks are willing to take up. Between 2012 and 2015 the ECB saw its balance sheet shrink by about a trillion euros, through no decision of its own (see Figure 8.1). The ECB's bank-centred modus operandi delayed its willingness to use the balance sheet actively as an instrument for monetary stimulus. While it had engaged in 'open-market operations' (direct securities purchases and sales) before 2015, that was largely to address malfunctions in specific markets, in particular for troubled sovereign bonds, not to alter general monetary conditions. That history buttressed scepticism about asset purchases

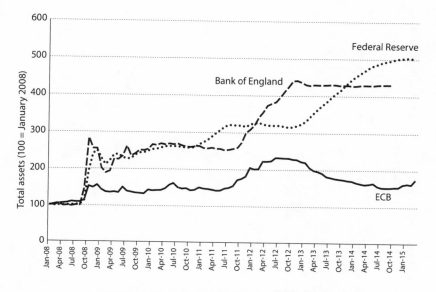

Figure 8.1. Size of central bank balance sheets.
Sources: Central banks via Federal Reserve Economic Data via St. Louis Fed.

because of how they alter relative financial costs for different countries, quite separately from their overall aggregate demand effect. The
Bundesbank more than anyone has vocally opposed eurozone quantitative easing. Germans are often painted (including by themselves) as
having an irrational phobia of inflation. It is closer to the truth to say
they are wary of policies, ostensibly for the common good, that might
subsidise other countries at their expense.

Along either dimension – interest rates or the size of the balance sheet
– the ECB long did much less than it should. Under Mario Draghi it
has been edging in the right direction, and the launch of quantitative
easing is helping to bring the eurozone economy back to health. The
central bank's defenders are, however, right that there are limits to what
monetary stimulus can achieve when its effects are blunted by neglected
problems in the banking sector (allowing zombie banks to stay alive) and
fiscal policies that destroy aggregate demand.

That is, of course, a reason for the central bank to do more rather
than less. But the point is its ability to do more. The euro is not to
blame for bad monetary policy; bad monetary policymakers are.

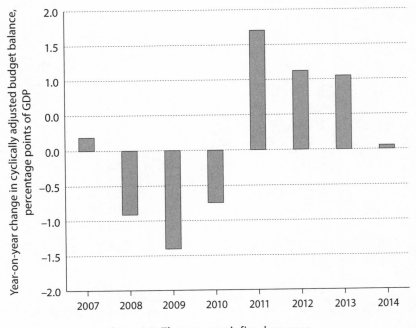

Figure 8.2. The eurozone's fiscal squeeze.
Source: EC Annual Macroeconomic Database.

Fiscal policy. For the eurozone taken as a whole, the fiscal deficit has been around 2.5 per cent of aggregate GDP since late 2013[14] – far from any danger zone for the sustainability of public debt, and far too tight for a stagnant economy still marked by a private sector unwilling to borrow and spend. Between 2010 and 2013, the eurozone's structural fiscal balance was tightened by more than one percentage point per year, just when the recovery needed all the help it could get. (See Figure 8.2.)

Astonishingly, amid all the talk of coordinating their economic policies, the euro's members have not seen fit to coordinate their national fiscal policies to achieve a collectively rational outcome – in this case a more growth-friendly level of government deficits. This would not require sophisticated institutional frameworks (though these might help). In 2009, a simple political agreement by the leaders of the G20 produced the coordinated fiscal stimulus that ended the global downturn. And in August 2014, Mario Draghi named the unnameable in a speech arguing not only that the eurozone needed to set its aggregate fiscal stance as a matter of explicit policy but also that the right policy would be to loosen the stance.[15]

A decision to expand the overall eurozone deficit to, say, 4 per cent would do wonders by prompting an immediate growth spurt. Given that virtually all government spending in Europe still happens at the national level or below, however (the EU budget amounts to just 1 per cent of EU GDP), achieving such a goal would require changes to national government spending and taxation plans. This is not an argument for a fiscal union in the form of a larger common budget. Using such a budget for fiscal stabilisation would still require the political will – and if the will existed, a large common budget would not be needed. That brings us to the failures of aggregate demand policy at national level.

Needed: Aggregate Demand Policy in Each Member State

To retrieve the euro's prosperity, its members must rediscover the national room for manoeuvre they possessed but neglected during the boom. That includes the control over credit cycles, as discussed in Chapter 2, but of particular importance is countercyclical fiscal policy.

The effects of austerity policies were much broader than simply killing off domestic demand in the countries that implemented them. Austerity in one country reduces aggregate demand in the economies it trades with as well, and European economies trade a lot with one another. As countries cut their deficits, ostensibly to make debts more manageable, they also cut demand for each others' exports. This is why those with no immediate need to consolidate their public finances (Germany above all) caused so much damage when they went ahead and did so anyway: it made things a lot harder for those with little other choice (see note 16 from Chapter 1).

It is possible for national governments to be a lot smarter about domestic demand management, even without running foul of the tighter European rules they have imposed on themselves. The one redeeming feature of the updated rules is that they pay attention to structural deficits as well as headline deficits. There is room, therefore, for countries to let the gap between the two widen considerably and pass reforms now that create significant savings in the long run, when the economy has recovered, but amount to deficit stimulus in the short run. Possibilities include higher but more progressive taxes so as to close the deficit faster in normal economic times but leave more in people's pockets in bad times; or bigger payments to the short-term unemployed (of which there will, by definition, be fewer at a better point in the business cycle) paid for by permanent but less variable savings elsewhere in the budget. Another kind of tax reform that would mimic the sort of price adjustment many call for is 'fiscal devaluation', which involves cutting taxes on labour and employment and increasing them on sales and consumption. Such changes could leave government revenues unaffected even as they favoured domestic production over imports, effectively shifting demand away from trading partners to the domestic economy.[16]

So there are many unused opportunities that national governments should and could take to improve lacklustre aggregate demand in their economies. The most powerful tool at their disposal, however – plain deficit-financed fiscal stimulus – is heavily constrained by the stability and growth pact and its associated rules. This has got the eurozone into a situation where choosing a good fiscal policy – or even one that does not do too much harm – poisons the politics further, and, conversely, where keeping the peace must lead to bad fiscal policy. To deal properly with its economic stagnation, Europe must free itself of these constraints.

A Pact Long in Need of Reform

As Chapter 1 discussed, there is a strong case for coordinating national fiscal policies to manage their spillovers across borders. In eurozone economic policymaking, however, 'coordination' has come to mean instead that everyone should do the same thing – and that the thing they should all do is to borrow less. By progressively narrowing the room for countercyclical fiscal policy, the eurozone has been digging itself deeper and deeper into a sandtrap. To get out of it, the fiscal rules need to be exchanged for something more fit for purpose.

What would a well-designed fiscal framework, untrammelled by politics, look like? It would have to satisfy three criteria:

- restore national governments' ability to run effective counter-cyclical policies,
- restore domestic responsibility for the outcomes of fiscal choices, and
- ensure macroeconomic coordination, properly understood – that is to say, get the eurozone's overall fiscal stance right.

Each change is desirable in its own right, but the three can best be achieved together. That is not just because of politics. The economic consequences of achieving only one of these three goals may be to make things worse with respect to the others. Only done together can the three changes produce a significant improvement in eurozone fiscal demand management.

Given that the stability and growth pact's prohibitions on excessive deficit spending have come to look more and more set in stone, how could European governments realistically be freed to pursue better fiscal management? The misguided institutional reforms during the crisis tightened the screws on fiscal demand management in two principal ways: through the Commission's enhanced powers of surveillance over national budgets, and through the fiscal compact. But neither need block a widening of the national room for fiscal manoeuvre.

The Commission's dominion over national governments is in large part a discretionary one. It is from Brussels that the 'medium-term objectives' and 'stability and convergence programmes' that fence national governments into fiscal contractions are assessed; and it is the Commission's prerogative to initiate recommendations and sanctions against those it considers wayward. In addition, the rules themselves allow for a range of interpretations. While one requirement is to stay clear of the Maastricht overall deficit limit of 3 per cent of GDP, others emphasise moving towards a sustainable debt position and leaving room for budgetary manoeuvre. The consolidation programmes, moreover, are supposed to be set out in structural terms.

All this leaves a Commission minded to use its discretion constructively formally free to judge debt sustainability in a more Keynesian way. By acknowledging that cutting spending in a recession makes debt less, not more, sustainable (recall Figure 5.9), Brussels could allow a country to expand its headline deficits to fund a time-limited stimulus programme while changing structural tax and spending policies so as to gradually improve the cyclically adjusted deficit.

The new Commission that took office in November 2014 under Jean-Claude Juncker has already shown that it understands its power to interpret the fiscal rules in light of its political priorities. To drum up support for his flagship investment plan, Juncker implicitly promised governments that the Commission's monitoring of their deficits would turn a blind eye to spending contributing to the plan:

> Importantly, in the context of the assessment of public finances under the Stability and Growth Pact, the Commission will take a favourable position towards such capital contributions to the Fund.[17]

The Commission should exercise this discretion much more broadly.

The fiscal compact, which echoes the stability and growth pact, lends itself to similar reinterpretation by national authorities. The deficit target of no more than 0.5 per cent of GDP is set in structural terms. There are also quantitative benchmarks for how much excessive debt stocks or deficits should be reduced on average per year. A government with a Keynesian bent could reason as follows. Because of the harm fiscal contraction does to an economy whose private sector has curtailed its spending, the *average* progress towards lower debt and deficit ratios of GDP could be faster if debts and deficits are allowed to rise before they fall. Buoying, or at least protecting, growth through fiscal stimulus would speed up progress towards the target by having the economy recover faster.

This sort of interpretation might quickly face scrutiny from the European Court of Justice if it displeased Berlin. But given that it is vindicated by the eurozone's experience in the crisis – where fiscal consolidation may have reduced deficits but made the debt mountains larger than ever – this is a test it should pass. Furthermore, since the fiscal compact is an intergovernmental treaty rather than an integral part of EU law, the extreme option of pulling out of it is available, as it can be done without jeopardising the legal underpinnings of the euro or the EU itself. Unusually, there are no explicit provisions for withdrawal in the fiscal stability treaty itself, but the Vienna Convention on the Law of Treaties allows a party to withdraw if such a right 'may be implied by the nature of the treaty'. The Keynesian reasoning above offers an argument why that may indeed be the case: the policies it ostensibly requires run counter to the treaty's own explicit purpose of 'sound and sustainable public finances', let alone the 'proper functioning of the euro area' and 'stronger economic growth'. The fiscal compact, moreover, explicitly subordinates itself to the 'Treaties on which the EU is founded'. If its rules, as a matter of economics, threaten the EU's fundamental goals – which include 'balanced economic growth' and 'economic and social cohesion' – that gives a legal justification for renouncing them.

A negotiated reform of both the stability and growth pact and the fiscal treaty, with the aim of making countercyclical fiscal policy more straightforwardly available as a national policy choice, would of course be preferable to unilateral violations of what Germany, at least, surely sees as the spirit of the fiscal rules. The point here is simply that even without such a renegotiation, the scope for national action is not as limited as most seem to think.

This solution would, however, leave us with the original problem of policy coordination: national fiscal policies have spillover effects that must be managed collectively to achieve the best fiscal stance and the best fiscal–monetary policy mix for the eurozone as a whole. Hence the desirability of the third change set out above: to a system that does ensure the coordination (as opposed to the uniformity) of different countries' fiscal policies. There were proposals for a real coordination mechanism at the time of the euro's birth. It is high time to dig them out of the dustbin in which the eurozone's designers left them.

In 1999, Alessandra Casella, a Columbia University economist, pointed out that the problem of spillover effects from national fiscal policy choices was analogous to the economic problem of pollution. The efficient solution, she suggested, is analogous too: set the overall optimal fiscal deficit and issue 'tradable deficit permits' to the member countries.[18] Each permit would correspond to a euro's worth of deficit spending, but a country that did not want to use up its full allocation could sell its permit to one that wanted to run a bigger deficit than its original quota permitted. There would be a built-in incentive against deviating from the quota; and incentives for discipline could be further built in by making the price of permits vary with existing indebtedness. The fiscal stance for the currency union as a whole would have to be set by a technocratic body, much in the way the ECB decides the appropriate interest rate, or by a simple automatic rule (Casella's own preference). That would facilitate an overall deficit that varied according to economic conditions, making effective countercyclical policy and the correct fiscal–monetary policy mix achievable at the eurozone level.

With such a scheme, fiscal policy autonomy could be restored to national governments while holding them accountable for the effects of their choices on others (letting sovereign restructurings happen when necessary would also hold them accountable for their effects on themselves). The market in permits would charge a price for making the monetary union's desired overall fiscal stance harder to achieve, and it would reward those that contributed to realizing it. Coordination and collaboration could be achieved without the political disempowerment on which anti-European political forces feed.

Encouraging Long-term Growth

Belatedly and partially, the eurozone has been redressing its bungled responses to the two most urgent economic challenges of financial instability and economic stagnation. The result can be seen in slowly improving growth rates. But beyond the short term, there is too little clarity of vision about where the eurozone's economic future lies. Even in normal economic times – which these are not and have not been for seven years – this should exercise minds. At a time of continuing crisis, it should inform the short-term policy steps as well.

Chapter 1 stated the main facts about economic development in Europe since the 1980s: productivity growth has declined, leading to lower growth per capita combined with an increase in inequality. A large proportion of Europeans have experienced stagnant or falling living standards coupled with more uncertainty in their economic lives – a drastic break with the post-war era, which delivered on its promise of prosperity for all. That Europe has a supply-side problem is as undeniable as its shortfall in aggregate demand.

The eurozone is not alone in struggling to find the conditions for growth that is sustained, broad-based and shared. Most developed nations face similar difficulties. (See Table 8.1.) But if the euro is not at fault for this predicament, nor has it offered much in the way of dealing with it. Ending the eurozone's crisis is therefore only the beginning of the work. No country in the eurozone has as yet found an economic strategy that reliably brings increasing prosperity to all its citizens in today's global economy. What Europe's monetary

Table 8.1. Global productivity slowdown.

	Average annual growth in total factor productivity				
	1985–1990	1991–1995	1996–2000	2001–2005	2005–2010
Austria	2.20	2.52	1.34	0.66	0.94
Belgium	1.28	1.38	0.72	0.48	−0.14
Canada	−0.42	0.72	1.22	0.56	0.06
Denmark	0.77	1.42	0.02	0.16	−0.62
Finland	2.55	1.72	2.80	1.88	0.16
France	1.88	1.06	1.26	0.72	0.00
Germany		1.43	1.22	0.68	0.58
Ireland	2.95	3.46	5.28	1.64	0.08
Italy	1.47	1.26	0.36	−0.34	−0.46
Japan	3.43	0.68	0.58	0.96	0.58
Korea	5.55	3.80	3.58	3.08	3.50
Netherlands	0.82	0.12	0.94	0.58	−0.04
Portugal		1.30	0.84	−0.44	0.24
Spain	1.13	0.94	−0.12	−0.06	0.18
Sweden	0.18	0.94	1.68	2.16	0.12
Switzerland		−0.74	0.76	0.46	0.48
UK	0.90	2.04	1.70	1.48	−0.22
US	0.88	0.74	1.48	1.70	0.82

Source: OECD.

experiment will ultimately be tested on is whether its participants, individually or collectively, succeed in restoring Europe's old ideal of solidarity in prosperity. At a minimum, euro membership must not become synonymous with preventing them from doing so.

The next chapter addresses the political aspects of this challenge. We complete this one with a few thoughts on what long-term future Europe, and the eurozone specifically, can realistically aim for, and what sort of economic policies can help to bring it there.

Two important decisions about what a desirable economic future for Europe should look like have big implications for how best to come out of the crisis. The first is whether, at the end of the economic changes underway, we expect the capital flows that marked the euro's first decade to be eliminated or even reversed. The second is whether the least successful eurozone economies should chart a future in which they pay their way by adjusting their cost levels to their productivity levels or the other way around. It is important to treat these as separate questions: it is not as if lower costs necessarily go with surpluses and higher ones with deficits. It is possible to be a high-cost, high-productivity economy in permanent surplus (think of Germany) or a low-cost, low-productivity country that lives – while lenders permit – beyond its means. Conversely, fast productivity growth may well both require and justify large external deficits in the medium term.

In large part, austerity advocates and demand boosters give the same answer to these questions: the eurozone needs to 'rebalance', that is to say that the deficit countries must stop running a deficit. Their current accounts must be redressed at least to the point of balance, and perhaps significantly into surplus, if their debts are to be reduced. Where the two camps differ is in how surplus Europe should accommodate this change. Some say it must (at least) eliminate its current account surplus in parallel with the shrinking deficit in the periphery; they are the loudest critics of a Germany that has racked up current account surpluses exceeding 7 per cent of GDP since 2013.[19] By insisting on exporting products and capital, they complain, Germany is making it harder for the crisis-hit economies in the euro to adjust. This is a vision of a balanced eurozone in which each country exactly pays its way – and it is a vision, they say, that Germany is as responsible as deficit Europe for bringing about. Most German commentators, in contrast, bristle at the idea of reducing their national savings (which are what their current account surplus amounts to). Whether they spell it out or not, their vision is one where other countries follow Germany's track of becoming a net saver. In other words, they want a eurozone that looks like Germany writ large – exporting to the rest of the world more than it imports from it – though without much thought as to whether the rest of the world will accept the role of net importer.

If demand is constrained in the short run, there can be a case for 'balancing' it fairly (though Germany's critics too often ignore that its surplus vis-à-vis other euro countries has already shrunk sharply). In the long run, however, is the ideal destination for the eurozone really as a grouping of economies that are all in external balance vis-à-vis each other and either balanced or in surplus vis-à-vis the rest of the world? More extremely still, is it one where the former deficit countries run permanent surpluses to service their debts?

The answer should be 'no'. That outcome would give up on one of the main promises of monetary integration: namely, the most efficient allocation of capital across the currency union as a whole. Academic studies of Europe's faltering productivity show that even an ideal set of reforms at the national level can only be expected to give a modest boost to productivity growth.[20] Scepticism has also been voiced that higher investment rates will do Europe all that much good.[21] That makes it all the more important that whatever capital is invested is deployed where it produces the greatest return. As Chapter 2 argued, the problem of the eurozone boom was not large flows of capital from core to periphery per se, but the waste of that capital. It ought to have financed activities that would lift long-term growth rates in the European periphery and accelerate its catch-up with Europe's richest countries. But it failed to do so.

Financing growth in the relatively undeveloped parts of Europe with savings from its richer parts must surely remain the goal. Rather than eliminating the imbalances of the boom, therefore, the eurozone should consciously aim for a growth path that restores these asymmetric capital flows: a German-centred core that is running current account surpluses and a poorer periphery that finances growth-promoting domestic investments through current account deficits. For this to be doable, two things must happen.

The first is the recurrent theme of this book: existing external debt, whether public or private, must be restructured to lighten the burden of debt service on the current account. If, as could realistically be the case for Greece or Spain if debts are not written down, 5–10 per cent of GDP must eventually be devoted to external debt service, domestic absorption (the economic production enjoyed within the country) will be so squeezed that investment can only happen with an unrealistic sacrifice of current consumption. Wiping the debt slate clean would allow new capital flows to fund investment while maintaining living standards.

The second is to ensure that this time round, the capital is indeed put to productive use. That is why the insistence of Germany and the troika on structural reforms is not misplaced. But the reforms need to be more intelligently designed, with a view to achieving productivity increases rather than wage reductions and fiscal savings. As the next chapter suggests, this is more likely if national governments again become more accountable to their own citizens.

In particular, the peripheral countries must make their product markets more competitive, and find ways for more workers to be employed and to be employed productively. Uncompetitive product markets, whether because of monopolistic market power or legal barriers to competition, reduce the living standards of the majority and weigh on real wages because of the excessive prices those with market power can charge. The dual labour markets common across southern Europe and France offer sometimes extravagant protections for those in permanent jobs but discourage companies from offering such jobs to new workers. This ties up workers, skills and the capital used by them in the sectors and firms that were dominant in the past, even if new industries and start-up firms would be able to employ these resources more productively. Often, onerous regulations for larger companies discourage businesses from growing and reaping the efficiencies of large scale, with the result that the economy's resources are trapped in the least productive organisations.

Worse still, it makes things more precarious for the young, who are disproportionately hired on temporary contracts. The system discourages new or growing businesses from cultivating their workforce with a long-term perspective. This is a big reason behind the spectacularly high unemployment rates in countries such as Spain, which long predate the euro. It inhibits the growth of new firms, which are where jobs are disproportionately created. A study of seventeen Organisation for Economic Co-operation and Development (OECD) countries found that, in general, all net job creation (the difference between new jobs created and old ones eliminated) is done by young small and medium-sized firms; established firms, on average, destroy more jobs than they create. This held up even through the financial crisis, when small young firms continued to be net job creators albeit it at much lower rates than before.[22]

That many countries need better-functioning labour markets does not mean they need the policies Germany has pursued. The German reforms of the early 2000s, known as the Hartz plan, focused straightforwardly on reducing disincentives to work by rationalising the benefits system. The German system of decentralised wage bargaining pulled in the same direction.[23] A predictable consequence was downward pressure on wages and thus on unit labour costs. This effort is held up as a model for the European periphery today, especially by those who blame the diverging development of unit labour costs in Germany and other eurozone countries for the debt crisis (rather than, as this book does, attributing it to the financial promiscuity of the 1999–2007 era). But the results of the Hartz plan are mixed at best. It may well be credited for bringing down Germany's unemployment rate, but it was followed by a decade of stagnant wages and investment, and lacklustre productivity growth (see Figure 8.3 and Table 2.1). The redistributive effect of shifting income from workers to capital owners may well have been an important cause of the country's low domestic demand and consequent large foreign savings, as well as a rise in inequality. The German model, then, has involved making work more precarious and less well paid even in an era of economic growth. Rather than being a model for how to defend Europe's social values in the face of globalisation, this is an abdication of them.

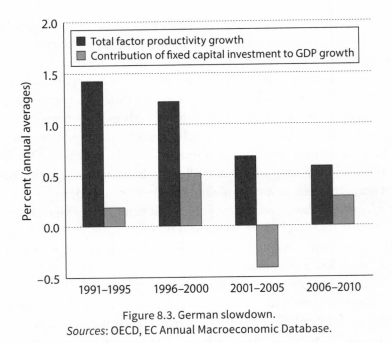

Figure 8.3. German slowdown.
Sources: OECD, EC Annual Macroeconomic Database.

The troika-imposed reforms in the periphery, meanwhile, suffer from the overarching emphasis put on fiscal consolidation. That has directly squeezed public investment and, through the contraction and uncertainty it caused, discouraged private investment as well. The credit crunch brought on by financial fragmentation and monetary policy compounded the damage. Gross fixed capital formation in the eurozone on average lingers 17 per cent below where it was in 2008.[24] That average masks huge variations between countries, however. Unsurprisingly, investment has fallen the most in the most crisis-hit countries – which on the whole are those that need it the most. In Greece, investment is only one-third what it was before the crisis. Extreme underinvestment does nothing to put these economies on a sustainable footing. In contrast, Germany today invests slightly more than it did before the crisis.

Indirect harm aside, some structural reforms in the crisis-hit countries have been outright counterproductive. In Greece and Portugal, removing protections in the labour markets before making product markets more competitive has meant wages fell before excess profit margins did. The result was an unnecessarily big hit to workers' living standards, a deeper contraction in domestic demand, and naturally stronger resistance to the reform agenda. Ensuring greater competition between firms first would have made it easier to re-absorb workers losing their jobs as a result of the labour market reforms. The case for prioritising product markets before labour markets is also borne out by the IMF's own research department, which has found that labour market liberalisation can harm growth in the short run. Even in the long run, they do not usually lift growth more than marginally – and much less than product market reform. These insights do not, however, seem to have guided the IMF's operational teams in the field.

Another example is tax policy. To counteract high unemployment and promote exports during a balance-of-payments crisis, taxes on labour – especially in traded industries – should be eased and replaced by other taxes as necessary. But since 2007, the tax wedge on labour (the difference between what a firm pays for labour and what workers take home, accounted for by social security contributions and income taxes) has widened significantly for two-earner families in several eurozone countries, including Greece, Portugal, Spain, Ireland and Italy.[25] This is structural reform, but in exactly the wrong direction.

UNEXPLOITED OPPORTUNITIES

This litany of errors committed by the eurozone paradoxically gives cause for cheer. It means that the countries of the euro cannot be written off as doomed to failure, or that the only alternatives are interminable stagnation or the collapse of the euro itself. Nothing in the fact of monetary union, and very little in the particular form Europe has given it, stands in the way of much better economic policy. Even the tightened fiscal rules could fairly easily be reinterpreted and be substantially improved. It was through unforced policy errors, not because of the euro's structure, that the eurozone dug itself into its current hole. Different policy decisions – whether prompted by a more correct diagnosis of the economic problems or by pressure from voters who have had enough of the current course – can get it out of the hole again. We should not underestimate eurozone leaders' ability to make things even worse, but the opportunities for improvement are much greater. The eurozone is much more likely to surprise positively than negatively.

For that to happen, two political changes have to happen at once: the balance of power must begin to tilt back from centralised control towards national policy autonomy; and whatever influence the centre retains must be used to demand much more enlightened policies. The next chapter examines the political path by which these two changes might happen.

NINE
The Politics That the Euro Needs

CRACKS IN THE CONSENSUS?

THE DEPTH OF THE EUROZONE's policy failures and the incompleteness of their reversal were such that a political counterreaction had to happen. Even so, the consensus view on how to steer the euro through the crisis, and the collusion between traditional mainstream parties that it enabled, has been remarkably robust. It was not until 2014 that it came under serious threat from not just one but two significant political trends. These emerged most visibly in the May 2014 European elections, and they have strengthened since. The first is an electoral insurrection in favour of fringe parties, all of which oppose the eurozone's policies and some of which oppose the euro itself. The culmination of this trend so far was the coming to power of Greece's radical left-wing movement Syriza in January 2015. The other trend, less virulent but quite possibly more important in the end, is the arrival on the scene of politicians willing to challenge the mainstream consensus from within. The best hope for the eurozone is that the latter trend strengthens and accommodates the most constructive parts of the former.

A 'NEW DEAL'?

The palace revolution by which Matteo Renzi rose to the helm of Italy's centre-left Democratic Party and quickly became the country's prime minister was welcomed across Europe as a gust of youthful energy capable of sweeping away an ossified Italian establishment. When Renzi, who is barely half the age of many of the men who control Italy, struck a deal on electoral reform with one of them (his predecessor Silvio Berlusconi), promising to make Italy more governable, he was rewarded with landslide results in the May 2014 European elections. Although he has not yet contested a national election himself, he has a strong mandate to prove that Italy can indeed be reformed. For that, many Europeans have put their hopes in him not just to reinvigorate Italy's economy but to give impetus to reform across the eurozone.

But there is something paradoxical in the confidence placed in Renzi. It betrays, first of all, that the levers of economic growth do remain largely at the national level – otherwise why would it matter that Italy got a more congenial leader? It jars, in other words, with the idea of controlling more and more policy from the centre. What is more jarring still is that Renzi's electoral mandate, such as it is, derives in part from his willingness to challenge the eurozone orthodoxy – both on the substantive question of the primacy of fiscal discipline and on the procedural one of whether tight reins need to be kept on national governments to keep them from misbehaving.

Renzi and Pier Carlo Padoan, his finance minister, have signalled clearly that they want to be 'serious'. Padoan's appointment itself sent that signal: as chief economist of the OECD, he had been a strong proponent of fiscal austerity. Renzi and Padoan's Italy, the message is, will show the fiscal restraint needed to respect the eurozone's formal rules and Germany's political preferences. It might as well: the damage of excessive fiscal tightening was done in the years before Renzi's elevation, and reversing it straightaway may buy too little economic benefit to be worth the political cost of upsetting Berlin. Renzi is rightly playing a longer game.

Nevertheless, in several speeches he has come closer than any other European leader – before Syriza's victory in Greece – to challenging the way the eurozone currently does its economic business, even as his government stays religiously on side. In late 2014 he called for a 'European New Deal' – a renewed policy focus that makes growth a bigger priority. Renzi and Padoan have also lobbied to weaken the intellectual dominance of the austerity approach by challenging the European Commission's measurement of the agreed fiscal benchmarks and arguing that the benchmarks themselves are obsolete.

Most importantly of all, Renzi speaks out clearly against the view that the eurozone's crisis-hit countries must have reforms imposed on them by the German paymaster: 'No one should think that Europe is a school in which there is one teacher and all the others are students', he has said in interviews.[1]

These are encouraging noises. They suggest a sensible policy approach along some of the lines I set out in the previous chapter. More fundamentally, it shows a long-overdue reaction against treating nations like wayward children in need of a Teutonic governess and her Bruxelloise handmaiden. It is not just people in the periphery that are fed up with being dictated to: those in Italy and France, the euro's second and third countries and the EU's co-founders, are fed up too. The evidence is clear in the surge of fringe and often eurosceptic parties. Paris, which has uniquely declined to do much austerity at all, was in early 2015 openly flaunting the European rules, declaring flatly it would not meet its twice-extended deadline for bringing the budget deficit under 3 per cent of GDP.

The eurozone's approach of trading German money for peripheral discipline has blocked the proper working of political processes in their most democratic and transparent arenas, which remain the national ones. When one pretends there is no alternative, national democracy is reduced to a form of political stoicism: the only freedom that remains is to choose what you are forced to do anyway. That absurdity was particularly glaring in Greece's 2015 referendum, where a landslide rejection of the creditors' terms was followed in a matter of weeks by their unconditional adoption.

Even at the European level, politics has been hamstrung where it should have been the most powerful: in the government-to-government bargaining of the European Council and the eurogroup. There, too, statecraft and policymaking have been squeezed into the single dimension of how much creditor Europe – primarily Germany – should subsidise debtor Europe, and how much policy freedom the debtors must give up in return.

The result is that political conflict, instead of being resolved where it should, has migrated to the places of decision making where it least belongs, above all to the ECB. After politicians shirked their responsibility to decide where the losses from unpayable debts contracted in the boom should fall, monetary policy became the proxy for that unresolved conflict rather than technocratic decision making in the eurozone's common interest. When the same politicians revealed themselves to be unable as well to generate an appropriate fiscal policy for the monetary union – or indeed any holistic fiscal policy at all – the central bank, whose policy needed to be looser in order to compensate, became the battleground for political disagreements that should have been settled in the arena of fiscal policy. It is no coincidence that monetary policy has attracted the greatest controversy just when other policy decision processes have been stymied. And time and again we have seen the ECB act as the eurozone core's political enforcer.

It is still unclear whether Italian grumbles or French recalcitrance presage a big shift in mainstream policy thinking. Few leaders other than Renzi speak with conviction about an alternative. That task has been left to political insurgents, especially those of the left: Spain's Podemos and especially Greece's Syriza. In response, established parties and the Commission they have collectively installed in Brussels have mostly doubled down on the conventional approach. Renzi has nowhere near the international heft he would need to convert Europe to a 'New Deal'. Even in the best-case scenario where he succeeds in reforming the Italian economy and returning it to sustained growth – which very much remains to be seen – Italy's ageing, shrinking population and long history of mismanagement robs it of influence in the councils of Europe. The best Italy can do for now is to fix its own problems. That alone would be no small feat.

The greater task of shifting the direction of European policy around will have to be carried out, if at all, by the two countries on which the EU's development has always hinged: Germany and France. Since they and their mainstream elites have played the greatest part in institutionalising the policy consensus of 'there is no alternative', the prospects of a Damascene conversion may seem far-fetched. But on a closer look, the political interests of both powers speak in favour of a new approach. The interests of many of the smaller countries, as well as swelling political support for explicitly alternative political programmes, pull in the same direction. If the courage to achieve a different vision can be found in Europe's traditional Franco-German motor, then a political path towards realising that vision exists. It would involve Paris moving first.

CHOOSING AN ALTERNATIVE

France demonstrated that it was possible to take less-than-drastic action on the fiscal deficit without falling victim to an investor panic. In contrast with almost everywhere else in the eurozone, there has been little discernible austerity in the French public finances since the crisis. France tightened its structural balance less than any other big eurozone country in the 2010–13 period (see Figure 9.1). It could be said this has not brought the French economy much good, but it would be wrong to attribute its sluggishness to rebellious fiscal policy. France's post-crisis growth has certainly not been stellar, but its output

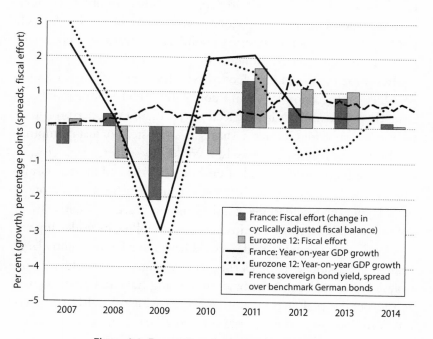

Figure 9.1. France: Less austerity, more growth.
Sources: EC Annual Macroeconomic Database, ECB.

per head has recovered at about the same rate as the United Kingdom's and only a little more slowly than Germany's. Even though France's seeming insouciance provoked a credit rating downgrade, it did not rattle markets, which have continued to finance the deficit at very low rates and acceptable spreads compared with Germany.

This reflects how the French establishment reserves a degree of national autonomy for itself that it has conspired with Berlin to deny other, less powerful nations. But it has also consistently been pushing the financial burdens of the crisis-hit periphery – and its own – onto the broader shoulders of the German economy. This has only been a partial success. France can take the biggest credit for securing Germany's participation in the fiscal rescue operations for the periphery, which disproportionately benefited French banks. French banks' relative exposure to Greece was larger than France's share of the rescue loans, which therefore effectively involved a bail-out of French banks by German – but also Italian and Spanish – taxpayers.[2] Paris did not, however, persuade Berlin to adopt the holy grail of fiscal union: shared responsibility for eurozone countries' public debt through jointly issued eurobonds. (German politicians retort that France will not give up the national autonomy that this would require.)

The eurozone would have looked very different today – and much healthier both economically and politically – had France more consistently preached what it practiced for itself, and practiced for itself what it preached for Germany. That is to say: instead of just exempting itself from the rulings of Brussels, it could have rejected tighter rules in the first place. And instead of pushing – in the end unsuccessfully – for Berlin to mutualise public debt, it could have gone ahead on its own, laying the foundations of a fiscal union based on jointly issued debt together with those countries willing to follow its leadership.

Had France taken the lead, it could have rallied a sufficiently large coalition of countries to block the push for centralisation of fiscal control. A French-led 'southern bloc' comprising Italy and Spain as well as the smaller peripheral countries, allied with other EU members politically opposed to concentrating more power in Brussels (above all the United Kingdom), could have rebuffed German pressure to strengthen the Commission's power over member states under the revamped stability and growth pact. Similarly, had France said no, Berlin would never have been able to get the fiscal compact off the ground.

In the face of such concerted opposition, Berlin would have needed to offer concessions to obtain a compromise that satisfied its main priority of protecting whatever taxpayer money it did put on the line. As the previous chapter suggested, a bargain was possible that would have achieved this without curtailing national autonomy and without inducing a recession through inappropriately countercyclical fiscal policy.

What a French-led southern bloc could have demanded was a rewritten fiscal code that prioritised the overall fiscal stance for the eurozone as a whole. Rather than blind deficit cutting by every country regardless of circumstances, a treaty-enshrined deal could have required every country to do its part to achieve a targeted aggregate fiscal deficit (or surplus, as the case may be in good economic times), and to compensate other countries for free-riding on their discipline. The best institutional solution for this would be Casella's tradable deficit permits (see Chapter 8), though other methods could be envisaged that would charge (or reward) countries for deviating (or overachieving) relative to the common fiscal target. Scholars at the Bruegel think-tank, for example, have proposed a 'Eurosystem of fiscal policy' with the authority to determine the fiscal balance a country would have to pursue.[3]

In such a deal, Germany's interests would be protected by reenshrining the no bail-out principle. No rescue lending would take place without restructuring outstanding sovereign debt first, and loans would be limited to financing a falling path of ongoing primary deficits, excluding any debt service or refinancing. The Cyprus approach would have been regularised from the start: no rescue loans would be available unless undercapitalised banks were bailed in to eliminate any need for public subsidy. As I explained in earlier chapters, these two moves would radically reduce the size of any money needed in a balance-of-payments crisis. Finally, German worries about a transfer union would be definitively put to rest by abandoning any push for eurozone-wide debt mutualisation. Instead, the southern bloc, led by

France, could have pursued eurobonds based on intergovernmental agreement between those willing to take the leap.

The main advantage of common debt issuance is often thought to be that the stronger economies would thereby underwrite the weaker – that is why Berlin resists it. But the more immediate, and arguably the more important, benefit from debt pooling in the eurozone would be the size of the pool that resulted from it. Consider this: at the end of 2014 the quantity of US and Japanese public debt outstanding amounted to about $18 trillion (€15 trillion) and ¥875 trillion (€6 trillion), respectively. Those markets are so big that there is nowhere else investors in them could realistically flee en masse. That helps make them reserve currencies and is a chief reason why neither Japan's massive deficit and debt nor Washington's brinkmanship with default have led to European-style debt panics. In contrast, the biggest European sovereign bond pools are Italy's at €1.8 trillion, France's at €1.7 trillion and Germany's at €1.6 trillion. The other eurozone governments' bond supplies are much smaller still. For every government whose creditworthiness is rightly or wrongly in doubt, there are other euro-denominated sovereign assets to shift into. Hence the ease with which capital flight can destabilise individual eurozone countries.[4]

This is the problem that debt mutualisation would solve. Suppose Paris left Berlin behind and simply invited interested countries to mutualise the public debt. Even if Germany's most like-minded partners – the Netherlands, Austria, Finland and Slovakia (and Greece, which needs special treatment) – were left out, the remaining thirteen eurozone countries could create a roughly €5 trillion bond market with macroeconomic figures only marginally worse than those for the eurozone as a whole. (If debt in other forms, such as loans, was converted into tradable bonds, the market would be even bigger.) That pool of debt would, moreover, be more than three times as big as the supply of German sovereign bonds, the main safe haven investment in euros. There is every reason to think that investors would finance such debt at interest rates close to German ones, and that the divide-and-rule vulnerability of individualised national debt pools would be a thing of the past. A long-time French policy goal would have been achieved.

There is no economic hindrance to gaining the advantages of size in this way, nor any insurmountable legal obstacles. A jointly issued bond could be modelled on the Bruegel think-tank's blue bond/red bond proposal, in which mutualised debt gradually replaces national debt up to a ceiling.[5] The willing states would need to sign a new treaty that was compatible with their existing treaty duties in respect of monetary union, and that would enshrine their promise to treat the mutualised debt as senior to other obligations. To further panic-proof the joint debt, its maturities could be spread evenly over, say, fifty years (or longer), which would avoid any of the refinancing 'spikes' that turned bond market stress into vicious cycles in the sovereign debt crisis. Indeed a mutualisation project would be the ideal occasion for launching perpetual bonds.

Such eurobonds need not run afoul of the 'no bail-out' rule, for to agree to borrow jointly is not to assume another country's debt. Politically, of course, it would fly in the face of Brussels etiquette for a subset of the eurozone to go it alone. But the fiscal compact already did so: on Berlin's insistence, an intergovernmental treaty was signed without UK or Slovak participation. And the European spirit is surely on the side of those who want to pool sovereignty rather than on the side of German recalcitrance. The latter would be justified if Berlin had to pay for the project – but the point is that here it would not.

As I have argued throughout the book, jointly issued bonds are not necessary for the eurozone to thrive; nor is any other form of fiscal union. But that is not to say it would not bring benefits; and some countries have expressed a desire for it. My assertion is simply that such countries can just go ahead of their own accord; neither the structure of the euro nor the politics of Germany need detain them.

This, then, is one alternative which it has been claimed does not exist: greater national autonomy to pursue countercyclical fiscal policies combined with a framework for orderly sovereign debt restructuring; a eurozone fiscal framework that prioritises the collective fiscal stance; and mutualised debt issuance by a coalition of the willing. Such an alternative, if it had been pursued early in the crisis, would have addressed the balance-of-payments vulnerability of weaker euro members, reduced the cost of stagnation by requiring less austerity, and avoided the strain that the 'no alternative' rhetoric has inflicted on Europe's democracies.

France: The Duumvir that Abdicated

France could have chosen to cast itself as a leader of the most crisis-hit countries and those who saw the merit of an alternative policy. Had it picked its goals wisely and negotiated cleverly with Berlin, it could have combined the role of protector of the eurozone's battered periphery with a restored position as Germany's equal partner in the process of European integration. Even as it has yearned for the old Franco-German duumvirate, however, Paris has consistently punched below its weight since the onset of the crisis.

Why has it not done better? There are three mains reasons.

The first is philosophical. The French elite are true believers in certain ideas that were inimical to better policy for the eurozone. The determining push for sovereign rescues – against the early German contemplation of letting Greece default or even leave the euro – came from a trio of French policymakers: Jean-Claude Trichet at the ECB, Dominique Strauss-Kahn at the IMF, and of course president Nicolas Sarkozy and his government. This reflected a particularly French aversion to markets getting the better of governments – a motivation as much behind France's support for monetary union in the first place as for rescue policies in the crisis. From this perspective it is anathema not just to restructure sovereign debt, but to let banks fend for themselves instead of bailing them out at taxpayer expense. In France, credit allocation – even though at the hands of nominally private banks – has always been an affair of state. This attitude, which it shares with Germany, has resulted in French and German banks being among the most highly leveraged in the world, safe in the hitherto-unchallenged belief that the state will always stand behind them.

A related, less lofty, ideological factor has been France's willingness to apply different standards to itself and smaller countries. The first to breach the original stability and growth pact (with impunity) in 2004 were precisely the eurozone's two leading governments. But while it left Berlin determined to set an example by showing excessive fiscal restraint later, Paris maintained its double standards, and this has led it to pursue contradictory and counterproductive diplomatic goals. Recall Deauville: in return for acquiescing to a fiscal stability treaty as well as a sovereign debt restructuring framework (the latter quite a concession for France), Paris secured only a weakening, later reversed, of the European Commission's power to sanction governments for breaking the tighter fiscal rules. The French priority, in other words, was not to improve the rules but to make it less likely that it would be stopped from breaching them. This betrays an old-fashioned approach to policymaking, which sees a rule-based order as secondary to the politics of the moment, but also a French desire to distinguish itself from the lesser powers of the EU. (The bilateral Deauville agreement itself, where France and Germany set the course of policy over the heads of everyone else, is a supreme manifestation of that approach.)

This leads to the second reason: vainglory, and the lack of confidence that so often underpins it. The idea of being leader of a southern bloc must have seemed humiliating to many French leaders, including Sarkozy. Especially in 2010–11, when Germany was thundering ahead in its recovery, in contrast with a periphery under constant assault from markets, there was strong envy of the German model in much of the rest of Europe. The vulnerability of French banks, and especially their large amount of US dollar-denominated borrowing, was a particular source of nervousness in Paris. In Brussels, meanwhile, a country's influence depends a lot on its domestic economic strength. So France under Sarkozy, sensing itself weak even as it pretended not to be, decided its credibility depended on emulating Germany in domestic policy and siding with it in European matters. Sarkozy was unsuccessful in domestic policy, where resistance to reform proved stronger than his zeal to pursue it. And he was ineffective on the diplomatic front, where France followed Germany when it should have opposed it and opposed it when it should have conceded. The result was to diminish French influence even further.

Finally, underpinning all of this was the same incorrect analysis of the eurozone's economic problem. France, like most others, accepted the conventional wisdom that the euro's survival depended on German money. From that followed a diplomatic priority to try to secure Germany's willingness to shoulder as much of other countries' risks as possible. In return, Paris endorsed Berlin's obsession with national 'competitiveness' and hence deflationary reforms, and paid lip service to the need for treaty-anchored fiscal discipline (even if France considered itself exempt in practice). Paris may also have misjudged what Berlin might actually be willing to accept, and acted unnecessarily timidly as a result. Only when the German leadership decided it had had enough of putting taxpayer money at stake for the sake of other countries and their banks did the eurozone move remarkably swiftly from bail-out to bail-in, something that France could have claimed as its victory two years earlier had it played its cards right.

GERMANY: THE RELUCTANCE OF THE HEGEMON

How would Germany have reacted had it faced more concerted opposition from its traditional EU partner against its austerity and reform drive? How might the country react if such opposition finally materialises in the future?

A superficial reading of German politics would predict a fierce resistance to rolling back the constraints on national governments' fiscal freedom along the lines proposed above. Greater fiscal discipline and structural reforms enforced from the centre have after all been the price exacted by Berlin for bankrolling the eurozone's fiscal rescue programmes, as well as for acquiescing in more aggressive monetary policy. Angela Merkel has demanded in unambiguous terms that the new rules be respected in full and in perpetuity; a reason for anchoring them in treaty law was to give the European Court of Justice the power to sanction offenders. 'All member states must accept in full the strengthened rules', she told the German parliament in October 2014, just as France was proposing to extend again its timeline for bringing its deficit down and Rome was enacting an overdue fiscal stimulus (though staying within the 3 per cent).[6]

But one should ask what Berlin could do to stop a determined French-led bloc from restoring the national capacity for countercyclical fiscal policy. As argued before, there is much scope for reinterpreting the current rules, as there is a good economic case to be made that a mechanical priority on austerity policies undermines rather than supports the rules' overarching goal of sustainable public finances. Politically, the austerity proponents would by hypothesis have little traction with the 'reinterpreters'; legally, their case is weaker than they might hope. And even the legal resort would only be available if Berlin or others were willing to pay the political cost of taking other sovereigns to court over fiscal policy.

Beyond this, why would Germany not learn to live with greater national fiscal autonomy? Its current insistence on fiscal rules is certainly easy to understand. Removing the fetters on national budgeting would permit some governments to live beyond their means again if lenders could be found to finance them. But that is only a problem to the extent it affects other member countries of the common currency. As Germany has itself been learning, allowing countries to incur larger deficits – even irresponsibly large ones – need not mean allowing countries to 'get away with it' if national room for manoeuvre is matched with national responsibility. Letting national governments borrow what they see fit can be made politically acceptable as well as economically reasonable if they have to confront the full cost of their borrowing decisions. Greater fiscal freedom therefore requires a framework for sovereign restructuring. The predictability that such a framework would bring would in turn sharply reduce the danger to others that the disciplinarians have always feared from unsustainable government finances. (As Chapter 7 showed, these dangers were in any case always exaggerated.) Eurozone countries have already come a long way towards making their economies safe from each others' fiscal crises.

In theory, Germany's nuclear option would be to withdraw from the eurozone if it found the unravelling of centrally enforced discipline intolerable. In practice, the most realistic German response would be to block any future rescues of an 'undisciplined' country unless such a country first restructured its sovereign and bank debt. It would not get to impose discipline, but it would also not have to pick up the bill, and the temporary lack of credit would itself discipline the offending sovereign. Taken together, a moderate renationalisation of fiscal policy coupled with strengthened national responsibility for its consequences are not as alien to German policy as many think. It moved much closer to such a position in its dealings with Greece in 2011–12 and with Cyprus in 2013. And Germany has hardly embraced with enthusiasm its role as the eurozone's paymaster and disciplinarian. On the contrary, the reluctance to order its neighbours about is such that, when Europe seemed most adrift in the crisis, it drove the foreign minister of Poland (not a country with fond memories of German activism) to practically beg Berlin to take up the mantle of leadership.[7]

The message that German policymakers constantly send is that they may consider pooling more budget resources with other euro member states, but only if national sovereignty is pooled in tandem so that there can be adequate control over how the money is used. Germany will, or says it will, countenance both fiscal and political union together, or neither. This is usually interpreted as a delaying tactic to avoid putting any more money up, or a sign that Germany's ultimate goal is to be able to shape all of Europe in its image. What it in fact suggests is that Germans would just as much prefer to be let off the hook – both of the responsibility to pay and of the burden of telling others what to do.

The choice is most articulately laid out by Jens Weidmann, the president of the Bundesbank. In speeches and interviews, Weidmann has formulated the distinction between full fiscal union and a 'return to Maastricht', in which there would be no fiscal transfers and in which sovereigns would recover both the freedom to borrow at will and the ability to go bankrupt if they overextend themselves. The choice, Weidmann suggests, is a deeply political one that all the peoples of the eurozone must make. But his own preferred route seems to be back to Maastricht. Consistently with this perspective, Weidmann campaigns for ending bank regulations that treat sovereign debt as completely safe, instead requiring banks to hold capital reserves against their holdings of government bonds depending on their riskiness, like they do with other risky securities.[8]

Weidmann is right about the choice; and there is good reason to think much of German public and political opinion leans in his direction as to which alternative is preferable. German policymakers rarely miss an opportunity to point out, in private, that France will never share sovereignty over its budget to an extent needed for fiscal union to be workable. Beyond that, Berlin's choices throughout the crisis suggest it prefers things this way.

Consider the record. In the early days of the crisis, Berlin was the capital most willing to contemplate letting Greece default. Shortly after, at Deauville, it insisted on putting in place a framework for restructuring troubled sovereign debt in the future. In the second half of 2011, it demanded that a default be engineered for the portion of Greece's debt that remained in private hands. And in 2013, it was German pressure that left Cyprus without any alternative to restructuring its banks so that the amount of rescue lending required could be limited. All along, the budgetary committee of the Bundestag has retained a veto, affirmed by the constitutional court, over any sovereign rescue commitments with German money, and it has let it be known that it will not rubber-stamp eurozone fiscal transfer requests. Throughout, the crisis fiscal or monetary support to other governments has faced opposition from a vocal and influential segment of public opinion inside Germany.

The most reasonable conclusion to draw from all of this is that the German establishment, as well as the German public, could live very well with a eurozone in which fiscal power – but also fiscal responsibility – is renationalised rather than federalised further, so long as it and the eurozone can be made safe from the restructuring of any government unable to service its debt. This book has argued, and experience has shown, that such safety is available and that some of Germany's wiser policies – the move towards an orderly sovereign restructuring mechanism and the support for bail-in rules for banks – have contributed to it. A French-led initiative to explicitly renationalise some fiscal policy would in some ways push Germany further along a road it has already freely taken.

INSURRECTIONS

The elites of Europe have not remained entirely unmoved by the evidence – persistent stagnation and, in the crisis-hit countries, desperate joblessness and a hollowed-out middle class – that their policies have failed. They have tilted away from an approach of bailing out debtors towards one of bailing in creditors. Paris and Rome bristle more demonstrably against their subjection to Brussels in fiscal matters than when they signed up to it a few years ago. The first big initiative from the new European Commission that took office in November 2014 was a plan, albeit imperfect, to boost private financing for capital investment. It is also, rightly, trying to move Europe slowly away from its addiction to bank debt financing. But these changes of heart remain far too timid compared with what is needed.

The timidity has made voters leave mainstream parties behind in droves. The rise of anti-establishment forces in almost every European country should not be surprising, given how disappointingly the traditional parties have performed, but it is no less impressive for that. Populists of the right and the left are making big inroads into electoral terrains traditionally held by the established centre-right and centre-left, making it increasingly difficult for those established elites to govern as before.

In the election to the European Parliament in May 2014, fringe parties with radical anti-establishment appeal received a quarter to a third of the vote in Italy, France and Greece; in the latter two, the biggest fringe party got the most votes overall. Greece's Syriza, of course, went on to win power in national elections eight months later. In Spain, the left-wing party Podemos, founded only months before the election, won 8 per cent and has frequently topped the polls of voting intentions for national elections in 2015. In Germany, the right-wing anti-euro *Alternative für Deutschland*, also barely a year old, won 7 per cent. Outside the eurozone, too, fringe parties surged. In the United Kingdom and Denmark, the openly eurosceptic and anti-immigrant parties Ukip and Dansk Folkeparti topped the ballots in May 2014; in national elections the following year, they won the third and second largest vote shares.

Mainstream politicians have reacted by ringing the wagons. There has been little attempt to differentiate between left-wing and right-wing fringes, or between rank populists and thoughtful radicals. To believe the besieged establishment centrists, outsiders represent a civilisational danger that can only be averted by returning to the convenient oligopoly where two or three well-behaved political blocs share the bulk of votes between them. To achieve this, they engage in the doomed effort of mimicking their challengers' populism. And sometimes, the mask slips and the gloves come off. In the run-up to Greece's July 2015 referendum, European leaders effectively made it a prerequisite for staying in the euro that Syriza must abandon its policy programme and, after the vote, that it must ignore the people's choice.

This defensiveness is wrong-headed on several counts. It confirms the main claim the various insurrectionist movements lay to electoral support: that the traditional forces are all the same and no longer offer a real choice, so they all need to be thrown out if change is to be achieved. This just increases the outsider parties' appeal to millions who were hurt by the crisis and feel abandoned by the 'system'. It also allows the fringe parties to reach across the traditional left–right dividing line by appealing to nationalism. Right-wing movements, in particular, have been successful at attracting working-class voters. That has left mainstream parties clinging to power either through minority governments that have a hard time getting anything done or through grand coalitions between social democrats and the centre-right. These protect the existing consensus but marginalise any real political opposition. Either way, the challengers can shout 'we told you so' from the fringes in the expectation of even greater support next time around.

But the most aggravating mistake establishment politicians have made is their absolute refusal to engage with the substantive policy proposals from the more thoughtful insurrectionists. Amid the rabble-rousing and xenophobia of the ascendant fringes there are oases of serious thinking. In particular, a proper hearing needs to be given to the agendas of two groups that have instead been stonewalled. Those are the moderate wings of Syriza in Greece and Podemos in Spain, which enjoy the support of more than a quarter of the electorate and, in the case of Syriza, high approval rates for its (short) record in government at the time of writing.

There are many similarities between the two. Both are broad left-wing radical movements managing a range of constituents from hard-left activists to disenchanted former supporters of the mainstream social democratic party (Pasok in Greece, the Socialist Party in Spain). Both present themselves as anti-system movements and irreconcilable critics of established political forces, and the only real alternative to politics as usual. Both have benefited from the dramatic drop in living standards after the boom and the conventional parties' complicity (the question is whether Spain's belated growth spurt comes too late to save prime minister Mariano Rajoy). Both are led by youthful politicians with TV charisma, Alexis Tsipras and Pablo Iglesias. And they recognise their mutual affinities: Tsipras addressed Podemos's founding conference.

Beneath these superficial parallels is a shared political agenda. It is hard to pin down the precise policy programme of movements trying to manage sudden popularity and either an imminent election campaign (in Podemos's case) or the task of governing amid an acute liquidity crisis (in Syriza's). Both have exposed flashes of irresponsible populism. But at the core of both movements is a serious commitment to three things: debt writedowns; ending fiscal austerity; and reversing the pursuit of competitiveness through squeezing labour, at least among the lowest paid. (Syriza has made moves to raise the minimum wage while Podemos has advocated a universal basic income – an unconditional stipend to all citizens.) Beyond these three tenets, which are those most crucially at variance with what the eurozone policy consensus prescribes, lie other left-wing policies like more redistributive tax and benefit systems – and in the more extreme flanks of the movements, an aim to topple capitalism altogether.

It is natural that the established parties dismiss these movements' policies as a recipe for taking Greece or Spain out of the euro. It is a good scare tactic, given that the majority of Greeks and Spaniards want to remain inside. When Tsipras called a referendum on the policies demanded by Greece's official creditors, other European leaders immediately insisted on equating it with a vote on euro membership. In fact Syriza and Podemos have both gone out of their way to state their support for staying in the euro (although Syriza's hard-left wing wants Greece to leave); their argument is that policies can be changed without breaking up the monetary union, and indeed that the euro will be better off for it. What is more surprising is how uncritically independent observers, especially in the international financial press, joined the chorus that Syriza's and Podemos's policies are incompatible with staying in the euro. Hugo Dixon of Reuters, for instance, has written:

> Podemos wants to clean up politics, which is good. But ... it wants to cut the retirement age to 60, audit the country's debt before writing part of it off, and guarantee everybody a minimum income. If such a programme ever became policy, Spain would be heading for default and exit from the euro zone.

The *Economist* magazine wrote of Syriza that its 'programme seems, to put it mildly, to sit uncomfortably with Greece's continuing membership of the single currency.'[9] One wonders whether these impeccably market-friendy commentators realise that such arguments turn them into the allies of Syriza's hard left.

The notion that radically left-wing policies are incompatible with the euro is such an attack on the possibility of democracy within a monetary union that it is curious it has not generated more outrage. And nobody should be under any illusion that it does not guide policy thinking at the highest level. Mario Draghi has used several speeches to call for centralised control of structural economic policies. Draghi's argument is that the euro's integrity is only safe so long as each member thinks it is better off inside than out, and ensuring this is therefore 'a legitimate interest of the whole union'.[10] It is a duty of euro membership, in other words, to reform so as to prevent an exit from ever looking attractive. The implication is clear: this is an argument to centralise authority over laws on labour relations, product market regulations, and a lot else besides. Family policy, housing policy and pensions are all structural policies that could potentially be caught in Draghi's dragnet.

But we should reject his argument. First, because it is an affront against democracy to disenfranchise national electorates from shaping the economic model they want to govern their lives, so long as they accept the consequences and costs. A nation may choose policies that lead to lower growth but achieve other political or social goals, and there is no reason why the euro should not accommodate this. Second, because the structural policies pushed by Draghi and much of the eurozone political elite do not always deliver what they promise. Even on plain economic grounds, there is value in having a diversity of approaches that allows countries to learn from one another which solutions work best. As this book has argued, the particular policies that creditor Europe has foisted on debtors (and to a large extent on itself) have often made a bad situation worse.

The eurozone's entrenched elite, however, has clung to the claim that there is no alternative to their policy programme, which new-found openness in Italy and France has so far not done much to alter. And the lack of flexibility has been firmest in the long stand-off with Greece's radicals in 2015. Syriza's coming to power ought to have been treated as a challenge but not a disaster (as it should be with any future Podemos election victory). These parties' inexperience and excessive enthusiasm for leftist economics will no doubt lead to some economic cost. On the other hand, their independence from existing social power structures gives them a stronger hand to crack down on tax evasion, which is how they promise to raise tax revenues.

Instead, the eurozone showed an inordinate stubbornness in response to the admittedly bungling diplomacy of the fresh Syriza government. That has already cost the country more in halted growth than leftist economic amateurism would have been likely to. Amid the wreckage of the Greek economy, Athens has been paying its way domestically since 2013. Government revenues have more than covered domestic public spending apart from debt service, and the debt stopped growing in euro terms after the 2012 restructuring. In this sense, the fiscal adjustment was largely complete. In 2014, austerity was paused (the structural primary budget balance was actually loosened slightly), and growth duly resumed as one would expect in such a depressed economy. There was no need for any additional loans – private investors were even dipping their toes in the water – and therefore there should have been no need to impose specific non-fiscal policies on Greece. Given this (primary) surplus, the only question that needed to be resolved was on what terms the no-longer-growing debt should be serviced and eventually whittled down.

Because of missed opportunities in the 2012 writedown, the ECB retained billions in unrestructured Greek bonds whose principal was due to be repaid in 2015 and 2016 (see Chapter 6). Without refinancing or rescheduling, Athens would not be able to repay these without drastically cutting expenditure and depressing the economy again. Until June 2015, that is what it did in order to repay mainly IMF loans. In 2014, it had looked as if Athens might finally have settled back into private bond markets, in which case it could privately refinance debt falling due. But the uncertainty caused by Syriza's stand-off with the eurozone scared international investors away again, and this uncertainty and the need to extract resources out of the economy to repay rather than refinance maturing loans combined to stifle the fledgling growth.

The right policy in early 2015 was always to do what should have been done in the 2012 restructuring (see Chapter 3): have the eurozone rescue fund relieve the ECB of its Greek bond holdings and replace them with a long-term loan. The eurozone should have refinanced the IMF loans, too, or convinced the IMF to roll them over on a long-term basis.

All obligations to official lenders should have been spread even further into the future than they already are, to avoid a return of the refinancing trap. Greece's debt service – including any net repayments of principal – should have been linked to growth and limited to a realistic proportion of GDP. This would have been bearable for the Greek economy, and since it would have removed the temptation of unilateral default, it would have reassured creditors as well. Together, this would have obviated the need to cut the nominal value of the debt, a political impossibility for some creditor states. Greek banks would have had to be restructured, writing down current ownership stakes and replacing them with equity for bailed-in bondholders and large depositors, who would have an incentive to make the banks work.[11] The economic boost from removing the debt overhang and rebooting the banking system would, in the long run, increase prospective returns for creditors, not reduce them.

This may, in the end, be where the eurozone and Greece end up. If so, they will have taken the worst way to get there. In the months following Syriza's election, the eurozone enforced a repayment schedule that was both unfeasible and entirely of its own making to force Athens into submission. The goal was never to see the ECB-held bonds repaid – their fate was always either unilateral default or an agreed rescheduling – but to force the left-wing radicals to continue with similar policies as the centre-right party they defeated in elections.

This was profoundly wrong-headed. To demand further budgetary tightening to pay down maturing debt, as well as structural reforms that are often counterproductive, is to compound the economic mistakes described earlier in this book. Worse, it repeats the political mistakes as well by making a mockery of democratic choice. Creditors have a legitimate stake in fiscal policy that strengthens the ability to repay debts, but not in the choice between different non-fiscal policies, which should rather reflect how Greeks want to arrange their affairs. The eurozone's policymaking record in any case has undermined any claim to superior economic management; and even if it had not, the choice of how much to prioritise growth over other economic and political priorities is one that should be democratically decided.

But the eurozone is back to its bad habits. A single economic vision has been mercilessly enforced – through the overlordship of creditors' technical staff, through the ECB's refusal to lend freely in the last resort to banks it itself deems solvent, through pressure to change the make-up of the government and – in a repeat of Papandreou's subjection in 2011 – through first violently rejecting a referendum then insisting it was a choice on whether to stay in the euro rather than on the specific local conditions the creditors had proposed.[12]

Much has been made of the political impossibility of letting Syriza have its way on debt writedowns, lest other crisis-hit countries with similar political insurrections (Spain, Ireland with Sinn Fein, later perhaps Portugal) opt for the same. But this political contagion argument makes little sense beyond being self-serving for established elites. For if restructuring is the right policy, why should it not be pursued elsewhere? Take Spain, which owes very little (a few per cent of GDP) to the troika and most of whose excessive debt is in the private sector.

Madrid could achieve private restructuring entirely through national legislation; in the case of banks this would be in line with the new common bail-in rules. How could this be bad for Europe? As for public debt, now that interest rates are low much can be achieved by swapping bonds with longer maturities on a voluntary basis for the participants. Ireland, as mentioned before, has a good case for being relieved of some banking-related losses by other eurozone countries. In both cases, any cross-border repercussions can and should be handled through the new rules for recapitalising banks (and restructuring them if necessary).

This would never be a conflict-free process, but it could be made an orderly one provided the will is there on all sides. And in any case, a permanent rejection of the more thoughtful insurrectionists' proposals leaves the field open for more extremist forces. This cannot be sustained forever. As Podemos-affiliated economists clearly articulate, debt restructuring and a reversal of austerity eventually become a matter of economic necessity – in other words, it may not be a question of if, but when.[13] Europe has been desperately lacking in politicians distinguished by their acceptance of such realities. The eurozone elite's refusal to let Syriza score points that would admit the eurozone's past policy mistakes, and its scaremongering about Podemos, are just further confirmation of that sad fact.

FROM RESTORED NATIONAL AUTONOMY TO RENEWED EUROPEAN INTEGRATION

The political alternative for the eurozone, then, is to reopen the space for more national freedom in policymaking, above all in fiscal affairs but also in reform policy. The necessary complement to regained autonomy is to re-establish national responsibility for the choices a country makes, including arrangements for an orderly restructuring of the government's debt when those choices have been sufficiently poor. One should expect that some governments would use their freedom to choose policies at odds with the austerity-and-price-competitiveness path taken almost universally since 2010. Greece's Syriza government is the first to try to do so explicitly, albeit incompetently.

This book has offered reasons why such a policy shift might lead to better economic results. I finish this chapter with three observations on how a policy shift may also change Europe's political economy for the better.

First, by eliminating the conditions for the current state of reciprocal blackmail where, explicitly or implicitly, Germany threatens not to pay, deficit Europe not to comply, and the price of disagreement is expulsion. This would remove the most significant cause of political resentment between eurozone countries. That would be a worthwhile prize in its own right for a region that has no need for more enmity between its nations. It would also be good for democracy. No longer would rulers be able to tell dissatisfied voters that their hands were forced by the invidiousness or harshness of supposed partners in the common currency. A country's fortunes would be more clearly the responsibility of national governments, for which they could be held to account by their own electorates. That, in turn, would require both incumbents and challengers for power to articulate better what they would do for their people; blaming the foreigners would have less resonance than it does today. The result would be more heterogeneity in policymaking, and occasional attempts at radically different policies. While such attempts may well fail, it is surely right for voters to be able to choose them.

Second, it would allow Europe to exploit the diversity between individual countries better. A deep problem with centralised policymaking is that it shrinks the scope for experimentation from which others can learn. In the United States, radical tax cutting in Kansas or the Massachusetts approach to universal health provision, to take just two examples, have provided valuable lessons to other states and to the federal government about what works and what does not. Europe should be similar, above all in how it addresses the challenge of equitable growth in the face of globalisation. In the crisis, however, the eurozone staked out a path that converges on a German model, not just in fiscal matters but more critically in the nature of structural reforms – precisely the competitiveness-through-wage-restraint strategy that Berlin implemented in the early 2000s. Those reforms are credited with growth and employment, but they also brought

precarious work, insufficient investment and a decade of wage stagnation. Germany can hardly claim to have found the answer to Europe's
(and indeed the whole rich world's) challenge. Unless different countries are allowed, indeed encouraged, to try out very different solutions – some of which will fail, perhaps badly – Europe will miss out
on the opportunity to learn which ones work best.

Finally, fretting less over how other governments behave would let
European countries pay rather more attention to what is in their common interest. Paradoxically, greater national autonomy may encourage more integration. That does not have to mean steps towards fiscal
and political union, though it could mean groups of countries voluntarily adopting elements of these. With less voter antagonism, countries may find it beneficial to deepen integration in specific areas with
'coalitions of the willing', subsets of likeminded European states. One
possibility is the aforementioned joint issuance of debt; eurobonds
could be launched by those who want them, without waiting for Germany's participation. There are other examples, the most significant
of which would be pursued by France and Germany on a bilateral
basis, but would be open to others to join, as many surely would.
In late 2014 the two countries' economy ministers commissioned a
report from Henrik Enderlein and Jean-Pisani Ferry, highly compe-
tent economists and committed Europeans, who produced one of
Europe's best policy documents since the crisis. Among their recommendations are for Berlin and Paris to create 'borderless sectors' in key
industries through bilateral harmonisation of regulations, taxes and
other structural policies. This is precisely the sort of policy harmonisation that Europe's nation states should be looking for, and that the
European Commission should be encouraging even if it is only for a
subset of interested states.

The work of European integration remains unfinished, and plenty
of opportunities for such bilateral or multilateral initiatives exist. The
only obstacles in their way are insufficient political attention and an
unwillingness to withstand domestic protectionist pressures. The
hope is that undoing some of the counterproductive centralisation
the eurozone has imposed on itself during the crisis could help get
both obstacles out of the way.

TEN
Great Britain or Little England?

The Real Choice for Britain in Europe

THERE IS ONLY ONE big economy in Europe that has stayed outside of the monetary union. Britain is nonetheless strongly affected by the euro's failure or success, and by how the eurozone manages its economy. More profoundly and less widely appreciated, the euro affects the United Kingdom's influence in Europe. Most neglected of all is how the British choice to stay out has made a difference to how the euro is run. For all these reasons, a book about the euro needs to discuss the United Kingdom's relationship with the monetary union on its doorstep and assess the decision not to take part.

It may seem eccentric to start a conversation about UK membership of the euro just when the battle is on over whether Britain should leave the EU altogether, and when the single currency itself is perceived as thoroughly discredited. Even the more level-headed commentators and voters who think 'Brexit' would be an act of gratuitous self-harm take it for granted that British euro membership is a crazy idea. The decision to be absent from the euro's creation in 1999 has, since the sovereign debt crisis, been a source of universal relief, and most of those who did once support membership have now recanted their views. Seventy per cent of the public disapprove of the euro.[1]

But in fact there is no better time to revisit the case for British euro membership. Doing so clarifies how much the United Kingdom's current status – in the EU but out of the euro – falls short of the potential benefits it could reap from closer European integration. That is relevant to the debate over membership of the EU overall. Establishing the cost Britain pays to stand apart from a core strand of the European project may cast light on how much bigger the cost could be from pulling out of it altogether. Alternatively, it may reveal that the status quo is an untenable position. If so, the real choice over the long term is not what David Cameron will ask Britons in a referendum, namely whether to stay in or leave an EU that possibly grants slightly more national autonomy than today. The real choice for Britain may be between leaving the EU and becoming a fully engaged member, including of the eurozone.

The discussion of British euro membership always had two parts to it. One was whether it would benefit the United Kingdom economically – the subject of Gordon Brown's 'five tests'. The other was whether it would enhance British influence.

Both are worth revisiting, and I will do so later in this chapter. But the crisis, and the way it has supposedly exposed the euro as a currency not fit for purpose, provides a third perspective from which to judge the question. That is, how would a Britain inside the euro have influenced the policies chosen before and during the crisis? In particular, are there reasons to think that the eurozone's crisis response would have been superior to what it actually was if the United Kingdom had been a member? And what, finally, would this have meant for Britain's own economy? Contrary to what most people think, I will argue that the crisis, far from destroying the euro's attractiveness for Britain for good, was a situation where sharing the euro would have made the country better off.

COUNTERFACTUAL HISTORY: CRISIS POLICY WITH BRITAIN IN THE EURO

The failures of eurozone policy in the crisis, as I have analysed them in this book, amount to four things: the mistake of not radically restructuring sovereign or bank debt before any rescue loans were granted; an excessively tight monetary policy; the inability to coordinate on the right fiscal stance for the monetary union as a whole which, coupled with an excessive priority on deficit cuts for debtor Europe, resulted in too much austerity everywhere and the failure to respect national political processes in setting fiscal and structural reform policies. On all four, it is likely that better policy compromises would have been struck with the United Kingdom at the table.

Rescues and Restructuring

Take the rescue loans first. I pointed out in Chapter 3 that when it became clear that the choice for Greece was between bail-out and default, HM Treasury acted swiftly to make clear it would exclude itself from any rescue operation. As the largest non-euro country, Britain was influential in establishing the conventional wisdom that Greece was the eurozone's responsibility because its implosion was caused by the flawed currency. As discussed above, this was a poor argument: if the main rationale for lending to Greece was the collateral damage of a Greek default on other countries, then all the economies in the line of fire had reason to contribute. That the potential repercussions were vastly exaggerated does not alter the fact that the United Kingdom was at least as exposed as many eurozone countries, and arguably more than most because of its huge financial sector. Banks and other financial companies would, after all, be the industry with the most to lose from the turmoil it was feared that a Greek default would trigger.

The Treasury washed its hands of Greece's liabilities. That was wise in terms of UK interests, and it would have been a wise choice for other eurozone countries to do the same. It is likely that inside the euro, too, the UK government would have expressed the same aversion to bailing out creditors that had foolishly lent to politicians in Athens. That may or may not have swayed the eurozone's collective decision in those fearful days in April and May 2010. But it would at least have pulled in the right direction.

Now it could be pointed out that after the first Greek loan, the United Kingdom did in fact participate in some of the later rescues, in particular that of Ireland, where it contributed a £3.2 billion loan to the overall eurozone rescue package. Like all EU members it also stood behind the European Commission's participation in rescue loans to Ireland and Portugal through the so-called European Financial Stability Mechanism (a junior partner to the EFSF). But these participations were minimal – much smaller than what eurozone countries had to contribute.[2] Within the euro, Britain could not have got away with putting up less than its proportional share or with picking and choosing which rescues to contribute to. It is of course possible that the UK government would have folded and paid as much into the kitty as other similarly sized economies. But given the country's special allergy to contributing to EU funds, manifest in its unique rebate from the EU budget, as well as the acute feeling in the new coalition government that it, too, was vulnerable to market attack, it is more probable that it would have done whatever it could to minimise its outlays. That would suggest minimising the cost of the rescues by requiring outstanding debt to be restructured.

British policymakers also had a more clear-eyed view of what ailed the banking system. While the government blinked on the question of bailing out big banks with taxpayer money, it had at least put in place a special resolution regime for restructuring and resolving bankrupt banks as early as February 2009. This would have put UK policymakers in a strong position to correct the eurozone's dogmatism over whether Ireland's taxpayers should pay to protect the bondholders in the country's private banks from losses.

Monetary Policy

A UK seat on the ECB's Governing Council would have brought outsize influence. Not just because bigger countries in practice carry more weight in the deliberations than the voting key suggests.[3] But also because the Bank of England, one of the world's oldest central banks, is an intellectual leader in monetary policy thinking, and its experience with the City of London makes it the most attuned of all the European central banks to how securities markets can be harnessed for monetary policy goals.

While there is much to criticise about the Bank of England's behaviour before and during the crisis – like most others, it did not see it coming – it has been consistently more aggressive than the ECB in trying to loosen monetary and credit conditions. It cut its policy rate to 0.5 per cent in March 2009 and has kept it there since. In the same month it began 'quantitative easing' – buying government bonds to provide further monetary loosening. It has added more inventive policies, such as low funding costs specifically targeted at bank lending to households and businesses (the ECB copied this policy in late 2014, and finally followed suit with the large-scale asset purchases in January 2015, six years after the Bank of England).

The Bank of England could have done more than it did. But its activism contrasts with an ECB constantly behind the curve, and its expertise lends it intellectual heft. So there is every reason to think that the British members of the ECB leadership would have had considerable influence, which would have made the euro's central bank lean towards lower interest rates and an earlier adoption of bond purchases. The monetary contraction and credit crunch in the eurozone would have been less onerous as a result. It is quite possible that if the ECB had bought bonds in large quantities in 2009, the eurozone would have been spared self-fulfilling panics in the bond markets and the sovereign debt crisis might never have happened.

Otherwise, it is quite likely that the United Kingdom would have fallen on the wrong side of the market panic in 2010–11. While the public debt was moderate by eurozone standards, the government's deficit was second only to Greece's when the sovereign debt crisis first spun out of control. Britain's metastasised banking system, like that of Ireland, was an additional vulnerability. It is therefore quite possible that, had the United Kingdom been in the euro, its governments and its banks would have faced the same rise in borrowing costs as Italy, an economy of roughly the same size. In contrast with Italy, however, the United Kingdom would have had the political heft to demand that the eurozone's collective policy tools be used to stabilise the gilt (UK government bond) market. The most likely outcome is that, rather than preferentially buying the bonds of crisis-hit countries including the United Kingdom, the ECB would have resolved to start big and broad-based purchases of all member countries' sovereign bonds years before Frankfurt finally resolved to do so in January 2015.

Fiscal Policy

The coalition government that took office in Westminster in May 2010 could match Berlin in its enthusiasm for cutting deficits. While comparisons with Greece were far-fetched – the United Kingdom is a richer and much-better-run country, and it entered the crisis with much less public debt – the deficit was worryingly high. David Cameron and George Osborne declared that the state should balance its finances like a thrifty household, much as Angela Merkel praised the proverbially prudent Swabian housewife. But their commitment to austerity was more parochial than hers. The coalition government's plan for economic recovery was predicated on exports to Britain's trading partners – above all the eurozone – picking up the slack (together with private investment) from the cutbacks to public spending.

It was always in the United Kingdom's interest that its European neighbours should not take the same medicine as it did, or at least not to the same degree. But Cameron and Osborne could hardly preach to other Europeans the Keynesian anticyclical policies they refused to practice at home. Nor, as outsiders to the common currency, could they claim much of a stake in the euro countries' decisions on fiscal policy. Even so, it is worth noting that David Cameron refused to sign up to Angela Merkel's fiscal compact, forcing her into an inter-governmental, rather than an EU, treaty with twenty-six countries (the Czech Republic declined as well). It may have been for the wrong reasons (largely to satisfy eurosceptics in his own Tory party), and it was of little consequence for the rest of Europe, but had the United Kingdom been inside the euro, it would have mattered enormously.

The whole purpose of the compact was to regulate more tightly the spending behaviour of eurozone members; and it was Angela Merkel's quid pro quo for acquiescing to a permanent, treaty-based rescue fund (the ESM). The British government, however, acutely aware that its own fiscal consolidation plans relied on growth in continental Europe, would have pushed for more relaxed budget limits in countries with room to spend in order to compensate for fiscal contraction by countries with no other choice (including the United Kingdom itself). UK economic interests, as well as domestic politics which

militated against accepting more centralised rules on budgetary freedom, would have made it much harder for Germany to secure the
policy combination Berlin did, in the event, obtain: sizeable financial
aid from creditor to debtor countries in return for much tighter limits
on how the recipients – and, in principle, the donors – would be
allowed to run their finances.

National Autonomy

Significantly smaller financial transfers than actually transpired
would by themselves have reduced the grip creditor Europe exercised
through the troika. The troika itself may not have existed in its actual
form, or at all (Britain may well have preferred a pure IMF operation). But no doubt there would still have been a push for centralised
control of policies among the core euro countries of the eurozone, in
particular France and Germany and their closest allies. Berlin would
still have wanted to keep debtor countries in line; Paris would still
have pushed for a common 'economic government' for the eurozone;
and both would still have adhered to a policy analysis that said the
monetary union could only function properly with greater sharing of
resources across countries.

A UK presence inside the euro would have served as a strong
counterweight to this centralising bias. For cultural and historical
reasons – and partly because of the way the EU is depicted in the
press – the British public is much more averse to the idea of closer
union than most continental European countries. That, more than
any economic consideration, is why the United Kingdom has stayed
out of the euro, and why Britain is the only country that is seriously
contemplating a departure from the EU. But it is also why the United
Kingdom, had it been part of the monetary union, would have resisted
the accumulation of power by the Commission in the interests of the
big creditor countries. To much of Britain's elite, let alone its electorate, the centralisation would have seemed wrong in principle and
the institutionalisation of creditor power inimical to British interests.
Eurozone governance would not have moved as far in that direction if
the United Kingdom had had a say.

Britain's Benefit from Membership

In all of these ways, a United Kingdom that had participated in the single currency would have pulled the eurozone's crisis response in a better direction. Not because British policymaking is more enlightened (though on some issues, such as monetary policy, there is a case for claiming this) or more concerned with the European interest. But the particular substance of what the United Kingdom would have pursued in its own selfish interests, and the way these interests happen to relate to those of other countries, would have tilted the scales of compromise in the monetary union's councils towards a less devastating economic and political trajectory. Less excessive austerity (in the rest of Europe, not necessarily in the United Kingdom itself) and more accommodating monetary policy would have avoided at least some of the lost growth; there is a good chance the eurozone's second recession, perhaps even the sovereign debt crisis, would have been avoided altogether. The financial fragmentation that contributed to the economic downturn and ended up threatening the euro's survival would have been nipped in the bud. Much smaller rescue packages would have contained the erosion of political goodwill between eurozone members, and this – together with better economic performance – would have left Europe's electoral grounds much less fertile for populists and extremists of the left and the right.

The benefit from all this to the United Kingdom should be obvious. Had the eurozone been growing in 2011–12, the boost to British exports would most likely have returned the economy to solid growth much earlier (as it was, it stagnated until 2013). The banking sector would not have had to contend with the uncertainty involved in the prospect of a euro break-up. To guess how British politics would have evolved as a result is recklessly speculative, but it is fair to suppose that with the eurozone less discredited by economic failure and the coalition government benefiting from stronger domestic growth, there would have been less for Ukip's eurosceptic insurgency to feed on before the 2014 and 2015 elections, and the Tory right wing's pressure on its own prime minister would have been weaker as a result.

Brown's Five Tests Today

In the 1990s, there was a real debate about whether the United Kingdom would be well served by euro membership. The decision was taken, of course, to stay out. After the crisis, however, what was once an open if uneven debate (scepticism was always dominant) turned into a non-existent one. The unquestioned consensus is now that the crisis demonstrated how deeply flawed the euro was and that the United Kingdom should breathe a sigh of relief that it had not joined. Those who were against it back then barely manage to keep themselves from gloating, while most of those who were in favour make a point of expressing their contrition. Official policy, too, changed when the coalition took office in 2010. Labour's policy was to be open in principle to joining when it was judged to be in Britain's economic interest – as determined by the Treasury's five tests. David Cameron's government swept even the theoretical prospect of joining into the dustbin along with the five-tests framework.

The argument above suggests that both gloating and contrition are misplaced. Properly understood, the crisis showed that the benefits to the United Kingdom from euro membership would have been greater, not smaller, than seemed to be the case before 2008. That does not clinch the argument in favour of joining the euro, but it does show the idea that the crisis should bury the debate for good is all wrong. The political reasons for taking euro membership off the agenda are clear enough, but they do not reflect a dispassionate consideration of what would be best for Britain.

How euro membership might have benefited the United Kingdom during the crisis is, however, an argument about the past. What is done is done, and even if Britain joined the euro tomorrow, it would be too late to save it from the effects of Europe's self-inflicted economic losses. Instead we should ask: how do things stand today?

In the political and economic debate, the original five tests have been superseded by the conviction that a monetary union cannot work economically without a fiscal union, and that a fiscal union is politically impossible without a political union. This has become an unquestioned axiom in the British political debate, as was quite visible in the Scottish referendum campaign. The pro-independence camp never gave a satisfactory answer to how an independent Scotland could keep the pound without subjecting itself to precisely the kind of fiscal and economic suzerainty that independence was supposed to do away with.

Since both fiscal union and political union with the rest of Europe are unacceptable to a majority of the British people, this seems to rule out monetary union with it too. But that, as I have argued, is a non sequitur, although one believed almost universally.[4] Its main function is to make the five tests look irrelevant, for if it were true that only a fiscal and political union could make the euro safe from balance-of-payments crises, then Britain would conclude that the euro was not in its interest even if the five tests were all satisfied.

Given that this is not true, however, the tests remain worthwhile. They have stood the test of time fairly well, as far as they go. The problem is that they do not go very far. What happened in the crisis reveals the extent to which the tests, whether or not they are met, ask the wrong questions in the first place.

The tests are as follows.[5]

Convergence. Are business cycles and economic structures compatible so that we and others could live comfortably with euro interest rates on a permanent basis?

Flexibility. If problems emerge, is there sufficient flexibility to deal with them?

Investment. Would joining EMU create better conditions for firms making long-term decisions to invest in Britain?

Financial services. What impact would entry into EMU have on the competitive position of the United Kingdom's financial services industry, particularly the City's wholesale markets?

Growth, stability and employment. In summary, will joining EMU promote higher growth, stability and a lasting increase in jobs?

The decisive tests are really the first two. The government's own assessment was that the UK economy would benefit according to the last three criteria if 'sustainable and durable convergence' was achieved, as defined by fulfilling the convergence and flexibility tests. From either of these two, Britain has less to fear than is commonly thought.

How Bad Would It Be to Lose Monetary Independence?

We have already noted that the freedom to have very different interest rates from those set by a much larger trading partner can only be exercised within very tight limits, regardless of the currency regime. And within those limits, countries that do have independent monetary policy have tended to use it largely to reproduce the interest rates of larger neighbours. That is why I noted in Chapters 1 and 2 that for European countries monetary independence is not as grand as it is sometimes made out to be.

In the case of the United Kingdom, those who favoured entering the euro at the outset or in the early 2000s pointed to the fact that British and euro area interest rates tracked one another quite closely, as Figure 10.1 shows. This was true for real short-term rates and both real and nominal long-term rates. (The real rate is the nominal rate adjusted for inflation, which better represents the true cost of borrowing and reward for lending. Nominal short-term rates have also moved closely in step, with a gap between them reflecting the United Kingdom's higher inflation rate.) As for Britain's economic cycle, it has become much more synchronised with the eurozone countries' than it used to, to the point where the UK economy tracks the eurozone economy as closely as Germany and more closely than for instance Finland.[6] Since the end of the recession in the early 1990s the distance between the 'output gap' of the UK economy and that of the euro area (a measure of an economy's distance from its normal potential, indicating its position in the economic cycle) has hovered around 1 percentage point of GDP (see Figure 10.2). That is hardly an unbridgeable difference.

The current moment is the harshest test of monetary policy compatibility, because after a decade and a half of convergence, the United Kingdom and the eurozone have diverged in the last two years. Since 2013

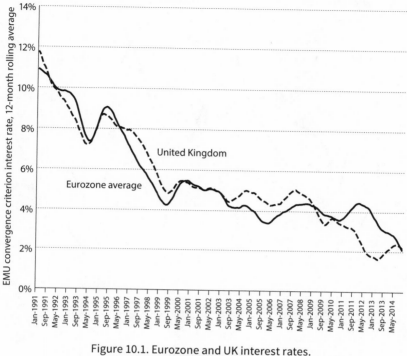

Figure 10.1. Eurozone and UK interest rates.
Source: Eurostat.

the Bank of England has been making noises about rising rates after a good economic growth spurt, whereas the ECB is keeping rates around zero and has belatedly launched additional monetary stimulus. Similarly, the UK output gap outperforms that of the eurozone by 2 percentage points of GDP, the largest difference in twenty-five years. The UK recovery, which gained speed in 2013, is clearly ahead of the eurozone's. But this divergence is not one caused by external 'asymmetric shocks' – events that call for different monetary policy in the two economies. It is the other way round: difference in policy has caused the divergence. Specifically, the contrast is due to the ECB's mistakes – as explained before, it should have followed the Bank of England's lead towards a bond-buying programme much earlier. Such policy-generated divergence is not an argument for having separate monetary policies, but for having the right monetary policy (in the years since 2009, one more like the United Kingdom's). As I argued above, that would have been more likely for the eurozone had Britain been a member.

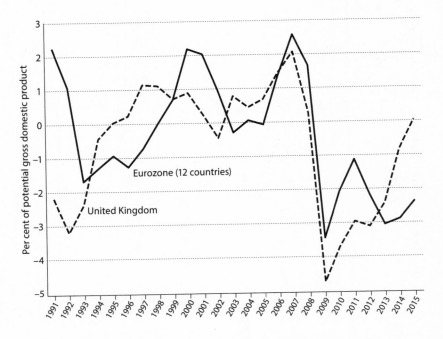

Figure 10.2. Output gaps in the UK and the euro area economies.
Source: EC Annual Macroeconomic Database.

In any case, if sterling and euro market interest rates do diverge for a while, it does not prove that Britain is better off for having its own monetary policy. As we have seen, other stabilisation tools are available, and could be used more actively if interest-rate setting could not. In the five-tests frameworks, the Treasury recognised that fiscal policy can and should play a role in macroeconomic stabilisation. Even when government budgets are constrained, we know since the crisis that the effect of monetary policy depends on broader credit conditions, or the ease with which actual people (as opposed to the Bank of England's circle of counterparties) can borrow money. These broader credit conditions remain amenable to national policy action even without domestic control of the central bank rate; indeed there is now broad agreement that the interest rate is a poor tool for financial stabilisation. The United Kingdom has been at the forefront of developing policies and institutions to better control credit creation

– what is now called 'macroprudential' policy. This consists of rules aiming to tighten the reins on the financial system if credit grows too fast and causes economic overheating, or to give freer rein if credit becomes too dear and holds economic activity back. If the price of predictable export and import prices (a fixed exchange rate) is to give up fine-tuning the national official interest rate, the existence of fiscal and macroprudential stabilisation tools makes that sacrifice a lot cheaper.

Because foreign exchange prices can move instantaneously whereas prices of goods and services only change gradually, floating exchange rates would overreact to the economic shocks they are supposed to cushion against even if foreign exchange markets were fully rational and driven only by economic fundamentals.[7] And in fact, nominal exchange rates are set by financial exchanges whose participants behave in volatile and short-term ways. In the words of Willem Buiter:

> Like most other financial markets, the market for foreign exchange ... reflects not just [economic] fundamentals (or people's view of fundamentals) but all the fears, phobias, hopes and impulses that drive foreign exchange traders and their principals. Bubbles, sudden mood swings from euphoria to despondency, from irrational exuberance to unwarranted depression, herding behaviour and bandwagon effects are the rule, not the exception.[8]

A floating exchange rate is as likely to be a source of instability as an instrument of stabilisation.

A Common Fallacy of 'Flexibility'

Now consider the second of the five tests.

Discussions of flexibility too often assume that the only thing that matters is *price* flexibility: the tendency, after an economic disturbance, of relative prices to fall for goods and services that find themselves in less demand (or greater supply) and to rise in response to greater demand (or curtailed supply). But the flexibility of the *reaction* to price changes matters just as much. There is little benefit in a falling exchange rate if unemployed workers and idle capital cannot move into the export activities that the cheaper domestic currency makes more profitable. While this may narrow a trade deficit by reducing imports, it would not in such a situation increase exports or overall output. Since a depreciation impoverishes consumers – that is what more expensive imports mean – exchange rate flexibility without the flexibility to move resources from one sector to another could cause a fall in living standards without a swift compensation of more jobs and higher production. This is often missed by optimal currency area-based arguments.

This point is illustrated very vividly by two European countries whose real exchange rates fell sharply in the crisis, but where the depreciation failed to have the effects you would predict if resources were reallocated smoothly in response to price changes. One is the United Kingdom itself (see Figure 10.3). The pound fell from an average value of about €1.45 in the three years before the crisis to about €1.15 in the three years following 2008, a nominal depreciation of

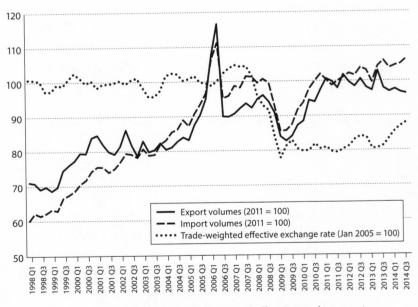

Figure 10.3. UK goods trade volumes and effective exchange rate.
Source: Office of National Statistics.

more than 20 per cent. The trade-weighted exchange rate (which measures sterling's value against all trading partners' currencies) depreciated by the same amount. The government naturally expected the trade balance to improve, with a boost to exports and a shift of domestic demand away from imports towards domestic goods and services. One reason why the economic recovery and fiscal deficit reduction failed to materialise as planned was that trade did not respond this way. The trade balance remained stubbornly negative. Export volumes regained their previous level, then stagnated. Even though the eurozone's own goal hurt the United Kingdom's biggest export market from spring 2011, the depreciation against the euro should have helped; in any case, sales volumes to non-euro markets stagnated as well. The UK export market share held up no better than those of Spain, Portugal and the Netherlands.[9] The most likely reason is that instead of increasing sales, exporting companies left prices in foreign currency unchanged and pocketed the increased profit margin. This could be a consequence of the floating exchange rate itself: if exporters do not know whether a depreciation reflects a permanent change or a temporary windfall, it is risky to expand. Import volumes, too, returned to their previous levels and remained there, unaffected by their higher cost.

The other example may come as a surprise to many. Greece, despite its membership of the eurozone, has achieved a large real exchange rate depreciation through swingeing cuts in average wages. In nominal terms, the wage per hour worked in Greece fell from €7.60 to €6.30, a 17 per cent cut, between 2007 and 2014. In every other eurozone country, the nominal hourly wage rose in the same period. In Germany, it grew (albeit after years of stagnation) by 15 per cent from €21.60, or almost three times the Greek wage, to €24.90, almost four times as high. Greece effectively devalued – economists call it an internal devaluation – by lowering the labour cost of production in Greece relative to its trading partners. But much like in Britain this real exchange rate depreciation had little to show for it. Greek export volumes tumbled by one-fifth with the global crisis in 2008–9 and have remained depressed since (see Figure 10.4).[10]

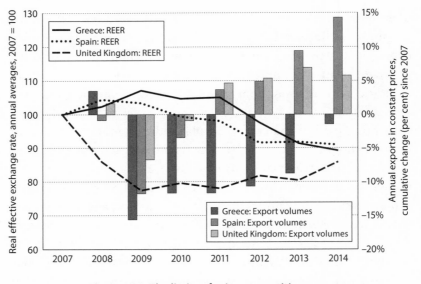

Figure 10.4. The limits of price competitiveness.
Source: EC Annual Macroeconomic Database.

Contrast those two cases with Spain. Also in the euro, it had no more room for a nominal depreciation than Greece did, though it, too, has seen real wages fall. But not on the same scale, and by nowhere near the amount that British wages have fallen in international terms. Yet its trade performance has left Britain's in the dust. While imports have been pared back by Spain's recession, exports have grown fast – faster than its export markets, where Spanish companies have increased their share. Clearly price flexibility does not guarantee the adjustment of quantities; and a lot of quantity adjustment can take place while prices remain rigid. Without the flexibility that really matters – the ability to move resources from failing sectors to more productive ones – price flexibility may do more harm than good, at least in the short run. If real flexibility exists, moreover, it is unclear how much one needs nominal exchange rate changes at all. As in Spain, capital and labour can respond quickly to their underemployment in unprofitable industries and move elsewhere. (Such a response could result in lower wages if the new industries pay less well. The point is that the flexibility that matters most is the quantity adjustment – resources moving from one sector to another – not the price adjustment.)

To sum up, little in the UK crisis experience suggests that either the convergence test or the flexibility test is further from being met than ten or fifteen years ago. If anything, the opposite is the case.

Greater Guernsey?

The five tests in any case encourage a rather narrow perspective on the euro question. It is becoming clear that the consequences of the single currency relate to institutional and structural conditions as much as they do to the classic challenges of short-to-medium-term economic stabilisation that concern optimal currency area theory. This fact alters the relative importance of each of the five tests. The first two – which in the light of stabilisation concerns trump and largely determine the others – are more easily met than they once were, and than many think they still are. The institutional evolution of the eurozone, however, increases the significance of the fourth test: how euro membership would affect Britain's enormous financial sector. It was always to be expected that monetary union might align its members' interests in how the financial industry is governed, and the eurozone's travails have accelerated that alignment. The existence of the euro, in other words, means that its members will increasingly shape the environment in which UK financial companies have to do business.

One can question exactly how much benefit the United Kingdom at large derives from hosting Europe's largest financial centre in the City of London. On the one hand, it doubtlessly plays an outsize role in the British economy.[11] Since 2009, financial and insurance services have accounted for about one-tenth of UK GDP, having doubled in size (measured by economic value added) in the decade before the crisis. The financial sector employs more than a million people, and both financial and insurance services generate persistent and large export surpluses. They pay more than £30 billion a year in taxes. On the other hand, the large banking sector (with assets about five times Britain's annual GDP) exposes the country to financial instability. This proved costly for the taxpayer in the crisis, when several of the biggest banks were rescued from bankruptcy by the government. A seemingly never-ending string of scandals, from rate-rigging to fraudulent sales of payment protection insurance, also shows that some of the banks' presumed value added consisted of ill-gotten gains that should not be counted as a contribution to the economy.[12]

For the purpose of passing judgment on Britain's self-exclusion from Europe's monetary union, let us take it as given that providing financial services to the rest of the world provides the country with a net benefit. What are the consequences for the success and profitability of this business of whether Britain is within or outside the euro? Two implications of monetary union are particularly important: the existence of a large market of financial products denominated in the single currency and related to counterparts whose home is a euro member state; and the evolution of unified rules, regulations and supervisory authorities for the eurozone as a whole.

The first is, in principle, positive for the UK financial industry, which is well-placed to supply the new and deeper markets with its services, as it has been doing successfully so far. But a push exists to require more euro-denominated financial activity to be carried out from within the eurozone. The UK government has already had to take the ECB to court over the central bank's desire to prohibit companies located in non-euro countries from clearing or settling transactions in euro-denominated derivatives. While the ECJ sided with the United Kingdom, British leaders are justified in seeing this as an attempted ECB land grab, and one can barely fault them for sensing behind it a more general threat of business-snatching by euro countries with significant financial sectors. That threat, while not very great, would be smaller if the United Kingdom itself was a euro country.

A much greater challenge for the UK financial industry is the very rapid development of supranational rules for banking and finance. Regulatory harmonisation had already been proceeding at the EU level for some time, but it picked up speed when the financial crisis exposed just how inadequate a nationally fragmented system of financial regulation is for dealing with an integrated market in financial services.

The sorry saga of Icesave illustrates how badly things can go. For a long time before the crisis, EU banks have enjoyed the right of 'passporting': offering banking services to customers in any other EU country without opening a local subsidiary company. That means the activity is governed by the banks' home regulator rather than by the host country. The Icelandic bank Landsbanki offered deposit accounts under the Icesave brand in the United Kingdom and the Netherlands. (Iceland is not in the EU but is a member of the European Economic Area, by which it gains access to the single market.) These promised better rates than local banks, but as it turned out were protected – or rather not protected – by a much punier deposit guarantee scheme than the British or Dutch ones. When Iceland's banks collapsed in October 2008, there was nowhere near enough money in the guarantee scheme for depositors to get their money back, and the Icelandic government rejected responsibility for the losses. This caused a minor diplomatic crisis (Landsbanki's UK assets were seized under terrorism legislation) but the courts ultimately agreed with Iceland's stance. The EU's 1994 Deposit Insurance Directive, passed when EU countries worried about too much government support (which would lure business away) rather than too little, required governments to make sure the banking sector put in place a deposit insurance scheme, but proscribed backing it with public money. The result was unprotected British and Dutch depositors.

The Icesave affair is just one example of why, by 2009, it was necessary to choose between 'more Europe or less Europe' – more common regulation or re-erected barriers to capital flows between EU countries. For obvious reasons, the UK financial sector overwhelmingly preferred 'more Europe'. A bigger market with homogenous regulation – provided it is not *too* onerous – is preferable to smaller markets, each with its own rules.

But if common rules are generally preferable to fragmented ones, some common rules are much more strongly preferred than others. The more financial regulation is decided at the European level, the more it matters for Britain that the rules are as compatible as possible with a thriving UK financial sector. And that depends on UK influence when the rules are made. That influence has been waning: since the crisis, a number of decisions have gone the wrong way from a British perspective. One example is the imposition of upper limits on the capital buffers national regulators could require from the banks in their jurisdiction.[13] This means the Bank of England – which has been at the forefront of regulatory reform to make banks safer since 2009 – might be at the mercy of European Commission approval to rein in a future credit bubble. Another example is how the European Parliament successfully insisted on a cap on bankers' bonuses to be included in the EU's updated capital regulations. Both measures go against what UK authorities consider to be the best way to regulate banks.

The main worry for Britain and its financial sector is that the euro area countries 'gang up' against them, using their numerical advantage to dominate. As one critical think-tank puts it, there is a risk that the United Kingdom will be 'out of the euro but run by the euro'.[14] The community of interest forged by their common currency could increasingly mean that euro members systematically find their interests in financial policy aligned – and aligned against UK interests. As their number is set to rise, it will become increasingly easy for them to impose their will. The eurozone's banking union – which lifted some bank supervision and resolution power to the supranational level – reinforces this process. The UK government is highly alert to the risk, which is why it insisted that decisions by the European Banking Authority must be passed by a 'double majority' of both euro and non-euro countries.[15] (David Cameron's so-called veto of the fiscal compact was also triggered by his attempt – and failure – to secure 'safeguards' for the City of London.) But as more countries join the euro, it is hard to see how this arrangement can be sustained, let alone broadened to other EU or eurozone decision-making bodies with influence over how finance is regulated in Europe and thus on how the UK financial sector must conduct a large part of its business.

That makes it increasingly likely that a decade or so from now, euro non-membership will leave the United Kingdom's financial industry at the mercy of rules set predominantly by a group with little reason to care about its interests and which the Westminster government is ever less able to influence. Of course the United Kingdom can and will fight hard to protect the fundamental principle of the single market that the same rules should hold for all EU members, whether in or out of the euro. But common rules for all does not entail rules that help the City thrive. There is much talk of the British government appealing to the so-called Luxembourg compromise, a political understanding dating back to the 1960s that no member state should be outvoted on matters of essential national interest. But the fiscal compact, which circumvented the British 'veto' with a separate intergovernmental treaty, should cast doubt on the eurozone's willingness to be held back from the harmonisation it thinks (in that case wrongly) it requires.

The logical end of this process, especially if Britain continues to contemplate leaving the EU altogether (let alone if it proceeds to do so), is that its financial services industry will have to live by rules made overwhelmingly by others, who moreover are not particularly sympathetic to the sector. That is not the end of the world, but it is probably the beginning of the end of the City's dominance in European financial markets. Once the eurozone finds itself setting banking rules as a collective, with little need for the United Kingdom's acquiescence, it will set those rules as it collectively sees most fit. Such common policy positions may not exist in a systematic form today, but they will surely develop, and develop differently from the views of a Britain outside the common currency.

Even without influence, and as a consequence with less dominance within the eurozone market, the UK financial services sector can still do thriving business with the rest of the world. It could, in other words, become the world's largest offshore financial centre; Britain would effectively turn into not even Little England but a Greater Guernsey. This slightly insulting quip became a talking point for German officials in 2012, after David Cameron's insistence on protecting the City from continental Europe's plan for banking union. But even Greater Guernsey may be too optimistic. Every offshore financial centre depends for its success on the patronage of the bigger economies that provide them with capital; Guernsey itself has depended on British tolerance of its financial activities and tax secrecy. As long as Britain remains in the EU, it will be subject to European majority decisions on its financial business with the rest of the world. If it left, it would have to hope that the rest of the EU would tolerate a giant offshore financial centre on its immediate borders rather than decide to make life harder for it. Either way, the loss of UK influence entailed by its non-membership of the euro – a loss that is already visible and will only intensify – makes for a precarious economic model.

The Euro and National Power

The loss of influence is not limited to financial sector policy.

The deepest political consequence of the euro's creation, at least for the United Kingdom, is that it spelt the end of centuries of British foreign policy aimed at maintaining a balance of power in Europe. The history of English and British alliances since early modern times has been one of preventing the formation of a dominant power centre on the European mainland. When most of western Europe proved willing to pool sovereignty by giving up their national currencies for the euro, it was going to create a community of interests that the United Kingdom could never hope to counterbalance. The eurozone's disastrous policy choices have partly camouflaged the power that monetary union collectively creates for its members, but the episodes listed in the previous section show that even now, that unity is a muscle to be flexed. If the argument of this book is right, Europe's monetary union is more robust than many think and will become more influential in European affairs with time, marginalising those who remain outside of it. The evolution of banking union, and the likely entry into the euro of most of the remaining 'outs', are steps in that direction.

This means that the creation of the euro left the United Kingdom with just one choice: between resigning itself to marginalisation or joining the eurozone. Monetary union in Europe meant that the United Kingdom's interests – no longer just in an economic sense, but its deepest national interests in terms of power and influence over its own circumstances – would incontrovertibly be best served by having a seat at the table. The country's most impressive politicians in the last half-century, Margaret Thatcher and Tony Blair, both clearly understood this deeply political point. That is why Thatcher never wanted the euro to see the light of day and why, once it was going to happen anyway, Blair was determined that Britain should join it.

ELEVEN
Remembering What the Euro Is For

WHAT IS AT STAKE

I WROTE AT THE BEGINNING of this book that the euro was the ultimate test of Spinelli's belief in the need to tear down the barriers behind which the nation state was erected. The entire European project has been premised on the gradual pursuit of this goal: the removal of national barriers one by one. Monetary unification is the last and most ambitious step in this process.

Today's conventional wisdom, whether in its eurosceptic or pro-integrationist guise, has it that Spinelli was fundamentally mistaken. Both shades have been on garish display in the stand-off between Greece and its creditors. The sceptics blame the euro for the economic failure and financial turmoil and condemn the folly of 'ever closer union'. Those committed to deeper European integration defend Spinelli by radicalising him: they say that monetary union is failing not because it tore down national barriers but because it did not tear them down comprehensively enough it left the nation-state with too much margin for error. If only the single currency could be bolstered by fiscal and political union, they say, the federalist credo would be proved right: you cannot cross a chasm in two jumps. The problem with this view is that this is a chasm the peoples of Europe are not willing to cross at all. If the critics are right, then the degree of union that the euro requires is incompatible with democracy in Europe. If integration cannot be gradual enough for voters to condone it, then it has already gone too far.

Can Europe have both monetary union and democracy? That is what is at stake in my main claim that the conventional wisdom is false in both its eurosceptic and pro-European versions. We will only be in a position to ask how the euro may strengthen Europe – and this should have been the most important question all along – once we have refuted those who say the euro must necessarily weaken it.

Exonerating the Euro: A Summary of the Argument

Before suggesting an answer to that question, let us sum up the refutation. The economic problems of the countries that have thrown their lot in with the single currency were not caused by the euro. Nor has monetary union stopped them from getting out of the quagmire their bad policy choices landed them in.

The current account asymmetries between the euro's member economies before the crisis did not constitute a problem with the currency itself. They did not reflect a problem of export competitiveness but credit-fuelled import binges. The debt accumulations they amounted to would have happened anyway, as they did within and between other, non-euro, economies. In any case, capital flows from richer to poorer countries are no bad thing: they are not a problem to be avoided but a challenge to be harnessed better than the eurozone deficit countries did.

The debt crisis that exploded in 2010 necessitated neither the international rescue loans nor the associated fiscal austerity at anywhere near the scale they were pursued. Public and private debt restructurings could and should have been carried out instead and before any rescue programmes.

Default and restructuring were never in themselves a danger to the euro or any individual country's membership of it. Unless a country freely chooses to exit, the euro can only disintegrate if the ECB expressly forces this outcome to happen. Even the danger of ECB overreach could have been and still can be neutralised with a comprehensive restructuring of vulnerable banks (combined with temporary capital controls if necessary). By dispelling any doubts about the restructured banks' solvency, this would remove the ECB's legal ability to threaten to cut off liquidity support. At the root, the eurozone's crisis is a result of ideological resistance to writing down debts – whether those of banks or those of sovereigns.

In the first phase of the crisis, Germany should therefore be blamed not for giving too little but for giving too much. It was best placed to insist that Greece's sovereign debt in private hands should be written down and, half a year later, that Irish banks should be restructured, before it acquiesced to rescue loans. In the ensuing years Berlin demanded and obtained restructurings in Greece and Cyprus. Its failure to do so at the outset, buckling instead to pressure from France and others, was the single most damaging mistake in the entire eurozone crisis.

The political economy of the rescue loans then combined with outright economic misdiagnosis to produce the harmfully tight fiscal and monetary policies that pushed the eurozone back into recession. Again, nothing in the euro's structure required this. Monetary union was not a disaster waiting to happen, it had disaster thrust upon it.

Looking forward, the prospects for the eurozone, and for Europe more generally, are brighter than they appear to most people.

Since the lack of fiscal and political union is not what caused the eurozone's economic stagnation, it is wrong to think that this is a permanent flaw that will continue to weigh on the economy. Nothing in the structure of the euro stops the eurozone from correcting the policy mistakes that have made its economy stagnate: removing excessive debt overhangs, loosening fiscal and monetary policy, and letting the euro's mechanisms for dealing with balance-of-payments crises – emergency liquidity assistance and Target2 balances – work freely instead of punishing the countries assisted by them.

The eurozone has already gone some way towards correcting its mistakes. From late 2011, it reversed the monetary tightening, slowed down fiscal austerity, and took steps to end the fragmentation of the eurozone financial markets. It dealt definitively with a part (but too small a part) of the Greek debt. In 2014–15 monetary policy was loosened further. In the spring and summer of 2015, however, the bad old habits reemerged in the Greek loan negotiations.

The rising political support for parties opposed to austerity and supportive of debt restructuring puts pressure on the mainstream establishment to move further in that direction. Doing so would make a stronger recovery more likely.

And finally, many countries have reformed the supply side of their economies, and will reap the rewards when demand finally picks up.

Even to readers who find this argument convincing, it still only makes a negative claim: that the euro was not as bad for its members as is usually claimed: no 'giant historic mistake'. A positive case for the euro, in contrast, is something most Europeans have forgotten. That is a natural consequence of how the euro has been disowned even by its closest kin, who have conspired with the sceptics to dump the blame for Europe's stagnation onto the single currency. In the concluding pages, then, I want to revive an idea about what the euro, that orphaned currency, is for.

THE EURO AND ECONOMIC STRENGTH

Europe is small – 7 per cent of the world's population, as Angela Merkel so often points out. There is no question of the region ever again dominating the world as it once did. But a question remains over whether it will at least defend a space in which it can run its own affairs, let alone retain – or regain – a leadership role in global politics.

When Syriza won the Greek election in January 2015, it was rightly seen as a sign of European disunity – and this was initially more acutely appreciated by outsiders than by the Europeans whom that disunity directly affects. Here is how *The Economist* described the Russian reaction:

> For the Kremlin, which sees the disintegration of the euro zone and the weakening of the European Union as among its main strategic interests, the Greek election results were a gift. Vladimir Putin was quick to congratulate Alexis Tsipras on his victory, and Russian state television gleefully reported that Syriza's landslide means the end of the EU's hold over Greece, which 'brought the country nothing but unemployment and misery'.[1]

The glee of a Russian president who is literally waging a war against European integration should remind Europe what is at stake. His claim that the EU's policies have weakened it economically is, unfortunately, correct. The EU has inflicted unemployment and misery on itself. More frighteningly, Putin and his claques see this, again rightly, as undermining Europe's political functioning as well as its economic prowess. The conflict between creditors and debtors has debilitated the monetary union's economies. But it also robs the eurozone, and by extension all of Europe, of its unity of purpose. Both make it harder for Europe to stand up for itself against powers that are either hostile or simply want to shape the world as they see fit. Many countries have made this observation, none more keenly than the emerging economic powerhouses of what used to be called the third world. If these ever looked to Europe (and the United States) for inspiration, advice or leadership, that credibility is gone after the financial crisis. Europe has not fully appreciated how deeply its prestige has been dented, and how much influence it has lost as a result.

European economic prowess and unity of purpose are goals towards which the euro can and should make a contribution, even if its leaders' policy choices have prevented that from happening so far. Let us quickly recall the economic arguments from earlier chapters. First, a single currency makes prices predictable for businesses across a market of 330 million people, and extends the safety of trading in your own national currency to trade with other countries that previously used different monies. Monetary union is good for trade, and trade is good for productivity and growth. Second, it makes it easier to invest across borders (even if cross-border capital flows needed no helping hand in the euro's spectacularly bubbly early years). The euro, at least when bubbles are kept under control, can help channel savings from the older, richer parts of Europe to investments in the younger, poorer, and potentially faster-growing, parts. In both these ways, the 'one market, one money' slogan got it right: letting both trade and capital work on larger stages lifts the limits that a small scale imposes on productivity. And, finally, the removal of the devaluation 'quick fix' encourages both companies and governments to address the sources of low productivity – except, of course, when a historic credit bubble throws cheap credit at anything that moves.

Paradoxical as it sounds today, the euro has also offered stability. The 1970s and 1980s featured competitive devaluations and haggles over the central bank swap lines and exchange rate supports needed to prevent them. These pitted countries against one another and exposed governments as not in control. Overcoming that divisiveness was an important motive for the politicians who brought the euro into being. It may not look that way, but they largely succeeded in this. It is an amazing fact about the euro that five years of massive balance-of-payments crises did not break it to pieces. At the time of writing, even Greece is still clinging on. As I pointed out in Chapter 5, thanks to the euro's central banking and cross-border settlement systems, immense flows of capital could flee the periphery countries without ending their participation in the euro. That political leaders through gratuitous action added economic pain and instability, to the point of putting the euro's survival in jeopardy, is a responsibility that must rest on their shoulders rather than be blamed on the single currency.

Unity in Diversity

It has been a long time, however, since Europe's place on the world stage was secured mainly by its economic power. While Europe still accounts for a quarter of the world economy, that share will certainly diminish – not because Europeans get poorer but because the rest of the world will gradually become as rich as they are. Europe's greatest and most sustainable source of political power is of the soft kind: the power of cultural, intellectual and political attraction.

It took Pope Francis to remind Europe's leaders of this in a speech to the European Parliament. Europe seems 'elderly and haggard' like a 'grandmother', he observed, 'feeling less and less a protagonist in a world which frequently regards it with aloofness, mistrust and even, at times, suspicion.' He went on to say that after the economic crisis,

> there has been growing mistrust on the part of citizens towards institutions considered to be aloof, engaged in laying down rules perceived as insensitive to individual peoples, if not downright harmful… The great ideas which once inspired Europe seem to have lost their attraction, only to be replaced by the bureaucratic technicalities of its institutions.[2]

The pope's message was that the grand European vision and the institutions charged with implementing it have ceased to appeal either to Europeans or to the rest of the world. The implication is that Europe was once capable of inspiring people both at home and abroad with its ideas. The hope is that it can become capable of doing so again.

What are those ideas? They include, of course the Enlightenment tradition, though this by now is the birthright of the entire world and Europeans have little claim to be its only standard-bearer. But there are two other specifically European achievements that deserve to be a source of pride for Europe and a source of inspiration for others. One is the social market economy. While it comes in many shades in different countries, they all share a common and distinctively European commitment to combining market capitalism with an unquestioned public responsibility to ensure decent material conditions for all. The second is precisely the commitment to creating peace and prosperity by sharing sovereignty – the greatest example of which is the EU itself – that is being tested by the euro crisis. Both constitute enormous political, cultural and intellectual contributions to human progress that should serve as a source of pride in Europe and a source of inspiration elsewhere.

What does this have to do with the euro? The current despondency over monetary unification – the widespread view that it was a mistake – has sapped Europe's own faith in these broader ideals. Worse, the prevailing diagnoses of what it takes to end the euro crisis involve actions that actively harm both ideals. The social market economy is threatened by the conflation of productivity with competitiveness, since this elevates lower wages to a policy goal and competition on the basis of price rather than quality to an economic strategy for Europe. The peaceful, democratically endorsed sharing of sovereignty is undermined when politics is defined by a zero-sum game between creditors and debtors. It turns all European countries into debt slaves – literally, in the case of the most troubled debtor countries, but intellectually too. Even Germany is acting against its own best interest, because it is in the grip of a logic putting debt relationships above all other considerations.

Europe needs to regain confidence in its own achievements, and that includes the euro. This is not an appeal for unfounded positive thinking. As this book has shown, there is in fact little wrong with the euro itself. Intellectually and politically disowning it is not a harmless miscomprehension: it leads to wrong policy prescriptions, some of which make the crisis worse and all of which distract attention from the real problems. The first step to regaining confidence in the European project is to see these things for what they are.

That would enable Europe to transcend the current infertility of eurozone politics. Paradoxically, as Chapter 9 argued, a reinvigoration of national autonomy is a necessary political condition both to overcome productivity stagnation and to encourage deeper collaboration between states. Monetary union has opened the door to much further integration – eurobonds, fiscal pooling and common economic governance are all possibilities. But these need to be chosen by each country as being in its interest, not imposed as necessary to avert disaster. To heal the politics of the euro, it must be admitted that it is compatible with more national self-determination than conventional wisdom has it.

It is in this paradox – a willingness to integrate further by nations whose national room for manoeuvre is restored – that the hope lies for the euro's political purpose, and Spinelli's vision, to be fulfilled. The promise of the euro was, and remains, that with one market and one money, Europe will move closer to speaking with one voice.

NOTES

Whenever a referenced article includes a web address, the publication date is the one stamped on the online version. For newspaper articles, this will often be the day before they appeared in print.

CHAPTER ONE

1. *Eurobarometer 82*, Autumn 2014 (http://ec.europa.eu/public_opinion/arc hives/eb/eb82/eb82_en.htm).
2. Angela Merkel, speech to the Bundestag, 26 October 2011 (www.bundesk anzlerin.de/ContentArchiv/DE/Archiv17/Regierungserklaerung/2011/ 2011-10-27-merkel-eu-gipfel.html).
3. Chris Giles and George Parker, 'Osborne urges eurozone to "get a grip"', *The Financial Times*, 20 July 2011 (www.ft.com/cms/s/0/e357fe94-b2ec-11 e0-86b8-00144feabdc0.html).
4. Robert Mundell, 'A theory of optimum currency areas', *American Economic Review* 51(4) (1961): 657–665 (www.jstor.org/discover/10.2307/1812792).
5. The political point is not part of the (purely economic) theory of OCAs, but it naturally follows once one thinks fiscal transfers are economically beneficial or necessary. A good review of the OCA arguments as well as their weaknesses is Franscesco Paolo Mongelli, 'European economic and monetary integration, and the optimum currency area theory', European Commission ECFIN Economic Papers 302, February 2008 (http://ec.europa .eu/economy_finance/publications/publication12081_en.pdf). Mongelli also presents a quick history of European monetary integration and an account of the economic policy debates surrounding its construction.
6. Rogoff made the comment in a panel on 'Is Europe back' at the World Economic Forum conference at Davos in January 2014, which can be watched at www.weforum.org/sessions/summary/europe-back. The panel was widely reported in the press, for example by Ambrose Evans-Pritchard in 'Crippled eurozone to face fresh debt crisis this year, warns ex-ECB strongman Axel Weber', *The Telegraph*, 22 January 2014 (www.telegraph .co.uk/finance/financetopics/davos/10590134/Crippled-eurozone-to-face -fresh-debt-crisis-this-year-warns-ex-ECB-strongman-Axel-Weber.html).

Famous critiques of the European project of monetary unification include Nicholas Kaldor, 'The dynamic effects of the common market', *New Statesman*, 12 March 1971, and Milton Friedman, 'The euro: monetary unity to political disunity?', *Project Syndicate*, 28 August 1997 (www.project-syndicate.org/commentary/the-euro--monetary-unity-to-political-disunity). For contemporary negative verdicts on European monetary union, see for example Vivien A. Schmidt, 'Saving the euro will mean worse trouble for Europe', *Foreign Affairs*, 28 November 2011 (www.foreignaffairs.com/articles/136694/vivien-a-schmidt/saving-the-euro-will-mean-worse-trouble-for-europe), and Paola Subacchi, 'The euro was a bad idea from the start', *Foreign Policy*, 25 February 2015 (http://foreignpolicy.com/2015/02/25/the-euro-was-a-bad-idea-from-the-start/).

7. Martin Wolf, 'Greek debt and a default of statesmanship', *The Financial Times*, 27 January 2015 (www.ft.com/cms/s/0/44c56806-a556-11e4-ad35-00144feab7de.html).

8. See Herman van Rompuy with José Manuel Barroso, Jean-Claude Juncker and Mario Draghi, 'Towards a genuine economic and monetary union', 5 December 2012 (www.consilium.europa.eu/uedocs/cms_data/docs/pressdata/en/ec/134069.pdf) and the so-called Five Presidents' Report: Jean-Claude Juncker with Donald Tusk, Jeroen Dijsselbloem, Mario Draghi and Martin Schulz, 'Completing Europe's economic and monetary union', 22 June 2015 (http://ec.europa.eu/priorities/economic-monetary-union/docs/5-presidents-report_en.pdf). See also Mario Draghi, 'Structural reforms, inflation and monetary policy', Speech to ECB Forum on Central Banking, Sintra, Portugal, 22 May 2015 (www.ecb.europa.eu/press/key/date/2015/html/sp150522.en.html).

9. Versions of such claims are put forward by many of the most respected policymakers and observers inside and outside the eurozone. See, for example, Mario Draghi, 'Stability and prosperity in monetary union', Speech at the University of Helsinki, 27 November 2014 (www.ecb.europa.eu/press/key/date/2014/html/sp141127_1.en.html), and Adair Turner, 'Hubris, realism and the European project', *Centre for European Reform Bulletin*, Issue 100, February/March 2015 (www.cer.org.uk/sites/default/files/bulletin_100.pdf).

10. Thomas Hanke, 'Die Dolchstoßlegende', *Die Zeit*, 7 May 1998 (www.zeit.de/1998/20/Die_Dolchstosslegende/).

11. Andrew Rose's 'One money, one market: estimating the effect of common currencies on trade' (*Economic Policy* 15(30) (April 2000): 8–45 (http://dx.doi.org/10.1111/1468-0327.00056)) was an influential estimate of the significant boost to trade monetary union would bring. Richard Baldwin's 'The euro's trade effects' (ECB Working Paper 594, March 2006; www.ecb.europa.eu/pub/pdf/scpwps/ecbwp594.pdf) provides an exhaustive

overview of later research, and finds that the euro may have boosted intra-eurozone trade by 5–10 per cent, much less than Rose's and other estimates implied. See also Jeffrey Frankel, 'The euro at ten: why do effects on trade between members appear smaller than historical estimates among smaller countries?', *VoxEU.org*, December 2008 (www.voxeu.org/article/euro-ten-why-such-small-trade-effects). Rose revisited the issue of the euro's effect on trade with Reuven Gluck in 'The currency union effect on trade: Redux', *VoxEU.org*, 15 June 2015 (www.voxeu.org/article/currency-union-effect-trade-redux). They conclude that the evidence is confusing but suggests a small boost to exports.

12. European Commission, 'Report on economic and monetary union in the European community' (The Delors Report), April 1989 (http://ec.europa.eu/archives/emu_history/documentation/chapter13/19890412en235repeconommetary_a.pdf).

13. The original 'overshooting' analysis is Rudiger Dornbusch, 'Expectations and exchange rate dynamics', *Journal of Political Economy* 84(6) (December 1976): 1161–1176 (www.jstor.org/stable/1831272). For the literature that followed, see for example Kenneth Rogoff's Mundell–Fleming lecture, 'Dornbusch's overshooting model after twenty-five years', IMF Staff Papers 49, 2002 (www.imf.org/external/pubs/ft/staffp/2001/00-00/pdf/kr.pdf).

14. Mongelli (note 5) gives a good account of this. Jeffrey Frankel and Andrew Rose's 'The endogeneity of the optimum currency area criteria' (*Economic Journal* 108 (1998): 1009–1025 (http://doi.org/10.1111/1468-0297.00327)) found that the OCA criteria themselves were affected by monetary integration, which cast doubt on the theory's ability to assess whether a common currency was economically beneficial even on its own criteria.

15. The euro founders' understanding of the problem is succinctly set out in C. Boyd and Marc Vanheukelen, 'The need for constraining national budgetary autonomy in an economic and monetary union', European Commissions Directorate-General for Economic and Financial Affairs Memo, 17 August 1988 (http://ec.europa.eu/archives/emu_history/documentation/chapter12/19880818en22needconstrainnatio.pdf).

16. The case for coordinating fiscal policy between integrated economies is explained, for example, by Gerald Carlino and Robert Inman, 'Spillovers: why macro-fiscal policy should be coordinated in economic unions', *VoxEU.org*, 24 June 2013 (www.voxeu.org/article/spillovers-why-macro-fiscal-policy-should-be-coordinated-economic-unions). The spillovers described in the main text are large, as shown for example by Alan Auerbach and Yuriy Gorodnichenko, 'Output spillovers from fiscal policy', *VoxEU.org*, 10 December 2012 (www.voxeu.org/article/output-spillovers-fiscal-policy).

17. European Commission, 'One market, one money: an evaluation of the potential benefits and costs of forming an economic and monetary union', *European Economy* 44 (October 1990): 100–347 (http://ec.europa.eu/econ omy_finance/publications/publication7454_en.pdf). See also the last part of Boyd and Vanheukelen (note 15).

18. At the same time, there was optimism that the single currency might inure economies' private sectors from the problems of overindebted governments. With a seamlessly integrated financial market, it was thought, private sector companies' access to credit would no longer lumber under whatever financing woes their governments might go through. 'A major effect of EMU,' the European Commission (note 16) wrote at the time, 'is that balance of payments constraints will disappear in the way they are experienced in international relations. Private markets will finance all viable borrowers, and savings and investment balances will no longer be constraints at the national level.' This remains the right aspiration for the euro, although it obviously did not transpire as the Commission had foreseen. I argue later that the reason why is eurozone leaders' willingness to countenance the break-up of the euro, more than any flaw in the single currency itself.

19. On the slowdown in productivity growth across Europe, see Chapter 8 and McQuinn and Whelan (note 1 from Chapter 8).

20. Cf. Tony Judt, *Ill Fares the Land* (Penguin, London, 2010).

21. Quentin Peel, 'Merkel warns on cost of welfare', *The Financial Times*, 16 December 2012 (www.ft.com/cms/s/0/8cc0f584-45fa-11e2-b7ba-00144fe abdc0.html).

22. Wolfgang Schäuble, 'We Germans don't want a German Europe', *The Guardian*, 19 July 2013 (www.theguardian.com/commentisfree/2013/jul/ 19/we-germans-dont-want-german-europe).

23. See Paul Krugman, 'Competitiveness: a dangerous obsession', *Foreign Affairs*, March/April 1994 (www.foreignaffairs.com/articles/1994-03-01/ competitiveness-dangerous-obsession), and 'Making sense of the competitiveness debate', *Oxford Review of Economic Policy* 12(3) (1996): 17–25 (http://doi.org/10.1093/oxrep/12.3.17).

24. Cf. Raghuram Rajan, *Fault Lines* (Princeton University Press, Princeton, NJ, 2010).

25. Alan Greenspan and James Kennedy, 'Sources and uses of equity extracted from homes', Finance and Economics Discussion Series Working Paper 20, March 2007 (www.federalreserve.gov/pubs/feds/2007/200720/2007 20pap.pdf).

26. Charles Calomiris and Stephen Haber, *Fragile by Design* (Princeton University Press, Princeton, NJ, 2014).

Chapter Two

1. Jean-Claude Trichet, 'The euro@10: achievements and responsibilities', Speech, 13 January 2009 (www.bis.org/review/r090119a.pdf).

2. Christian Dustmann, Bernd Fitzenberger, Uta Schönberger and Alexandra Spitz-Oener, 'From sick man of Europe to economic superstar: Germany's resurgent economy', *Journal of Economic Perspectives* 28(1) (Winter 2014): 167–188 (http://doi.org/10.1257/jep.28.1.167).

3. Karl Brenke, 'Real wages in Germany: numerous years of decline', German Institute for Economic Research Weekly Report 28/2009 (www.diw.de/sixcms/media.php/73/diw_wr_2009-28.pdf).

4. Paco Cabaña, 'Las tres primas de riesgo', 25 August 2012 (http://pacogcabana.blogspot.co.uk/2012/08/las-tres-primas-de-riesgo.html).

5. See, for example, Fernanda Nechio, 'Monetary policy when one size does not fit all', FRBSF Economic Letter 2011-18, 13 June 2011 (www.frbsf.org/economic-research/publications/economic-letter/2011/june/monetary-policy-europe/). Nechio constructs 'Taylor rules' separately for the eurozone core and the periphery which show the result mentioned in the main text.

6. For a detailed exploration of this argument, see Paul de Grauwe, 'Design failures in the eurozone: can they be fixed?', London School of Economics 'Europe in Question' Discussion Paper 57, February 2013 (www.lse.ac.uk/europeanInstitute/LEQS/LEQSPaper57.pdf).

7. Sebastian Edwards, 'The illusion of monetary policy independence under flexible exchange rates', *VoxEU.org*, 4 February 2015 (www.voxeu.org/article/illusion-monetary-policy-independence-under-flexible-exchange-rates); Sebastian Edwards, 'Monetary policy independence under flexible exchange rates: an illusion?', NBER Working Paper 20893, January 2015 (www.nber.org/papers/w20893); Guillermo Calvo and Carmen M. Reinhart, 'Fear of floating', NBER Working Paper 7993 (www.nber.org/papers/w7993).

8. Hélène Rey, 'The international credit channel and monetary autonomy', IMF Mundell–Fleming Lecture, 13 November 2014 (www.imf.org/external/np/res/seminars/2014/arc/pdf/Mundell.pdf).

9. Philippe Martin and Thomas Philippon simulate how the eurozone peripheral economies would have fared with different policies in the run-up to the crisis. They find that Greece, Ireland and Spain would have performed much better in terms of employment and debt during the crisis with a better fiscal policy beforehand, and in terms of employment (but not debt so much) had bank regulation been better. Combining both would of course have led to better results still. See 'Inspecting the mechanism: leverage and

the great recession in the eurozone', October 2014 (http://pages.stern.nyu
.edu/~tphilipp/papers/MartinPhilippon.pdf).

10. See Maurice Obstfeld and Kenneth Rogoff, *Foundations of International
Economics*, pp. 210–216 (MIT Press, Cambridge, MA, 1996).

11. We should note a deep conceptual problem with economy-wide unit
labour costs. Since the measure focuses on wage costs, it can go up because
the balance of rewards shifts from capital to labour, even without any
underlying change in productivity. This is instead a matter of distribution. Unit labour costs conflate productivity and distributive changes, and
that encourages an excessive focus on workers' responsibility for productivity erosion, neglecting the share of profits in production costs. This is
especially important when, as in most countries, the labour share of value
added has been falling, with the share going to capital correspondingly rising. Any observed rise in unit labour costs may simply reflect a correction
of that distributional shift. To illustrate the point, one might calculate the
unit capital cost or unit profit margin in an equivalent way to unit labour
cost and find that countries that have 'lost competitiveness' on the unit
labour cost measure have 'gained competitiveness' on the capital measure.
For the shortcomings of unit labour costs as a competitiveness measure,
see Jesus Felipe and Utsav Kumar, 'Unit labor costs in the eurozone: the
competitiveness debate again', Levy Economics Institute Working Paper
651, February 2011 (www.levyinstitute.org/pubs/wp_651.pdf). For the
fall in the labour share, see Loukas Karabarbounis and Brent Neiman,
'The global decline of the labor share', *The Quarterly Journal of Economics*
129(1) (February 2014): 61–103 (http://dx.doi.org/10.1093/qje/qjt032).

12. See Joong Shik Kang and Jay C. Shambaugh, 'The evolution of current
account deficits in the euro area periphery and the Baltics: many paths
to the same endpoint', International Monetary Fund Working Paper
13/169, July 2013 (www.imf.org/external/pubs/ft/wp/2013/wp13169.pdf);
Guillaume Gaulier, Daria Taglioni and Vincent Vicard, 'Tradable sectors
in Eurozone periphery countries did not underperform in the 2000s',
VoxEU.org, 19 July 2012 (www.voxeu.org/article/tradable-sectors-eurozo
ne-periphery); and Guillaume Gaulier and Vincent Vicard, 'The signa-
tures of euro-area imbalances: export performance and the composition of
unit labour cost growth', European Central Bank CompNet Policy Brief
02/2013, July 2013 (www.ecb.europa.eu/home/pdf/research/compnet/poli
cy_brief_2_export_performance_and_composition_of_ulc_growth.pdf).
These papers also show that the Baltic countries, which were not in the
euro at the time, did lose price competitiveness in their traded sectors in
the 2000s boom. So even if the euro periphery had experienced a loss of
export competitiveness, it is far from clear that staying out of the euro
would have made a difference.

13. On the Greece–Bulgaria comparison, see Guntram Wolff, 'A tale of floods and dams', *Bruegel.org*, 19 March 2015 (www.bruegel.org/nc/blog/detail/article/1597-a-tale-of-floods-and-dams/).

14. Through the so-called Vienna Initiative, these banks coordinated their practices in the crisis to mitigate capital flight from the affected countries. See http://vienna-initiative.com.

15. See Salvatore Dell'Erba, Ricardo Hausmann and Ugo Panizza, 'Debt levels, debt composition, and sovereign spreads in emerging and advanced economies', *Oxford Review of Economic Policy* 29(3) (2013): 518–547 (http://doi.org/10.1093/oxrep/grt026); and Paul De Grauwe and Yuemei Ji, 'Self-fulfilling crises in the eurozone: an empirical test', *Journal of International Money and Finance* 34 (2013): 15–36 (http://doi.org/10.1016/j.jimonfin.2012.11.003).

16. For the theory of why a country may choose to default on its domestic-currency debt, see Jesse Schreger and Wenxin Du, 'Sovereign risk, currency risk, and corporate balance sheets,' Harvard University Working Paper, December 2014 (http://scholar.harvard.edu/schreger/publications/sovereign-risk-currency-risk-and-corporate-balance-sheets-job-market-paper-be). Philippe Bacchetta, Elena Perazzi and Eric van Wincoop identify limits on a central bank's ability to prevent self-fulfilling runs on domestic sovereign in 'Self-fulfilling debt crises: can monetary policy really help?', NBER Working Paper 21158, May 2015 (www.nber.org/papers/w21158). For cases of default risk on such debt, note that credit rating agencies often rank it below the safest grade; and see the catalogue of domestic-currency sovereign defaults in Carmen Reinhart and Kenneth Rogoff, *This Time Is Different: Eight Centuries of Financial Folly* (Princeton University Press, Princeton, NJ, 2009).

17. Banks in much of central and eastern Europe – which were largely subsidiaries of western banks – carry out the bulk of their business in non-domestic currencies. This includes a large share of retail deposits in euros, which surveys show are demanded by customers who distrust the stability of their domestic currency. This suggests similar behaviour could have emerged in peripheral eurozone states had they remained outside of the single currency. See Martin Brown and Helmut Stix, 'The euroization of bank deposits in eastern Europe', *Economic Policy* 30(81) (January 2015): 95–139 (http://dx.doi.org/10.1093/epolic/eiu002). Another study has measured the share of banks' foreign currency debts that are not covered by matching foreign currency investments (or are matched with foreign currency loans to domestic borrowers who, with only domestic currency incomes, are likely to default in a significant depreciation). In Poland, Hungary, Bulgaria, Romania, Serbia, Croatia and Latvia, this percentage varied between 14.3 per cent and 44.3 per cent – far larger than banks'

typical capital ratios. See Pınar Yeşin, 'Foreign currency loans and systemic risk in Europe', *Federal Reserve Bank of St. Louis Review* 95(3) (May/June 2013): 219–236 (http://research.stlouisfed.org/publications/review/13/03/219-236Yesin.pdf).

CHAPTER THREE

1. For an account of Greek misrule, see Pavlos Eleftheriadis, 'Misrule of the few: how the oligarchs ruined Greece', *Foreign Affairs*, November/December 2014 (www.foreignaffairs.com/articles/142196/pavlos-eleftheriadis/misrule-of-the-few).

2. John Maynard Keynes, *The General Theory of Employment, Interest and Money*, Chapter 12 (Macmillan, London, 1936).

3. It is important to note that this way of massaging the figures was both legal and widespread enough to be called standard practice. See, for example, Tyler Durden, 'Step aside Greece: how Gustavo Piga exposed Europe's Enron in 2001 – focusing on Italy's Libor MINUS 16.77 per cent swap; was 'counterpart N' a threat to Piga's life?', *Zerohedge.com*, 28 February 2010 (www.zerohedge.com/article/step-aside-greece-how-gustavo-piga-exposed-europes-enron-2001-focusing-italys-libor-minus-16).

4. In the early 1990s, Greece sabotaged the international recognition of Macedonia, seeing irredentist designs in the name, until it prefixed its official name with 'Former Yugoslav Republic of'. The foreign minister at the time, who made this his personal obsession to the point of leaving his party and bringing the government down, was Antonis Samaras. He was elected Greece's prime minister in 2012.

5. Quoted in Tyler Durden, 'UST-Bund spread at three year wides as ECB warns IMF involvement would be beginning of end for eurozone', *Zerohedge.com*, 24 March 2010 (www.zerohedge.com/article/ust-bund-spread-three-year-wides-ecb-warns-imf-involvement-would-be-beginning-end-eurozone).

6. A good account of the IMF's role in the deliberations and its internal conflicts is Paul Blustein, 'Laid low: the IMF, the euro zone and the first rescue of Greece', Centre for International Governance Innovation Papers 61, April 2015 (www.cigionline.org/sites/default/files/cigi_paper_no.61web.pdf). See also 'IMF document excerpts: disagreements revealed', Real Time Economics Blog, *The Wall Street Journal*, 7 October 2013 (http://blogs.wsj.com/economics/2013/10/07/imf-document-excerpts-disagreements-revealed/).

7. Pascal Bruckner, 'Gloomy France', *City Journal*, Winter 2014 (www.city-journal.org/2014/24_1_france.html).

8. See Stefan Avdjiev, Christian Upper and Karsten von Kleist, 'Highlights of international banking and financial market activity', BIS Quarterly Review,

September 2010, 11–23 (www.bis.org/publ/qtrpdf/r_qt1009b.pdf). See also Christian Weistroffer and Jochen Möbert, 'Monitoring cross-border exposure', Deutsche Bank Research Current Issues, 26 November 2010 (www.dbresearch.com/MAIL/DBR_INTERNET_EN-PROD/PROD 0000000000266643.pdf). Karl Otto Pöhl, former Bundesbank president and the German member of the Delors Committee, said publicly at the time of the first Greek rescue that its purpose was to save French and German banks and rich Greek individuals. See www.spiegel.de/international/germany/former-central-bank-head-karl-otto-poehl-bailout-plan-is-all-ab out-rescuing-banks-and-rich-greeks-a-695245.html. Pöhl is an example of the broad support for a Greek debt writedown in the German economic policy elite.

9. The IMF later publicly stated it was a mistake not to have restructured at the outset; see International Monetary Fund, 'Ex post evaluation of exceptional access under the 2010 stand-by arrangement', IMF Country Report 13/156, June 2013 (www.imf.org/external/pubs/ft/scr/2013/cr13156.pdf). On Strauss-Kahn's opposition to restructuring, and more generally the pressure on Greece not to contemplate this option, see Blustein 'Laid low' (note 6).

10. See Tim Geithner, *Stress Test: Reflections on Financial Crises* (Crown, New York, 2014); and Peter Spiegel, 'How the euro was saved', *The Financial Times*, 11 May 2014 (www.ft.com/cms/s/0/f6f4d6b4-ca2e-11e3-ac05-001 44feabdc0.html).

11. For examples of the moral abhorrence of sovereign debt restructuring among European leaders at the time, see Karl Whelan, 'Sorry Olli, the IMF were being nice about Europe's role in Greece', *Forbes*, 10 June 2013 (www.forbes.com/sites/karlwhelan/2013/06/10/sorry-olli-the-imf-were-be ing-nice-about-europes-role-in-greece/).

12. The IMF in its own evaluation admitted that the programme was too detailed and lacked sufficient 'ownership' in Greece. See IMF, 'Ex post evaluation' (note 9).

13. The original expectation was that public debt would top out around 150 per cent of GDP, which at an average interest rate of 4 per cent would cost 6 per cent of GDP in interest only, with principal repayment coming in addition. The IMF forecast that interest service alone could reach 8 per cent of GDP before the interest on the official loans was cut, but some of that would have been to domestic creditors and not been taken out of the country.

14. Olivier Blanchard and Daniel Leigh, 'Growth forecast errors and fiscal multipliers', IMF Working Paper 13/1 (www.imf.org/external/pubs/ft/wp/2013/wp1301.pdf).

15. For a guide to academic research predicting such effects, see Jérémie Cohen-Setton, 'Supply policies at the zero lower bound', Bruegel Blog, 30 March 2015 (www.bruegel.org/nc/blog/detail/article/1599-supply-polici es-at-the-zero-lower-bound/. The essential feature of these models is that when monetary policy does not offset the deflationary effect of wage-reducing reforms, real interest rates rise and reduce aggregate demand.

16. On the collective bargaining point, see Barry Eichengreen, 'Lessons of a Greek tragedy', *Project Syndicate*, 13 June 2013 (www.project-syndicate .org/commentary/what-greece-should-have-done-differently-by-barry-ei chengreen). A thorough and even-handed assessment of the social consequences of the adjustment programme concludes that privileged groups managed to protect themselves – see Tassos Giannitsis and Stavros Zografakis, 'Greece: solidarity and adjustment in times of crisis', Institut für Makroökonomie und Konjunkturforschung Study 38, Hans-Bökler-Stiftung, March 2015 (www.boeckler.de/pdf/p_imk_study_38_2015 .pdf).

17. See, for example, IMF, 'World economic outlook', Chapter 3, April 2015 (www.imf.org/external/Pubs/ft/weo/2015/01/), and the more detailed analysis it draws on in Era Dabla-Norris, Si Guo, Vikram Haksar, Minsuk Kim, Kalpana Kochhar, Kevin Wiseman and Aleksandra Zdzienicka, 'The new normal: a sector-level perspective on productivity trends in advanced economies', IMF Staff Discussion Note 15/03, March 2015 (www.imf.org/ external/pubs/ft/sdn/2015/sdn1503.pdf). This research, which examines the effect on total factor productivity of reforms, finds relaxing labour market protection, as the troika demanded from Greece, has no effects in the long run and has negative effects in the short run. Product market liberalisation and lower taxes on labour, in contrast, have largely positive effects. See also Derek Anderson, Bergljot Barkbu, Lusine Lusinyan and Dirk Muir, 'Assessing the gains from structural reforms for jobs and growth', in Martin Schindler *et al.* (eds.), *Jobs and Growth: Supporting the European Recovery*, International Monetary Fund, April 2014, Chapter 7 (www.imf.org/external/np/seminars/eng/2014/eurbook/#7). They find that while product market reforms increase a country's consumption by 10 per cent in the long run, a standard set of labour market reforms adds only up to 1.5 per cent after ten years, and reduces consumption in the first five years after implementation. Moreover, this set includes publicly provided childcare and active job-matching policies, not just the deregulatory and cost-cutting reforms emphasised by the troika.

18. Adjusted for inflation and expressed in the euro's 2012 value.

19. IME GSEVEE, Household income and expenditure survey, December 2013 (www.imegsevee.gr/imesurveys/796-households-income-expediture).

20. Athens's deficit was about €25 billion in 2010, €20 billion in 2011, €12 billion in 2012, €6 billion in 2013 and projected at €5 billion in 2014, excluding money spent on bailing out banks in 2012 and 2013 (which could have been avoided with a Cyprus 'bail-in' policy as discussed below). Its interest payable was about €13 billion in 2010, €15 billion in 2011, €10 billion in 2012, €7 billion in 2013, and projected at €8 billion in 2014. The resulting primary deficit was roughly €12 billion in 2010, €5 billion in 2011, €3 billion in 2012, and then a €1.5 billion surplus in 2013 and a projected €3 billion surplus in 2014. See the Eurostat deficit notification tables (http://ec.europa.eu/eurostat/web/government-finance-statistics/ex cessive-deficit-procedure/edp-notification-tables) for 2010 and the IMF's fifth programme review (www.imf.org/external/pubs/ft/scr/2014/cr14151. pdf), p. 45 for the remaining years. The €25 billion estimate in the main text reflects the total €20 billion in 2010–2012 primary deficits with a buffer for accumulated arrears. It is comparable to a January 2015 accounting of how the rescue loans had been spent, which found that out of €226.7 billion disbursed by then, only about €26 billion, or 11 per cent, of the total went to cover the Greek state's 'operating needs' (primary deficits and arrears). See Yiannis Mouzakis, 'Where did all the money go?', *MacroPolis*, 5 January 2015 (www.macropolis.gr/?i=portal.en.the-agora.2080). The rest (89 per cent) largely went to debt service and bank recapitalisation.

21. This assumes a €12.5 billion primary deficit in 2010, and a cut of €2.5 billion every year thereafter, adding up to €37.5 billion.

22. Thomas Philippon considers a much more modest proposal – simply that the savings from the 2012 debt restructuring had been had two years earlier – and estimates that this would have left Greek GDP 5–10 per cent higher: 'Fair debt relief for Greece: new calculations', *VoxEU.org*, 10 February 2015 (www.voxeu.org/article/fair-debt-relief-greece-new-calculations).

23. There were precedents for GDP-linked debt repayment, such as Iceland's agreement with the United Kingdom and the Netherlands over compensation for its failed banks. Proposals that Greece's debt should be indexed to its GDP include Zsolt Darvas, 'The Greek debt trap: an escape plan', Bruegel Policy Contribution 2012/19, 9 November 2012 (www.bruegel.org/ publications/publication-detail/publication/759-the-greek-debt-trap-an -escape-plan/), and Marcel Fratzscher, Christoph Große Steffen and Malte Rieth, 'GDP-linked loans for Greece', DIW Economic Bulletin 9/2014 (www.diw.de/sixcms/detail.php?id=diw_01.c.488651.de). See also Barr *et al.*, 'GDP-linked bonds and sovereign defaults' (note 13 from Chapter 7).

24. See, for example, Nouriel Roubini, 'Greece must exit', *Project Syndicate,* 17 May 2012 (www.project-syndicate.org/commentary/greece-must-exit), or Hans-Werner Sinn, 'It is wrong to portray Germany as the euro winner',

The Financial Times, 22 July 2013 (www.ft.com/cms/s/0/bbb2176a-ed70 -11e2-8d7c-00144feabdc0.html).

25. Matthew Yglesias, 'They saved the eurozone; they just forgot to save the people', *Vox.com*, 28 May 2014 (www.vox.com/2014/5/9/5675398/they-sa ved-the-eurozone-they-just-forgot-to-save-the-people).

26. One study estimates a 40 per cent devaluation and a similar spike in inflation, as well as a 5 per cent drop in GDP in the first year after 'Grexit'. See Guillaume Menuet, 'What if Grexit were to happen?', *Citi Research Euro Economics Weekly*, 17 April 2015 (https://ir.citi.com/6s4hW1RMrfRh2rqs PDTdXCitg7A2wikPKrOohjdg6s14hl4Tct9wwQ%3D%3D).

27. Jens Hilscher, Alon Raviv and Ricardo Reis have shown that it is not so easy to inflate away debt. Because of short maturities, inflation may have to be very high to make a significant difference. See 'Inflating away the public debt? An empirical assessment', NBER Working Paper 20339, July, 2014 (www.nber.org/papers/w20339). See also Bacchetta *et al.*, 'Self-fulfilling debt crises: can monetary policy really help?' (note 16 from Chapter 2).

28. Guntram B. Wolff, 'Why Grexit would not help Greece: debunking the myth of exports', *Bruegel.org*, 6 January 2015 (www.bruegel.org/nc/blog/ detail/article/1530-why-grexit-would-not-help-greece/).

29. See Eduardo Levy Yeyati, 'How Argentina left its eurozone', *VoxEU.org*, 2 October 2011 (www.voxeu.org/article/how-argentina-left-its-eurozone).

30. Emmanuel Farhi, Gita Gopinath and Oleg Itskhoki, 'Fiscal devaluations', Federal Reserve Bank of Boston Working Paper 12-10 (www.bostonfed .org/economic/wp/wp2012/wp1210.pdf). See also their op-ed summarising the research: 'A devaluation option for Southern Europe', *Project Syndicate*, 1 March 2012 (www.project-syndicate.org/commentary/a-deval uation-option-for-southern-europe).

31. Miranda Xafa estimates that the net reduction in the face value of Greece's debt amounted to €68 billion (a gross reduction of €106 billion less a €38 billion loss by Greek banks for which the government would bail them out). See 'Sovereign debt crisis management: lessons from the 2012 Greek debt restructuring', Centre for International Governance Innovation Papers 33, June 2014 (www.cigionline.org/publications/sovereign-debt-cri sis-management-lessons-2012-greek-debt-restructuring). The burden of debt service was lifted more than the face value reduction suggests, since much of the remaining debt was significantly stretched out over time. It was still not enough.

32. A digest of the technical issues is Nick Malkoutzis, 'Is ELA the key to keeping the drachma at bay?', *Kathimerini*, 5 March 2012 (www.ekathime rini.com/4Dcgi/4dcgi/_w_articles_wsite3_1_05/03/2012_431268).

33. Ralph Atkins, 'The Bundesbank versus Greece', Money Supply Blog, *FT.com*, 22 May 2012 (http://blogs.ft.com/money-supply/2012/05/22/the -bundesbank-versus-greece/).

Chapter Four

1. Go to www.rte.ie/news/player/2010/1118/2856627-morning-ireland-talks -on-economy-to-start-today/ for a recording. Transcripts are available on www.theguardian.com/business/ireland-business-blog-with-lisa-ocarroll/ 2010/nov/18/ireland-central-bank-governor-transcript and http://web.dfa .ie/uploads/documents/embassy/Madrid%20EM/governor%20of%20the %20central%20bank%20patrick%20honohan.pdf. The same radio pro- gramme reported that several banks had lost more than 10 per cent of their deposits in just two months and that central bank liquidity to the Irish banking system amounted to some €130 billion, including €34 billion in emergency liquidity assistance from Honohan's own institution.

2. The last two paragraphs rely on the BBC radio documentary 'Bail-out boys go to Dublin', first broadcast on BBC Radio 4, 24 April 2011 (www.bbc .co.uk/programmes/b010mryv and www.youtube.com/watch?v=AAj7Sob 3cxg). Transcribed excerpts are available at www.thejournal.ie/the-bbc -bail-out-documentary-some-choice-quotes-126048-Apr2011/.

3. BBC World Service, Stephen Sackur interview with Partick Honohan, *Hardtalk*, 25 June 2014 (www.bbc.co.uk/programmes/n3csw9gd).

4. The property price figure is from the Permanent TSB/ESRI house price index (www.permanenttsb.ie/media/permanenttsb/pdfdocuments/house priceindex/8175+-+houseprice+index.pdf). The wage figure is from Jean- Claude Trichet, 'Competitiveness and the smooth functioning of EMU', Speech at the University of Liège, 23 February 2011 (www.ecb.int/press/ key/date/2011/html/sp110223.en.html).

5. These numbers are all from Erkki Liikanen (chair), 'High-level expert group on reforming the structure of the EU banking sector' (The Liika- nen Report), Brussels, 2 October 2012, pp. 11–14 and appendices 1 and 3 (http://ec.europa.eu/internal_market/bank/docs/high-level_expert_gro up/report_en.pdf).

6. European Systemic Risk Board, 'Is Europe overbanked?', Reports of the Advisory Scientific Committee 4, June 2014 (www.esrb.europa.eu/pub/ pdf/asc/Reports_ASC_4_1406.pdf). See also Sam Langfield and Marco Pagano, 'Bank bias in Europe: effects on systemic risk and growth' (www .aeaweb.org/aea/2015conference/program/retrieve.php?pdfid=1104).

7. Banks are encouraged to buy sovereign debt by intergovernmental stand- ards for banking regulations. The Basel rules for capital adequacy generally

treat the bonds of rich-country governments as risk-free. But while this can account for banks' tendency to lend to the public sector, it does not explain their eagerness disproportionately to finance their own governments. For the extraordinary extent of 'home bias' in a supposedly unified financial market, see for example Silvia Merler and Jean Pisani-Ferry, 'Hazardous tango: sovereign-bank interdependence and financial stability in the euro area', *Banque de France Financial Stability Review* 16 (April 2012): 201–210 (www.banque-france.fr/fileadmin/user_upload/banque_de_france/publications/Revue_de_la_stabilite_financiere/2012/rsf-avril-2012/FSR16-article-19.pdf).

8. See, for example, FDIC, 'Resolution handbook' (www.fdic.gov/bank/historical/reshandbook/).

9. An excellent primer on how to resolve failed banks quickly appeared on Willem Buiter's blog in March 2009 (http://blogs.ft.com/maverecon/2009/03/dont-touch-the-unsecured-creditors-clobber-the-tax-payer-instead/).

10. Liikanen Report (note 5), Box 2.2, p. 21.

11. A former chief economist at Ireland's central bank has testified to pressure from the government to suppress analysis showing that banks were fragile or house prices overvalued. See Padraic Halpin, 'Ex-Irish central bank economist says ordered to ask OECD to retract views', *Reuters.com*, 10 June 2015 (http://uk.reuters.com/article/2015/06/10/ireland-banks-inquiry-idUKL5N0YW3VL20150610).

12. See David Oakley and Sam Jones, 'Bond sell-off takes Ireland closer to tipping point', *The Financial Times*, 10 November 2010 (www.ft.com/cms/s/0/41815768-ecfa-11df-9912-00144feab49a.html).

13. At the end of 2010, the government's cash reserves were above €16 billion (see www.ntma.ie/download/press_releases/Funding_Q4_2010.pdf). The national pensions reserve fund still held €23 billion as of 31 March 2011 (see http://debates.oireachtas.ie/dail/2011/05/24/00050.asp). The 31 December 2010 value was €22.7 billion, which was after a €3.8 billion subscription of new AIB shares (www.nprf.ie/Publications/2011/NPRFReport2010.pdf).

14. 'Privatise Irish woes', *The Financial Times* (editorial), 12 November 2010 (www.ft.com/cms/s/0/c25b6d6e-edd2-11df-9612-00144feab49a.html).

15. See Jennifer Hughes and Anousha Sakoui, 'Anglo Irish ultimatum creates bail-in fears', *The Financial Times*, 26 October 2010 (www.ft.com/cms/s/0/9c57de0c-e12c-11df-90b7-00144feabdc0.html); Anousha Sakoui, Jennifer Hughes and John Murray Brown, 'Anglo Irish bondholders asked to share pain', *The Financial Times*, 21 October 2010 (www.ft.com/cms/s/0/6f3a949e-dd4b-11df-9236-00144feabdc0.html); and 'Ireland steps back into the ring', *The Financial Times* (editorial), 31 October 2010 (www.ft.com/cms/s/0/971c7582-e529-11df-8e0d-00144feabdc0.html).

16. Mary Watkins and Jane Croft, 'Court ruling poses questions for bondhold-ers', *The Financial Times*, 2 August 2012 (www.ft.com/cms/s/0/896697a4-dc87-11e1-a304-00144feab49a.html).

17. International Monetary Fund, 'Ireland: ex post evaluation of exceptional access under the 2010 extended arrangement', IMF Country Report 15/20, January 2015 (www.imf.org/external/pubs/ft/scr/2015/cr1520.pdf).

18. Morgan Kelly, the Irish economist famous for having warned against the real estate bubble, has argued that the guarantees could have been can-celled. See Kelly, 'If you thought the bank bail-out was bad, wait until the mortgage defaults hit home', *The Irish Times*, 8 November 2010 (www.irishtimes.com/opinion/if-you-thought-the-bank-bail-out-was-bad-wait-until-the-mortgage-defaults-hit-home-1.674081), and 'Ireland's future depends on breaking free from bail-out', *The Irish Times*, 7 May 2011 (www.irishtimes.com/opinion/ireland-s-future-depends-on-breaking-free-from-bail-out-1.565236). Richard Portes, president of the European eco-nomics network Centre for Economic Policy Research, argued the same; see 'Restructure Ireland's debt', *VoxEU.org*, 26 April 2011 (www.voxeu.org/article/restructure-ireland-s-debt).

19. John Murray Brown and Ralph Atkins, 'Dublin accepts ECB demands', *The Financial Times*, 29 November 2010 (www.ft.com/cms/s/0/819dce36-fbef-11df-b7e9-00144feab49a.html).

20. International Monetary Fund, 'Ireland: eighth review under the extended arrangement', IMF Country Report 12/336, December 2012 (www.imf.org/external/pubs/ft/scr/2012/cr12336.pdf).

21. 'Trichet letter revealed: ECB threatened to stop emergency funding unless Ireland took bail-out', *The Irish Times*, 6 November 2014 (www.irishtimes.com/news/ireland/irish-news/trichet-letter-revealed-ecb-threatened-to-stop-emergency-funding-unless-ireland-took-bail-out-1.1989869).

22. An excellent explanation of how emergency lending in the eurozone works is a report to the European Parliament by the University College Dublin economist Karl Whelan; see 'The ECB's collateral policy and its future as lender of last resort', November 2014 (www.karlwhelan.com/EU-Dialogue/Whelan-November-2014.pdf).

23. This was, incidentally, the only time the ECB had losses that needed to be covered proportionately by the members of the euro. Since, operationally, the secured loan to Lehman's European operations had been carried out by the Bundesbank, it was the German central bank that was entitled to compensation from its sister central banks for their share of the loss. Quite contrary to German fears that Germany would have to underwrite any losses at the ECB, Axel Weber could call on his colleagues to send him

cheques for their share of the €8.5 billion ECB loan Lehman's European operations had defaulted on.

24. From the 'Bail-out boys go to Dublin' documentary (see note 2).

25. Derek Scally, 'Bundesbank backed move to burn Irish bondholders', *The Irish Times*, 24 January 2014 (www.irishtimes.com/business/economy/ire land/bundesbank-backed-move-to-burn-irish-bondholders-1.1666162).

26. Jennifer Hughes, 'Bail-outs burden turns off bond investors', *The Financial Times*, 25 October 2015 (www.ft.com/cms/s/0/e95d0b90-dfa7-11df-bed9 -00144feabdc0.html).

27. Very small banks had of course also gone into normal bankruptcy in the past in Europe. One example was the Dutch DSB Bank, which failed in 2009.

Chapter Five

1. This is based on Sameer Khatiwada, 'Stimulus packages to counter global economic crisis: a review', ILO Discussion Paper 196/2009 (www.ilo .org/wcmsp5/groups/public/---dgreports/---inst/documents/publication/ wcms_193154.pdf), which puts the total size of Germany's fiscal stimulus at 2.8 per cent of 2009 GDP, and on Eswar Prasad and Isaac Sorkin, 'Assessing the G-20 stimulus plans: a deeper look', Brookings Institution, March 2009 (www.brookings.edu/research/articles/2009/03/g20-stimul us-prasad), which puts it at 3.4 per cent of 2008 GDP. Both studies find that Germany's stimulus was more than twice as large as a share of GDP than any other European country they examined.

2. See Daniel Schäfer and Ben Hall, 'Berlin calls for eurozone budget laws', *The Financial Times*, 16 May 2010 (www.ft.com/cms/s/0/5ff35db4-6117-11 df-9bf0-00144feab49a.html).

3. A good press account of the Deauville summit and the events surrounding it is Charles Forelle, David Gauthier-Villars, Brian Blackstone and David Enrich, 'As Ireland flails, Europe lurches across the Rubicon', *The Wall Street Journal*, 27 December 2010 (www.wsj.com/news/articles/SB100014 24052748703814804576035682984688312).

4. Other ECB policymakers, including the German and Portuguese executive board members Jürgen Stark and Vítor Constâncio, were also critical. See James Wilson, 'ECB's Stark cool on EU budget reforms', *The Financial Times*, 20 October 2010 (www.ft.com/cms/s/0/377fd11e-dc46-11df-a9a4 -00144feabdc0.html).

5. See Janis A. Emmanouilidis, 'The bumpy road to economic union', European Policy Centre Post-Summit Analysis, 2 November 2010 (www.epc.eu/pub_ details.php?pub_id=1164&cat_id=5). Rehn has travelled some distance. In

a valedictory interview shortly before finishing his tenure as commissioner, he said the eurozone's mistake had been not to set up an even more powerful rescue fund as early as 2010. See Stephen Fidler and Gabriele Steinhauser, 'Euro states wasted time in crisis, Commissioner Olli Rehn says', *The Wall Street Journal*, 29 June 2014 (http://online.wsj.com/articles/euro-states-wasted-time-in-crisis-commissioner-olli-rehn-says-1404076023).

6. All these numbers are from the IMF's Fiscal Monitor, April 2014 (www.imf.org/external/pubs/ft/fm/2014/01/fmindex.htm).

7. The 7.7 per cent estimate is from Sebastian Gechert, Andrew Hughes Hallett and Ansgar Rannenberg, 'Fiscal multipliers in downturns and the effects of Eurozone consolidation', CEPR Policy Insight 79, February 2015 (www.cepr.org/sites/default/files/policy_insights/PolicyInsight79.pdf). Simon Wren-Lewis covers a number of other estimates in 'The entirely predictable recession' (http://mainlymacro.blogspot.co.uk/2014/09/the-entirely-predictable-recession.html).

8. See www.ecb.europa.eu/stats/prices/indic/forecast/html/index.en.html.

9. This is according to the ECB's own euro area bank lending survey from April 2011 (www.ecb.europa.eu/stats/pdf/blssurvey_201104.pdf).

10. In the first three months of 2011 the stock of loans to businesses (non-financial corporations) did not budge from its level of €4700 billion. Household loans rose marginally from €5182 billion to €5225 billion. The data are available from the ECB statistical data warehouse at http://sdw.ecb.europa.eu/browse.do?node=bbn143 (sector codes S.11 and S.14/S.15). The money supply data are available at http://sdw.ecb.europa.eu/browseSelection.do?node=bbn141. Since inflation was running at close to 3 per cent year-on-year, this meant both lending and the money supply were contracting in real terms.

11. International Monetary Fund, 'Global financial stability report', April 2009 (www.imf.org/external/pubs/ft/gfsr/2009/01/). Table 4.1 gives $725 billion (about €550 billion at the contemporaneous exchange rate) as the estimated equity eurozone banks would need after expected writedowns to reduce leverage to 17, the average for US banks in the 1990s.

12. European Systemic Risk Board, 'Is Europe overbanked?' (see note 6 from Chapter 4).

13. For a good explanation of how Target2 works and how its balances should be interpreted, see Willem Buiter, Ebrahim Rahbari and Jürgen Michels, 'Making sense of Target imbalances', *VoxEU.org*, 6 September 2011 (www.voxeu.org/article/making-sense-target-imbalances).

14. Target2 data are available at www.eurocrisismonitor.com.

15. See, for example, 'The ECB's secret bail-out strategy', *Project Syndicate*, 29 April 2011 (www.cesifo-group.de/de/ifoHome/policy/Staff-Commen

ts-in-the-Media/Press-articles-by-staff/Archive/Eigene-Artikel-2011/med
ienecho_17561565_ifostimme-ps-29-04-11.html), and 'Why Germany is
threatened by a debt tsunami', Lecture at Humboldt University, 9 May
2011   (www.cesifo-group.de/ifoHome/events/individual-events/Archive/
2011/event-20110509-vortrag-berlin.html).

16. It did not help matters that the eurosystem charges interest on Target2 liabilities and pays it on claims. Ireland's central bank has been having to pay regular interest (at a mercifully low ECB rate), while the Bundesbank has been
receiving interest income on its Target2 credit. This gives the appearance of
a loan from Germany to Ireland to what were in reality massive movements
of euros from private Irish bank deposits to private German ones.

17. A detailed explanation of why is given in Karl Whelan, 'TARGET2: not
why Germans should fear a euro breakup', *VoxEU.org*, 29 April 2012
(www.voxeu.org/article/target2-germany-has-bigger-things-worry-about).

18. Peter Spiegel, 'How the euro was saved', *The Financial Times*, 11–16 May
2014 (www.ft.com/indepth/how-euro-was-saved).

19. See Christoph Trebesch and Jeromin Zettelmeyer, 'ECB interventions
in distressed sovereign debt markets: the case of Greek bonds', December 2013 (www.wiwi.uni-frankfurt.de/kolloquium/ws1314_/Zettelmeyer
.pdf). Karl Whelan summarises their findings in an article drawing lessons
for the ECB quantitative easing programme in 'How does QE work? A
picture worth a thousand words', 11 March 2015 (https://medium.com/
bull-market/how-does-qe-work-a-picture-worth-a-thousand-words-7fe0fc
a67ac4). ECB purchases drove up the price (and lowered the yield) of the
particular bonds it bought, but this had no effect on the bonds it did not
buy. So it did not cause a general fall in yields, in particular not for new
borrowing.

20. The limits on a central bank's ability to stop runs on sovereign debt are
analysed in Giancarlo Corsetti and Luca Dedola, 'The mystery of the
printing press: self-fulfilling debt crises and monetary sovereignty', CEPR
Discussion Paper 9358, September 2013 (https://ideas.repec.org/p/cpr/
ceprdp/9358.html). See also Philippe Bacchetta, 'Self-fulfilling debt crises:
can monetary policy really help?' (note 16 from Chapter 4).

21. A January 2015 opinion by the advocate-general of the European Court of
Justice says that any bond purchases cannot be pushed to a degree where
they make it impossible for a market price to be formed; see Court of Justice of the European Union, 'Advocate General's opinion in case C-62/14
Peter Gauweiler and Others v. Deutscher Bundestag' (http://curia.europa
.eu/jcms/upload/docs/application/pdf/2015-01/cp150002en.pdf).   This
suggests buying up the entire debt of a eurozone sovereign would indeed
fall under the Treaty prohibition of 'credit lines' to governments.

22. US fiscal transfers smooth the impact of state GDP fluctuations on local consumption by only 10–15 per cent. See Céline Allard, Petya Koeva Brooks, John C. Bluedorn, Fabian Bornhorst, Katharine Christopherson, Franziska Ohnsorge and Tigran Poghosyan, 'Toward a fiscal union for the euro area', Staff Discussion Note SDN/13/09, IMF, September 2013 (www .imf.org/external/pubs/ft/sdn/2013/sdn1309.pdf), and the associated technical notes at www.imf.org/external/pubs/ft/sdn/2013/sdn1309tn.pdf. While there is a lot of risk-sharing across US states, it mostly takes the form of financial flows through credit and capital markets, which cut the effect of GDP fluctuations on consumption by more than half.

23. See Roberto A. De Santis, 'A measure of redenomination risk', ECB Working Paper 1785, April 2015 (www.ecb.europa.eu/pub/pdf/scpwps/ecbwp 1785.en.pdf).

24. Daniel Gros instructively compares the cases of Greece and Puerto Rico in 'Puerto Rico and Greece: a tale of two defaults in a monetary union', High-Level Brief, CEPS, 30 June 2015 (www.ceps.eu/system/files/HLB5_DG_ PuertoRico_0.pdf). He finds that the reason for Puerto Rico's travails posing no threat to its use of the US dollar of the kind Greece's does to the euro is not fiscal union but rather banking union.

25. See the European Court of Justice's case-62/14, cited in note 21.

26. The letter to Berlusconi has been published by *Corriere della Sera* at www .corriere.it/economia/11_settembre_29/trichet_draghi_inglese_304a5f1e -ea59-11e0-ae06-4da866778017.shtml. The letter to Zapatero was later declassified by the ECB, which made it public at www.ecb.europa.eu/pub/ pdf/other/2011-08-05-letter-from-trichet-and-fernandez-ordonez-to-zapa teroen.pdf.

27. Alan Friedman, 'Italy: Monti's secret summer', *The Financial Times*, 10 February 2014 (www.ft.com/cms/s/0/b9474c88-8e98-11e3-b6f1-00144fe ab7de.html).

28. Marcus Walker, Charles Forelle and Stacy Meichtry, 'Deepening crisis over euro pits leader against leader', *The Wall Street Journal*, 30 December 2011 (www.wsj.com/articles/SB10001424052970203391104577124480046463576).

29. See James Mackenzie, 'Italy's Berlusconi says he was forced out by EU "plot"', *Reuters.com*, 14 May 2014 (www.reuters.com/article/2014/05/14/ us-italy-berlusconi-idUSBREA4D0N720140514), and Peter Spiegel, 'Draghi's ECB management: the leaked Geithner files', Brussels Blog, *The Financial Times*, 11 November 2014 (http://blogs.ft.com/brusselsblog/20 14/11/11/draghis-ecb-management-the-leaked-geithner-files/).

30. Paul Krugman and Martin Wolf are both among those who have used the 'morality play' moniker to criticise German economic policymaking.

See, for example, Krugman, 'Keynes's difficult idea', *NYTimes.com*, 24 December 2008 (http://krugman.blogs.nytimes.com/2008/12/24/keyne ss-difficult-idea).

31. Ralph Atkins, 'Germany and the eurozone: marked by a miracle', *The Financial Times*, 20 September 2011 (www.ft.com/cms/s/0/4d3c0b1e-e38c -11e0-8f47-00144feabdc0.html).

32. Consider the estimate that the eurozone's austerity policies reduced output by (rounding up) a cumulative 8 per cent. For a country with a 50 per cent debt-to-GDP ratio at the outset, that raises the ratio to 50/92 = 54 per cent. For a country with an original 100 per cent debt-to-GDP ratio, the ratio goes up to 100/92 = 109 per cent. For a country starting out at 130 per cent – similar to Greece and Italy early in the crisis – the contraction increases the burden to 130/92 = 141 per cent. And if austerity does more damage to the economy in already high-debt states, this counterproductive effect is worse still.

CHAPTER SIX

1. Commerzbank's Chief Executive Martin Blessing to *The Financial Times*, in Tom Burgis and James Wilson, 'German bank chief hits at Greek debt deal', 23 February 2012 (www.ft.com/cms/s/0/071d36a6-5e27-11e1-b1e9 -00144feabdc0.html).

2. Most likely, European policymakers inappropriately read across from the fall of US insurance titan AIG, which was toppled by all the CDSs it had written on mortgage-backed securities.

3. The last ECB Monthly Bulletin on Trichet's watch, in October 2011, included a box calling for eurozone governments to demonstrate their 'inflexible determination to fully honour their own individual sovereign signature' and making the extravagant claim that the willingness of any eurozone sovereign even to contemplate 'private sector involvement' could scare investors away from all euro-denominated assets. See www.ecb.euro pa.eu/pub/pdf/mobu/mb201110en.pdf, p. 44.

4. Jeromin Zettelmeyer, Christoph Trebesch and Mitu Gulati, 'The Greek debt restructuring: an autopsy', Peterson Institute for International Economics Working Paper 2013-13-8, 1 August 2013 (www.iie.com/publicat ions/wp/wp13-8.pdf).

5. Lee Buchheit and Mitu Gulati, 'How to restructure Greek debt', 7 May 2010 (http://dx.doi.org/10.2139/ssrn.1603304).

6. Robin Harding, 'IMF discusses third way over bail-outs', *The Financial Times*, 15 June 2014 (www.ft.com/cms/s/0/713abdb8-f4a9-11e3-bf6e-001 44feabdc0.html).

7. Manuel Altozano and Iñigo de Barron, 'Bankia salió a Bolsa apoyada en engaños', *El País*, 8 December 2014 (http://economia.elpais.com/economia/2014/12/04/actualidad/1417694060_120952.html); Raphael Minder, 'Former Bankia chairman Rodrigo Rato is accused of misusing company credit cards', *The New York Times*, 8 October 2014 (www.nytimes.com/2014/10/09/business/international/former-bankia-chairman-rodrigo-rato-is-accused-of-misusing-company-credit-cards.html).

8. An overview of the banking reforms is available on http://ec.europa.eu/finance/bank/crisis_management/index_en.htm.

9. Nicolas Verón's comprehensive essay on how banking union came and what it means makes clear how much its implementation depends on politics. 'Europe's radical banking union', Bruegel Essay and Lecture Series, 6 May 2015 (www.bruegel.org/publications/publication-detail/publication/880-europes-radical-banking-union/).

10. A good account of the negotiations is Peter Spiegel, 'Cyprus depositors' fate sealed in Berlin', *The Financial Times*, 17 March 2013 (www.ft.com/cms/s/0/f890566a-8f24-11e2-a39b-00144feabdc0.html).

11. Peter Spiegel, 'Cyprus rescue signals new line on bail-outs', *The Financial Times*, 25 March 2013 (www.ft.com/cms/s/0/68c9c18e-955e-11e2-a151-00144feabdc0.html).

12. The victims of these writedowns were therefore, unconscionably, the small savers to whom Bankia had unscrupulously sold its own subordinated debt when foreign institutional investors showed little interest in financing it. Similar shenanigans came to light in the Portuguese bank BES after its 2014 restructuring, mentioned below.

13. See Hans-Joachim Dübel, 'The capital structure of banks and practice of bank restructuring: eight case studies on current bank restructurings in Europe', Center for Financial Studies Working Paper, University of Frankfurt (www.finpolconsult.de/mediapool/16/169624/data/Bank_Restructuring/Eight_Bank_Case_Studies_Finpolconsult_for_CFS_FINAL.pdf).

14. Mervyn King, 'Monetary policy: practice ahead of theory', Bank of England Speech, 17 May 2005 (www.bankofengland.co.uk/archive/Documents/historicpubs/speeches/2005/speech245.pdf).

15. Brian Blackstone and Marcus Walker tell the riveting story behind Draghi's famous words in 'How ECB chief outflanked German foe in fight for euro', *The Wall Street Journal*, 2 October 2012 (www.wsj.com/articles/SB10000872396390443507204578020323544183926).

16. Paul De Grauwe, 'The European Central Bank as a lender of last resort', *VoxEU.org*, 18 August 2011 (www.voxeu.org/article/european-central-bank-lender-last-resort). See also the discussion on self-fulfilling runs in Chapter 2 and the papers cited in note 20 from Chapter 5).

17. Trebesch and Zettelmeyer, 'ECB interventions in distressed sovereign debt markets: the case of Greek bonds', cited in note 19 from Chapter 5.

18. Carlo Altavilla, Domenico Giannone and Michele Lenza, 'The financial and macroeconomic effects of OMT announcements', ECB Working Paper 1707, August 2014 (www.ecb.europa.eu/pub/pdf/scpwps/ecbwp1707.pdf).

19. Other doubters of the OMT programme include economics professor Tony Yates, who argues that the possibility of a self-fulfilling run still exists, since the ECB clearly would not buy sovereign bonds in all circumstances. See Yates, 'Why hasn't anyone called the ECB's bluff over OMTs?', 11 September 2013 (https://longandvariable.wordpress.com/2013/09/11/why -hasnt-anyone-called-the-ecbs-bluff-over-omts/). Simon Wren-Lewis has voiced the opposite doubt: that the ECB might be too willing to buy the bonds of a fundamentally insolvent government which should be forced to restructure first. See Wren-Lewis, 'How a Greek drama became a global tragedy', 13 June 2013 (http://mainlymacro.blogspot.co.uk/2013/06/how -greek-drama-became-global-tragedy.html).

Chapter Seven

20. Zettelmeyer, Trebesch and Gulati ('The Greek debt restructuring: an autopsy', note 4 from Chapter 6) show that although the writedown of Greek bonds ranks among the toughest sovereign restructurings, it still left considerable 'money on the table' for Athens. Even with the same parameters as the actual March 2012 writedown, a restructuring two years earlier would have cut the debt much more since the bonds were still all in private hands.

21. See ECB, 'Aggregate report on the comprehensive assessment', October 2014 (www.bankingsupervision.europa.eu/ecb/pub/pdf/aggregatereport onthecomprehensiveassessment201410.en.pdf). For shortcomings, see for example Viral Acharya and Sascha Steffen, 'Making sense of the comprehensive assessment', *VoxEU.org*, 29 October 2014 (www.voxeu.org/article/ making-sense-ecb-s-comprehensive-assessment). Note the wide discrepancy between regulatory capital ratios and simple leverage ratios (plain equity to total assets).

22. Peter Spiegel, 'Cyprus rescue signals new line on bail-outs', see note 11 from Chapter 6.

23. A comprehensive survey article on the ample legal and economic literatures on sovereign default was published in 2009, just in time for any eurozone policymaker in need of instruction. See Ugo Panizza, Federico Sturzenegger and Jeromin Zettelmeyer, 'The economics and law of sovereign debt and default', *Journal of Economic Literature* 47(3) (2009): 651–698 (http:// doi.org/10.1257/jel.47.3.651). A decade earlier, the experience of the Latin

American and Asian financial crises had produced a fertile debate on restructuring and refinancing in sovereign debt crises. See, for example, Stanley Fischer, 'On the need for an international lender of last resort', *Journal of Economic Perspectives* 13(4) (Fall 1999): 85–104 (http://pubs.aea web.org/doi/pdfplus/10.1257/jep.13.4.85), which discusses private sector haircuts and debt standstills for sovereigns. Anne Krueger advanced an important proposal for a regular sovereign bankruptcy procedure when she was a managing director at the IMF in the 2000s. See Krueger, 'A new approach to sovereign debt restructuring', IMF Report, April 2002 (www.imf.org/external/pubs/ft/exrp/sdrm/eng/sdrm.pdf). An updated discussion of these issues can be found in Committee on International Economic Policy and Reform, 'Revisiting sovereign bankruptcy', October 2013 (www.brookings.edu/research/reports/2013/10/sovereign-debt). Lee Buchheit and Mitu Gulati analyse the eurozone problems specifically in 'The eurozone debt crisis – the options now', 8 October 2012 (http://dx.doi .org/10.2139/ssrn.2158850).

24. See www.fdic.gov/bank/historical/bank/.

25. IMF Global Financial Stability Review, April 2009 (www.imf.org/Extern al/Pubs/FT/GFSR/2009/01/pdf/summary.pdf).

26. For data on outstanding debt securities in the eurozone see www.ecb.euro pa.eu/stats/money/securities/debt/html/index.en.html.

27. An ECB estimate puts the marginal propensity to consume out of wealth between 0.7 and 1.9 cents per euro (Ricardo M. Sousa, 'Wealth effects on consumption: evidence from the euro area', ECB Working Paper 1050, May 2009 (www.ecb.europa.eu/pub/pdf/scpwps/ecbwp1050.pdf)). Using the IMF's €550 billion figure as a guess of the potential wealth loss from bank restructurings, the resulting drag on consumption would be between roughly €4 billion and €10 billion – or less than 0.1 per cent of euro-zone GDP. The fiscal austerity applied in the eurozone was an order of magnitude larger, with structural primary deficit reductions of more than 1 percentage point of GDP per year from 2010 to 2013, as measured by the IMF's fiscal monitor.

28. Cf. Atif Mian and Amir Sufi, *House of Debt: How They (and You) Caused the Great Recession, and How We Can Prevent It from Happening Again* (University of Chicago Press, Chicago, IL, 2014). Even the United States did far too little restructuring – but it did more than the eurozone.

29. The total loan earmarked for bank recapitalisation purposes was actually about €50 billion – the unused amount was returned to the EFSF in February 2015.

30. According to the Bank of Greece, Greek credit institutions held about €34 billion worth of government bonds at the end of 2009. Their total

capital and reserves amounted to €32 billion, but banks had very few outstanding bonds, worth only about €2.4 billion. See Bank of Greece, 'Aggregated balance sheet of credit institutions' (www.bankofgreece.gr/ BogDocumentEn/Aggregated_balance_sheet_CI.xls).

31. Carmen Reinhart and Christoph Trebesch, 'Sovereign-debt relief and its aftermath: the 1930s, the 1990s, the future?', *VoxEU.org*, 21 October 2014 (www.voxeu.org/article/sovereign-debt-relief-and-its-aftermath-1930s-1990s-future) and 'A distant mirror of debt, default and relief', CEPR Discussion Paper 10195, October 2014 (www.cepr.org/active/publications/ discussion_papers/dp.php?dpno=10195).

32. See David Barr, Oliver Bush and Alex Pienkowski, 'GDP-linked bonds and sovereign default', Bank of England Working Paper 484, January 2014 (www.bankofengland.co.uk/research/Documents/workingpapers/2014/ wp484.pdf). The paper finds that GDP-linked debt can increase the amount of borrowing markets will tolerate by almost half compared with conventional bonds, which could increase consumption by 1 per cent to 9 per cent of GDP in perpetuity.

33. See Ashoka Mody, 'The ghost of Deauville', *VoxEU.org*, 7 January 2014 (www.voxeu.org/article/ghost-deauville); and also Ashoka Mody, 'Sovereign debt and its restructuring framework in the euro area', Bruegel Working Paper 2013/05, 12 December 2013 (www.bruegel.org/publications/pu blication-detail/publication/788-sovereign-debt-and-its-restructuring-fra mework-in-the-euro-area/).

34. Brent Glover and Seth Richard-Shubik, 'Contagion in the European sovereign debt crisis', NBER Working Paper 20567, October 2014 (www.nber .org/papers/w20567).

35. Madrid's rescue loan, which was only agreed in July 2012, was limited to 10 per cent of its GDP and was confined to bank recapitalisation costs and not general budget support.

36. See Reinhart and Trebesch (note 12).

37. Hugh Carnegy, 'Marine Le Pen launches European campaign with attack on EU', *The Financial Times*, 1 May 2014 (www.ft.com/cms/s/0/5907b5a6 -d128-11e3-bdbb-00144feabdc0.html).

Chapter Eight

1. Kieran McQuinn and Karl Whelan, 'Europe's long-term growth prospects', Working Paper, 25 March 2015 (www.karlwhelan.com/Papers/Mc QuinnWhelanMarch2015.pdf).

2. Giancarlo Corsetti, Lars P. Feld, Philip R. Lane, Lucrezia Reichlin, Hélène Rey, Dimitri Vayanos and Beatrice Weder di Mauro, *A New Start for the*

Eurozone: Dealing with Debt (CEPR Press, London, 2015) (www.voxeu .org/sites/default/files/Monitoring%20the%20Eurozone.pdf).

3. Viral Acharya and Sascha Steffen, 'Making sense of the comprehensive assessment', *VoxEU.org*, 29 October 2014 (www.voxeu.org/article/making -sense-ecb-s-comprehensive-assessment). See also Capital Issues, 'EU leverage ratio gap', *Capital Issues*, 27 October 2014 (http://capitalissues.co/20 14/10/27/eu-leverage-ratio-gap/).

4. Mario Draghi, for example, treated this as axiomatic in his recent speech in Helsinki (see note 9 from Chapter 1).

5. Jean Tirole, 'Country solidarity in sovereign crises' (http://idei.fr/doc/by/ti role/countrysolidarity042414.pdf).

6. Frankel and Rose, 'The endogeneity of the optimum currency area criteria', note 14 from Chapter 1.

7. See Céline Allard, Petya Koeva Brooks, John C. Bluedorn, Fabian Bornhorst, Katharine Christopherson, Franziska Ohnsorge, Tigran Poghosyan, 'Toward a fiscal union for the euro area', IMF Staff Discussion Note SDN/13/09, September 2013 (www.imf.org/external/pubs/ft/sdn/2013/ sdn1309.pdf), and the associated technical notes at www.imf.org/external/ pubs/ft/sdn/2013/sdn1309tn.pdf.

8. For discussions of how financial markets can fulfil the same function as formal fiscal union, see Mathias Hoffmann and Bent E. Sørensen, 'Don't expect too much from EZ fiscal union – and complete the unfinished integration of European capital markets!' (www.voxeu.org/article/hedging -macroeconomic-risk-eurozone-fiscal-union-versus-capital-markets), and Emmanuel Farhi and Iván Werning, 'Fiscal unions' (www.parisschoolofec onomics.eu/IMG/pdf/farhi-2.pdf).

9. For an illuminating comparison between Greece and Puerto Rico, see Daniel Gros, 'Puerto Rico and Greece: a tale of two defaults in a monetary union', CEPS High-level Brief, 30 June 2015 (www.ceps.eu/system/files/ HLB5_DG_PuertoRico_0.pdf).

10. Jakob von Weizsäcker and Jacques Delpla, 'The blue bond proposal', Bruegel Policy Brief, May 2010 (www.bruegel.org/download/parent/403-the -blue-bond-proposal/file/885-the-blue-bond-proposal-english/), and von Weizsäcker and Delpla, 'Eurobonds: the blue bond concept and its implications', Bruegel Policy Brief, March 2011 (www.bruegel.org/download/ parent/509-eurobonds-the-blue-bond-concept-and-its-implications/file/ 1370-eurobonds-the-blue-bond-concept-and-its-implications/).

11. See Benoît Cœuré, 'Life below zero: learning about negative interest rates', Speech, 9 September 2014 (www.ecb.europa.eu/press/key/date/2014/html/ sp140909.en.html).

12. Willem Buiter, 'Negative interest rates: when are they coming to a central bank near you?', Willem Buiter's Maverecon, 7 May 2009 (http://blogs.ft.com/maverecon/2009/05/negative-interest-rates-when-are-they-coming-to-a-central-bank-near-you/).

13. For the effects of central bank asset purchases, see Jack Meaning and Feng Zhu, 'The impact of recent central bank asset purchase programmes', Bank for International Settlements Quarterly Review, December 2011 (www.bis.org/publ/qtrpdf/r_qt1112h.htm), and Bank of England, 'Inflation report', May 2014, p. 43 (www.bankofengland.co.uk/publications/Documents/inflationreport/2014/ir14may.pdf).

14. See http://ec.europa.eu/eurostat/documents/2995521/5181810/2-24102014-AP-EN.PDF/a67248ec-1270-4277-8a1b-bb66cc133a89.

15. Mario Draghi, 'Unemployment in the euro area', Speech at Jackson Hole, 22 August 2014 (www.ecb.europa.eu/press/key/date/2014/html/sp140822.en.html).

16. See Farhi, Gopinath and Itskhoki, 'Fiscal devaluations' (note 29 from Chapter 3).

17. See http://ec.europa.eu/priorities/jobs-growth-investment/plan/docs/an-investment-plan-for-europe_com_2014_903_en.pdf.

18. Alessandra Casella, 'Tradable deficit permits: efficient implementation of the stability pact in the European monetary union', *Economic Policy* 14(29) (October 1999): 321–362 (http://dx.doi.org/10.1111/1468-0327.00052). Casella's original proposal was to require additional permits only for bigger deficits. The experience of overly tight fiscal policy in the post-crisis recession shows that the incentives ought to be symmetric – a permit should be needed both to exceed and to undershoot the common-best deficit-to-GDP ratio. A concern with the proposal is that where tradable permits have been used in other policy contexts, political pressures have caused too many permits to be issued. This has been a problem with the EU's Emissions Trading Scheme (ETS), which is widely seen to have issued too many emissions permits and thus driven their price too low to discourage carbon emissions sufficiently. The equivalent in a deficit permits scheme would be that collective deficit targets were set too high. In contrast, the European Central Bank defied concerns that it would give in to political pressure for loose monetary policy – if anything, it is guilty of the contrary. The model for a system of tradable deficit permits should be the ECB, not the ETS.

19. See, for example, John Springford and Simon Tilford, 'Why Germany's trade surplus is bad for the eurozone', Centre for European Reform Bulletin 93, December 2013/January 2014 (www.cer.org.uk/publications/archive/bulletin-article/2013/why-germany's-trade-surplus-bad-eurozone).

20. See McQuinn and Whelan (note 1).

21. Daniel Gros, 'Investment as the key to recovery in the euro area?', Centre for European Policy Studies Working Paper, 18 November 2014 (www.ce ps.eu/publications/investment-key-recovery-euro-area).

22. See Chiara Criscuolo, Peter N. Gal and Carlo Menon, 'The dynamics of employment growth: new evidence from 18 countries', OECD Paper, 21 May 2014 (http://doi.org/10.1787/5jz417hj6hg6-en), which found among other things that '[a]lthough they represent a small portion of the total employment, young firms create a disproportionate number of jobs. Conversely, the largest contribution to job destruction comes from the group of small (less than 250 employees) and mature (six years old or older) firms. These patterns ... are remarkably robust across countries and years' (p. 37). In every country, young firms contribute disproportionately to job dynamism and employment growth. Their shares of the total number of jobs both destroyed and created are many times bigger than their share of average employment, but the rate of creation outweighs that of destruction. The opposite is true for old firms (pp. 40–42). These findings generalise results established by the Kauffman foundation for the United States, which has found that 'net job growth occurs in the U.S. economy only through startup firms'. See Tim Kane, 'The importance of startups in job creation and job destruction', Kauffman Foundation Research Paper, July 2010 (www.kauffman.org/~/media/kauffman_org/research%20reports%20and%20covers/2010/07/firm_formation_importance_of_startups.pdf).

23. Dustmann *et al.*, 'From sick man of Europe to economic superstar: Germany's resurgent economy' (note 2 from Chapter 2).

24. See Citi Research, 'Euro economics weekly', 5 December 2014 (http://ir .citi.com/5lAnm6sIuNVRJAee9acqVE9iXrIa5Dpvu15EX0017U8tYGFb KTb6gA%3D%3D).

25. This refers to the OECD's measure of the tax wedge applying to a two-earner family with two children, where one earner makes 100 per cent and the other 33 per cent of the average wage. The remaining two countries that widened the tax wedge by more than one percentage point on this measure were Austria and Luxembourg. The latter, however, did so from a very low initial tax wedge (as, to be fair, did Ireland). See http://stats.oecd .org/index.aspx?DataSetCode=AWCOMP.

Chapter Nine

1. James Politi, 'Italy accuses Brussels of "shaky" accounting', *The Financial Times*, 20 November 2014 (www.ft.com/cms/s/0/86d522c8-70d5-11e4-85 d5-00144feabdc0.html); John Hooper, 'Italian finance minister: Europe

must act now to avoid stagnation', *The Guardian*, 12 December 2014 (www.theguardian.com/business/2014/dec/12/italian-finance-minister -padoan-europe-act-now-avoid-stagnation); ANSA, 'Renzi says EU must change in "dangerous moment"', 3 October 2014 (www.ansa.it/english/ news/2014/10/03/renzi-says-eu-must-change-in-dangerous-moment-upda te_b2c41cd5-284b-4e7a-a416-736730b61981.html).

2. See Benn Steil and Dinah Walker, 'Greece fallout: Italy and Spain have funded a massive backdoor bailout of French banks'. Council of Foreign Relations Geo-Graphics Blog, 2 July 2015 (http://blogs.cfr.org/geograph ics/2015/07/02/greecefallout/).

3. André Sapir and Guntram B. Wolff, 'Euro-area governance: what to reform and how to do it', Bruegel Policy Brief 01/2015, February 2015 (www.bruegel.org/publications/publication-detail/publication/870-euro -area-governance-what-to-reform-and-how-to-do-it/).

4. This and the following paragraphs draw on my *Financial Times* op-ed 'Europe need not wait for Germany', 17 August 2011 (www.ft.com/cms/s/ 0/d64f5702-c768-11e0-9cac-00144feabdc0.html), where I first proposed that a subset of eurozone countries issue debt jointly without German par- ticipation. For data on the United States, see www.treasurydirect.gov/NP/ debt/current; for Japan, see www.mof.go.jp/english/jgbs/reference/gbb/ 201412.html; for Europe, see http://appsso.eurostat.ec.europa.eu/nui/show. do?dataset=gov_10q_ggdebt. Note that the stocks of bonds outstanding are smaller than gross government debt because not all debt is incurred in the form of bonds. On the other hand, not all of the outstanding bonds are available in debt markets; a large portion is held by the issuers' own central banks as a result of monetary policy operations. The numbers in the text refer to the total amount of bonds issued.

5. See note 8 from Chapter 8.

6. Stefan Wagstyl and James Politi, 'Merkel defends fiscal rules as Paris and Rome put growth first', *The Financial Times*, 16 October 2014 (www.ft .com/cms/s/0/fedbfcfc-5518-11e4-b616-00144feab7de.html).

7. Radosław Sikorski, 'Poland and the future of the European Union', Speech in Berlin, 28 November 2011 (www.mfa.gov.pl/resource/33ce6061-ec12 -4da1-a145-01e2995c6302).

8. Ralph Atkins and Martin Sandbu, 'FT interview transcript: Jens Weid- mann', *The Financial Times*, 13 November 2011 (www.ft.com/intl/cms/s/0/ b3a2d19e-0de4-11e1-9d40-00144feabdc0.html); Jens Weidmann, 'Stop encouraging banks to buy government debt', *The Financial Times* (op-ed), 30 September 2013 (www.ft.com/intl/cms/s/0/81a505a4-278c-11e3-8feb -00144feab7de.html).

9. Hugo Dixon, 'Spain is a troubled country', *Reuters Analysis and Opinion*, 10 November 2014 (http://blogs.reuters.com/hugo-dixon/2014/11/10/spain-is-a-troubled-country/); 'The euro's next crisis', *The Economist* (leading article), 3 January 2015 (www.economist.com/news/leaders/21637334-why-early-election-spells-big-dangers-greeceand-euro-euros-next-crisis).

10. See Draghi, 'Stability and prosperity in monetary union' (note 9 from Chapter 1), and 'Structural reforms, inflation and monetary policy' (note 8 from Chapter 1).

11. I outline how this could be done in 'An alternative for Greece', *FT.com*, 26 February 2015 (www.ft.com/intl/cms/s/0/189d8aa4-bd9a-11e4-8cf3-00144feab7de.html). See also Sigrún Davíðsdóttir and Thórólfur Matthíasson, 'The good, the bad and the foreign: Icelandic lesson for stabilising the Greek banks', *A Fistful of Euros*, 25 February 2015 (http://fistfulofeuros.net/afoe/the-good-the-bad-and-the-foreign-icelandic-lesson-for-stabilising-the-greek-banks/).

12. Peter Spiegel and Kerin Hope, 'Frustrated officials want Greek premier to ditch Syriza far left', *The Financial Times*, 5 April 2015 (www.ft.com/intl/cms/s/0/04587d80-dbac-11e4-b693-00144feab7de.html).

13. See, for example, Juan Laborda, 'Sí a la reestructuración de la deuda' (http://vozpopuli.com/blogs/5118-juan-laborda-si-a-la-reestructuracion-de-la-deuda).

Chapter Ten

1. See *Eurobarometer,* October 2014 (http://ec.europa.eu/public_opinion/archives/eb/eb82/eb82_first_en.pdf).

2. The EFSM (which is guaranteed by all EU members) paid out about as much as the EFSF (the eurozone-only rescue fund) in the Irish and Portuguese rescues, implying that the United Kingdom would have been on the line for more than twice as much if it had been a euro member. That does not include the guarantees raised for the full €500 billion EFSF, later ESM, 'firewall', which would have multiplied UK financial commitments many times. For details about the various loan facilities, see European Commission, 'Financial assistance in EU member states' (http://ec.europa.eu/economy_finance/assistance_eu_ms/index_en.htm).

3. After a voting reform triggered by Lithuania's entry, big countries now formally enjoy greater voting weight than small ones in the ECB.

4. Bank of England governor Mark Carney made this claim during the Scottish referendum debate and has continued to make it. See, for example, Katie Hope, 'Eurozone needs to "share risks", warns Bank governor', *BBC.com*, 28 January 2015 (www.bbc.co.uk/news/business-31030425).

5. See the government's 2003 assessment of the five tests, of which it deemed the first two unfulfilled (http://news.bbc.co.uk/1/shared/spl/hi/europe/03/euro/pdf/final_assessment/03_1100.pdf).

6. See António Afonso and Davide Furceri, 'EMU enlargement, stabilisation costs and insurance mechanisms', *Journal of International Money and Finance* 27(2) (2008): 169–187 (http://dx.doi.org/10.1016/j.jimonfin.2007.12.010).

7. See note 13 from Chapter 1.

8. Willem H. Buiter, 'Why the United Kingdom should join the eurozone', *International Finance* 11(3) (Winter 2008): 269–282 (http://willembuiter.com/ifeuro.pdf).

9. See Zsolt Darvas, 'Export and unit labour cost adjustment' (www.bruegel.org/nc/blog/detail/article/1215-export-and-unit-labour-cost-adjustment-close-association-in-eu15/).

10. These numbers are taken from Guntram Wolff, 'Why Grexit would not help Greece' (note 28 from Chapter 3), and from Zsolt Darvas, 'Export and unit labour cost adjustment' (note 9).

11. House of Commons Library, 'Financial services: contribution to the UK economy', August 2012 (www.parliament.uk/briefing-papers/sn06193.pdf).

12. The benefits and dangers of a large banking sector are discussed in Oliver Bush, Samuel Knott and Chris Peacock, 'Why is the UK banking system so big and is that a problem?', Bank of England Quarterly Bulletin, 2014 Q4 (www.bankofengland.co.uk/publications/Documents/quarterlybulletin/2014/qb14q402.pdf).

13. This 'maximum harmonisation' was discussed in Chapter 6.

14. See Open Europe, 'Out of the euro but run by the euro?', 8 July 2014 (http://openeuropeblog.blogspot.co.uk/2014/07/out-of-euro-but-run-by-euro-uk-ecb.html).

15. See Alex Barker, 'UK demands hold up European banking union', *The Financial Times*, 11 October 2013 (www.ft.com/cms/s/0/0f2d8c8a-3281-11e3-b3a7-00144feab7de.html), and Barker, 'Eurozone agrees common bank supervisor', *The Financial Times*, 13 December 2013 (www.ft.com/cms/s/0/2946cbfe-44d4-11e2-8fd7-00144feabdc0.html).

Chapter Eleven

1. 'Greece turns, Europe wobbles', *The Economist*, 26 January 2015 (http://econ.st/1xYj6Fi).

2. Address of Pope Francis to the European Parliament, Strasbourg, 25 November 2014 (http://w2.vatican.va/content/francesco/en/speeches/2014/november/documents/papa-francesco_20141125_strasburgo-parlamento-europeo.html).

INDEX